# ACCOUNTING:
# The Language of Business
## Third Edition

**Sidney Davidson, Ph.D., CPA**
The University of Chicago

**James S. Schindler, Ph.D., CPA**
The State University of New York at Buffalo

**Clyde P. Stickney, D.B.A., CPA**
Dartmouth College

**Roman L. Weil, Ph.D., CPA, CMA**
The University of Chicago

Thomas Horton and Daughters, Inc. / 22 Appleton Place / Glen Ridge, New Jersey 07028

# For Our Children

Copyright © 1974, 1975, 1977 Thomas Horton and Company
All rights reserved
No part of this work covered by copyright hereon may be reproduced or used in any form or by any means—graphic, electronic or
mechanical, and photocopying, recording, taping, or information
storage or retrieval systems—without written permission of the
publisher.

**ISBN** 0-913878-13-8

**Library of Congress Cataloging in Publication Data**

Davidson, Sidney 1919–
  Accounting: the language of business, third edition

1. Accounting—Terminology.   2. Accounting.

I. Schindler, James Schwartz, 1917–    joint author.
II. Stickney, Clyde P., 1944–    joint author.
III. Weil, Roman Lee, 1940–    joint author.
IV. Title.
HF5621.D28   657.03     77-5974

Typography by The Composing Room
Grand Rapids, Michigan

Printed by R. R. Donnelley & Sons
Crawfordsville, Indiana, U.S.A.

# Preface

The study of accounting is both difficult and rewarding. Part of the difficulty stems from accounting's use of specialized vocabulary. Unlike many technical areas, however, accounting's vocabulary consists of many words that have other meanings in ordinary usage. Understanding the concepts and using accounting reports require that the reader know how to interpret the words used and their special meaning. The student of accounting and the reader of accounting reports will find the tasks easier the sooner he or she learns, for example, the difference between the meanings of *revenue* and *receipt,* between *expense* and *expenditure,* and between *fund* and *reserve.* The purpose of the Glossary is to define just how these and some 1,400 other terms are used or should be used, when describing an accounting event or reporting the results of that event. Because understanding the process of accounting is so essential to the understanding of business, the Glossary should prove useful to other functional areas of business as well.

A glossary is not a dictionary, so that we have given definitions of terms only as they are, or should be, used in accounting.

Students and readers of financial reports will not encounter all the terms in the Glossary. We have tried to include, however, all the terms that are used in a wide range of textbooks, problems, financial reports, financial periodicals and newspapers. Many textbook writers, not excluding ourselves, often include terms in problems that have not been carefully explained in the text preceding the problem. We suspect that students will find the Glossary particularly useful in understanding what the problems in a textbook are attempting to ask.

Many words and phrases in the Glossary are defined in terms of other entries in the Glossary. Terms in a given definition that are themselves explained elsewhere are *italicized.* Many of the entries in the Glossary are multiple-word phrases because much of the specialized terminology of accounting depends upon such phrases. We have tried to anticipate the most likely phrase that will occur to the reader and have used that phrase in the glossary. Nevertheless, we probably have failed in some cases to put the explanation by the word or phrase that occurs to you. Words and phrases are alphabetized using the letter-by-letter principle, not the word-by-word principle. Thus, the following terms are defined in the order shown: *account, accountancy, accounting, accounting standards, account payable, accounts receivable turnover.*

**WE ARE PROFIT-ORIENTED** and are eager to learn from you how we can make the book more successful. We will pay the first person who makes a given suggestion incorporated in subsequent editions. Such suggestions might include typographical errors ($1), additional cross references ($1), errors of fact or substance ($2), and additional terms with their explanation ($2).

There are a few words in accounting, most notably *cost* and *expense,* that mean different things to different people. Our own notions of learning lead us to the conclusion that the more precise the meaning of the words used, the easier is the understanding of accounting. Consequently, we give the restricted definition of, for example, *cost* that we think enhances the user's ability to understand but we also give the variants in meaning often used in practice. Further, certain terms used widely in the accounting profession, for example, *prepaid expenses,* seem to us to be self-contradictory given our preference for restricted and unambiguous definitions. We point out these contradictions knowing that many people, nevertheless, use these terms.

In addition, this book contains the following sections which we think useful for learning accounting and interpreting accounting statements.

**General Electric Company's Annual Report.** GE's annual report is consistently among the best published. We reproduce GE's annual report issued in 1977 along with our own comments and notes which should help in understanding it, and, we hope, other financial statements as well.

**Penn Central Transportation Company's Annual Report Just Before Its Bankruptcy.** One of the most widely known bankruptcies, and one of the largest, was that of the Penn Central. We reproduce excerpts from that report so that the reader can see the limitations of analyzing the stockholders' equity section of the balance sheet in forecasting bankruptcy. The annual report shows retained earnings of almost half a billion dollars and stockholders' equity of almost $2 billion. Yet soon after the report was issued, the company petitioned for bankruptcy because it could not meet its obligations.

**Excerpts from the Annual Report of Sears, Roebuck and Co.** We include the income statement, balance sheet, and some of the notes to financial statements from the Sears annual report issued in 1977. These excerpts are particularly interesting because of Sears' enormous amount of current liability for deferred taxes arising out of sales accounted for on the sales basis for financial statements but on the cash collection (installment) basis for tax returns. This "current liability" is likely never to be paid. We think this item should be considered to be a part of shareholders' equity; including it in shareholders' equity, contrary to generally accepted accounting principles, would increase shareholders' equity by about 17 percent.

**Accounting for Changing Prices.** In 1975 the Financial Accounting Standards Board proposed requiring that excerpts from general price level adjusted accounting statements be included in all annual reports issued in the near future. In 1976 the SEC required certain replacement cost disclosures. These bodies attempt to have companies show the effects of inflation on the conventional statements. We explain the nature of these items and show certain related illustrations.

**Pronouncements Governing Generally Accepted Accounting Principles.** We include a list of pronouncements governing generally accepted accounting principles, their dates of issuance, and a brief history of their development, including information about the promulgating organizations.

**Accounting Magic.** This example shows how generally accepted accounting principles allow a range of accounting treatments so that two firms, exactly alike in all respects except for their accounting methods, can report drastically different incomes.

**An Annual Report for the U.S. Government.** The government does not account for its operations in the same way that a corporation does. Arthur Andersen & Co. compiled financial statements for the government based on the accounting that corporations use. We reproduce, so that the reader can learn about the fiscal operations of the federal government.

We gratefully acknowledge the permission of The Dryden Press to reproduce material from our *Fundamentals of Accounting,* and *Financial Accounting: An Introduction to Concepts, Methods, and Uses,* published by them. We thank the General Electric Company, Penn Central Company, Shell Oil, Sears, American Telephone & Telegraph Co., Commonwealth Edison, Hilton Hotels, Koppers Company, Trans Union Corporation, and Arthur Andersen & Co. for their material. Nancy Vander Linde and Eli Worman designed the book and planned the layout. We thank them for their help.

S. D.
J. S. S.
C. P. S.
R. L. W.

# TABLE OF CONTENTS

# Glossary[1]

## A

**AAA.** *American Accounting Association.*

**Abacus.** A scholarly journal containing articles on theoretical aspects of accounting. Published twice a year by the Sydney University Press, Sydney, Australia.

**abnormal spoilage.** Actual spoilage exceeding that expected to occur under normal operating efficiency. Spoilage that should not occur if operations are normally efficient. Usual practice treats this cost as an *expense* of the period rather than as a *product cost.* Contrast with *normal spoilage.*

**aboriginal cost.** In public utility accounting, the *acquisition cost* of an asset incurred by the first *entity* devoting that *asset* to public use. Most public utility regulation is based on aboriginal cost. If it were not, then public utilities could exchange assets among themselves at ever-increasing prices in order to raise the rate base and, then, prices based thereon. *Historical cost* only to the first acquirer.

**absorption costing.** The generally accepted method of *costing* which assigns all types of *manufacturing costs* (direct material and labor as well as fixed and variable overhead) to units produced. Sometimes called "full costing." Contrast with *direct costing.*

**accelerated depreciation.** Any method of calculating *depreciation* charges where the charges become progressively smaller each period. Examples are *double-declining-balance* and *sum-of-the-years'-digits* methods.

**acceptance.** A written promise to pay which is equivalent to a promissory *note.*

**account.** Any device for accumulating additions and subtractions relating to a single *asset, liability, owners' equity* item, *revenue, expense,* and other items.

**accountancy.** The British word for *accounting.* In the United States, it means the theory and practice of accounting.

**Accountants' Index.** A publication of the *AICPA* which indexes, in detail, the accounting literature of the period.

**accountant's opinion.** *Auditor's report.*

**accountant's report.** *Auditor's report.*

**account form.** The form of *balance sheet* where *assets* are shown on the left and *equities* are shown on the right. Contrast with *report form.*

**accounting.** An *information system* conveying information about a specific *entity.* The information is in financial terms and is restricted to information that can be made reasonably precise. The *AICPA* defines accounting as a service activity whose "function is to provide quantitative information, primarily financial in nature, about economic entities that is intended to be useful in making economic decisions."

**accounting changes.** As defined by *APB Opinion* No. 20, a change in (a) an *accounting principle* (such as a switch from *FIFO* to *LIFO* or from *sum-of-the-years'-digits* to *straight-line depreciation*), (b) an accounting estimate (such as estimated useful lives or salvage value of depreciable assets and estimates of *warranty* costs or *uncollectible accounts*), and (c) the reporting *entity.* Changes of type (a) should be disclosed along with both the cumulative effect on *retained earnings* at the start of the period during which the change was made and the cumulative effect on the reported earnings for the period of change. Changes of type (b) should be treated as affecting only the period of change and, if necessary, future periods. The reasons for changes of type (c) should be disclosed and, in statements reporting on operations of the period of the change, the effect of the change on all other periods reported on for comparative purposes should also be shown. In some cases (such as a change from *LIFO* to other inventory *flow assumptions* or in the method of accounting for long-term construction contracts), changes of type (a) are treated like changes of type (c). That is, for these changes all statements shown for prior periods must be restated to show the effect of adopting the change for those periods as well. See *all-inclusive concept* and *accounting errors.*

**accounting conventions.** Methods or procedures used in accounting. This term tends to be used when the method or procedure has not been given official authoritative sanction by a pronouncement of a group such as the *APB, FASB,* or *SEC.* Contrast with *accounting principles.*

**accounting cycle.** The sequence of accounting procedures starting with *journal entries* for various transactions and events and ending with the *financial statements* or, perhaps, the *post-closing trial balance.*

**accounting entity.** See *entity.*

**accounting equation.** *Assets = Equities. Assets = Liabilities + Owners' Equity.*

**accounting errors.** Arithmetic errors and misapplications of *accounting principles* in previously published financial statements that are corrected in the current period with direct *debits* or *credits* to *retained earnings.* In this regard, they are treated like *prior-*

---

[1]Certain terms in the definitions are *italicized.* The *italicized* terms, or variants of them, are themselves explained in the glossary.

*period adjustments,* but, technically, they are not classified by *APB Opinion* No. 9 as prior-period adjustments. See *accounting changes* and contrast with changes in accounting estimates as described there.

**accounting event.** Any occurrence that is recorded as a transaction in the accounting records.

**Accounting Magic.** An illustration presented in another section of this book. Cross references to examples in *Accounting Magic* direct you to look at that section for further illustration and explanation.

**accounting methods.** *Accounting principles.* Procedures for carrying out accounting principles.

**accounting period.** The time period for which *financial statements* which measure *flows,* such as the *income statement* and the *statement of changes in financial position,* are prepared. Should be clearly identified on the financial statements. See *interim statements.*

**accounting policies.** *Accounting principles* adopted by a specific *entity.*

**accounting principles.** The concepts that determine the methods or procedures used in accounting for *transactions* or events reported in the *financial statements.* This term tends to be used when the method or procedure has been given official authoritative sanction by a pronouncement of a group such as the *APB, FASB,* or *SEC.* Contrast with *accounting conventions.*

**Accounting Principles Board.** See *APB.*

**accounting procedures.** See *accounting principles,* but usually this term refers to the methods required to implement accounting principles.

**accounting rate of return.** Income for a period divided by average investment during the period. Based on income, rather than discounted cash flows and, hence, is a poor decision-making aid or tool. See *ratio.*

**Accounting Research Bulletin (ARB).** The name of the official pronouncements of the former *Committee on Accounting Procedure* of the *AICPA.* Fifty-one bulletins were issued between 1939 and 1959. ARB No. 43 summarizes the first forty-two bulletins.

**Accounting Research Study.** One of a series of studies published by the Director of Research of the *AICPA* "designed to provide professional accountants and others interested in the development of accounting with a discussion and documentation of accounting problems." Fifteen such studies were published between 1961 and 1974. Abbreviated as *ARS.*

**The Accounting Review.** Scholarly publication of the *American Accounting Association,* which appears four times a year.

**Accounting Series Release.** See *SEC.*

**accounting standards.** *Accounting principles.*

**Accounting Trends and Techniques.** An annual publication of the *AICPA* which surveys the reporting practices of 600 large corporations. It presents tabulations of specific practices, terminology, and disclosures along with illustrations taken from individual annual reports.

**account payable.** A *liability* representing an amount owed to a *creditor,* usually arising from purchase of *merchandise* or materials and supplies; not necessarily due or past due. Normally, a *current* liability.

**account receivable.** A claim against a *debtor* usually arising from sales or services rendered; not necessarily due or past due. Normally, a *current asset.*

**accounts receivable turnover.** *Net sales* on account for a period divided by the average balance of net accounts receivable. See *ratio.*

**accretion.** Increase in economic worth through physical change, usually caused of a natural resource such as an orchard, caused by natural growth. Contrast with *appreciation.*

**accrual.** Recognition of an *expense* (or *revenue*) and the related *liability* (or *asset*) that is caused by an *accounting event,* frequently by the passage of time, and that is not signaled by an explicit cash transaction. For example, the recognition of interest expense or revenue (or wages, salaries, or rent) at the end of a period even though no explicit cash transaction is made at that time.

**accrual basis of accounting.** The method of recognizing *revenues* as *goods* are sold (or delivered) and as *services* are rendered, independent of the time when cash is received. *Expenses* are recognized in the period when the related revenue is recognized independent of the time when cash is paid out. Contrast with the *cash basis of accounting.*

**accrued.** Said of a *revenue (expense)* that has been earned (recognized) even though the related *receivable (payable)* is not yet due. This adjective should not be used as part of an account title. Thus, we prefer to use Interest Receivable (Payable) as the account title, rather than Accrued Interest Receivable (Payable). See *matching convention.*

**accrued depreciation.** An inferior term for *accumulated depreciation.* See *accrued.*

**accrued payable.** A *payable* usually resulting from the passage of time. For example, *salaries* and *interest* accrue as time passes. See *accrued.*

**accrued receivable.** A *receivable* usually resulting from the passage of time. See *accrued.*

**accumulated depreciation.** A preferred title for the *contra-asset* account that shows the sum of *depreciation* charges on an asset since it was acquired. Other titles used are *allowance* for *depreciation* (acceptable term) and *reserve* for *depreciation* (unacceptable term).

**accurate presentation.** The qualitative accounting objective suggesting that information reported in financial statements should correspond as precisely as possible with the economic effects underlying transactions and events. See *fair presentation* and *full disclosure.*

**acid test ratio.** Sum of *(cash, current marketable securities,* and *receivables)* divided by *current liabilities.* Some non-liquid receivables may be excluded from the numerator. Often called the *quick ratio.* See *ratio.*

**acquisition cost.** Of an *asset,* the net *invoice* price plus all *expenditures* to place and ready the asset for its intended use. The other expenditures might include legal fees, transportation charges, and installation costs.

**activity accounting.** *Responsibility accounting.*

**activity-based depreciation.** *Production method* of *depreciation.*

**actual cost (basis).** *Acquisition* or *historical cost.* Also contrast with *standard cost.*

**actuarial.** Usually said of computations or analyses that involve both *compound interest* and probabilities. Sometimes the term is used if only one of the two is involved.

**additional paid-in capital.** An alternative acceptable title for the *capital contributed in excess of par (or stated) value account.*

**adequate disclosure.** *Fair presentation* of *financial statements* requires *disclosure* of *material* items. This *auditing standard* does not, however, require publicizing all information detrimental to a company. For example, the company may be threatened with a lawsuit and disclosure might seem to require a *debit* to a *loss* account and a *credit* to an *estimated liability.* But the mere making of this entry might adversely affect the actual outcome of the suit. Such impending suits need not be disclosed.

**adjunct account.** An *account* that accumulates additions to another account. For example, Premium on Bonds Payable is adjunct to the liability Bonds Payable; the effective liability is the sum of the two account balances at a given date. Contrast with *contra account.*

**adjusted acquisition (historical) cost.** Cost adjusted for *general* or *specific price level changes.* See also *book value.*

**adjusted bank balance of cash.** The *balance* shown on the statement from the bank plus or minus appropriate adjustments, such as for unrecorded deposits or outstanding checks, to reconcile the bank's balance with the correct cash balance. See *adjusted book balance of cash.*

**adjusted basis.** The *basis* used to compute gain or loss on disposition of an *asset* for tax purposes. Also, see *book value.*

**adjusted book balance of cash.** The *balance* shown in the firm's account for cash in bank plus or minus appropriate adjustments, such as for *notes* collected by the bank or bank service charges, to reconcile the account balance with the correct cash balance. See *adjusted bank balance of cash.*

**adjusted trial balance.** *Trial balance* taken after *adjusting entries* but before *closing entries.* Contrast with *pre-* and *post-closing trial balances.* See *unadjusted trial balance* and *worksheet.*

**adjusting entry.** An entry made at the end of an *accounting period* to record a *transaction* or other *accounting event,* which for some reason has not been recorded or has been improperly recorded during the accounting period. An entry to update the accounts. See *worksheet.*

**adjustment.** A change in an *account* produced by an *adjusting* entry. Sometimes the term is used to refer to the process of restating *financial statements* for *general price level changes.*

**administrative expense.** An *expense* related to the enterprise as a whole as contrasted to expenses related to more specific functions such as manufacturing or selling.

**admission of partner.** Legally, when a new partner joins a *partnership,* a new partnership comes into being. In practice, however, the old accounting records may be kept in use and the accounting entries reflect the manner in which the new partner joined the firm. If the new partner merely purchases the interest of another partner, the only accounting is to change the name for one capital account. If the new partner contributes *assets* and *liabilities* to the partnership, then the new assets must be recognized with debits and the liabilities and other source of capital, with credits. See *bonus method.*

**ADR.** See *asset depreciation range.*

**advances from (by) customers.** A preferred term for the *liability* account representing *receipts* of *cash* in advance of delivering the *goods* or rendering the *service* (that will cause *revenue* to be recognized). Sometimes called "deferred revenue" or "deferred income."

**advances to affiliates.** *Loans* by a parent company to a *subsidiary.* Frequently combined with "investment in subsidiary" as "investments and advances to subsidiary" and shown as a *noncurrent asset* on the parent's *balance sheet.* These advances are eliminated in *consolidated financial statements.*

**advances to suppliers.** A preferred term for *disbursements* of cash in advance of receiving *assets or services.*

**adverse opinion.** An *auditor's report* stating that the financial statements are not fair or are not in accord with *GAAP.*

**affiliated company.** Said of a company controlling or controlled by another company.

**after closing.** *Post-closing;* said of a *trial balance* at the end of the period.

**after cost.** Said of *expenditures* to be made subsequent to *revenue* recognition. For example, *expenditures* for *repairs* under warranty are after costs. Proper recognition of after costs involves a debit to expense at the time of the sale and a credit to an *estimated liability.* When the liability is discharged, the debit is to the estimated liability and the credit is to the assets consumed.

**agent.** One authorized to transact business, including executing contracts, for another.

**aging accounts receivable.** The process of classifying *accounts receivable* by the time elapsed since the claim came into existence for the purpose of estimating the amount of uncollectible accounts receivable as of a given date. See *sales, uncollectible accounts adjustment* and *allowance for uncollectibles.*

**aging schedule.** A listing of *accounts receivable,* classified by age, used in *aging account receivable.*

**AICPA.** American Institute of Certified Public Accountants. The national organization that represents *CPA*'s. It oversees the writing and grading of the Uniform CPA Examination. Each state, however, sets its own requirements for becoming a CPA in that state. See *certified public accountant.*

**all capital earnings rate.** Net *income* plus interest charges, net of tax effects, plus minority interest in income divided by average total assets. Perhaps the single most useful ratio for assessing management's overall operating performance. See *ratio.*

**all financial resources.** All *assets* less all *liabilities.* Sometimes the *statement of changes in financial position* explains the changes in all financial resources rather than only the changes in *working capital.*

**all-inclusive (income) concept.** Under this concept, no distinction is drawn between *operating* and *nonoperating revenues* and *expenses;* thus the only entries to retained earnings are for *net income* and *dividends.* Under this concept all income, *gains,* and *losses* are reported in the *income statement;* thus, events usually reported as *prior-period adjustments* and as *corrections of errors* are included in net income. This concept in its pure form is not the basis of

*GAAP*, but *APB Opinions* No. 9 and 30 move very far in this direction. They do permit retained earnings entries for prior-period adjustments and correction of errors.

**allocate.**   To spread a *cost* from one *account* to several accounts, to several products, or activities, or to several periods.

**allocation of income taxes.**   See *deferred income tax*.

**allowance.**   A balance sheet *contra account* generally used for *receivables* and depreciable assets. See *sales* (or *purchase*) *allowance* for another use of this term.

**allowance for uncollectibles (accounts receivable).** A *contra* to Accounts Receivable that shows the estimated amount of *accounts receivable* that will not be collected. When such an allowance is used, the actual *write-off* of specific accounts receivable (*debit* allowance, *credit* specific account) does not affect *revenue* or *expense* at the time of the write-off. The revenue reduction is recognized when the allowance is credited; the amount of the credit to the allowance may be based on a percentage of sales on account for a period or determined from *aging accounts receivable*. This contra account enables an estimate to be shown of the amount of receivables that will be collected without identifying specific uncollectible accounts. See *allowance method*.

**allowance method.**   A method of attempting to *match* all *expenses* of a transaction with its associated *revenues*. Usually involves a debit to expense and credit to an *estimated liability*, such as for estimated warranty expenditures, or a debit to a revenue (*contra*) account and a credit to an asset (*contra*) account, such as for uncollectible accounts. See *allowance for uncollectibles* for further explanation. When the allowance method is used for *sales discounts*, sales are recorded at *gross invoice* prices (not reduced by the amounts of discounts made available). An estimate of the amount of discounts to be taken is debited to a *revenue contra account* and *credited* to an allowance account, shown contra to *accounts receivable*.

**American Accounting Association.**   An organization primarily for academic accountants, but open to all interested in accounting. See *The Accounting Review*.

**American Institute of Certified Public Accountants.** See *AICPA*.

**American Stock Exchange.**   AMEX. ASE. A public market where various corporate *securities* are traded.

**AMEX.**   *American Stock Exchange*.

**amortization.**   The general process of *allocating acquisition cost* of assets to either the periods of benefit as *expenses* or to *inventory* accounts as *product costs*. Called *depreciation* for *plant assets*, *depletion* for *wasting assets* (natural resources), and *amortization* for *intangibles*. Also used for the process of allocating *premium* or *discount* on *bonds* and other *liabilities* to the periods during which the liability is outstanding.

**analysis of changes in working capital accounts.** The *statement of changes in financial position* explains the causes of the changes in *working capital* during a period. This part of the statement, which may appear in footnotes, shows the net changes in the specific working capital accounts which have been explained in the main section of the statement.

**analysis of variances.**   See *variance analysis*.

**annual report.**   A report for stockholders and other interested parties prepared once a year; includes a *balance sheet*, an *income statement*, a *statement of changes in financial position*, a reconciliation of changes in *owners' equity* accounts, a *summary of significant accounting principles*, other explanatory *notes*, the *auditor's report*, and, perhaps, comments from management about the year's events. See *10-K* and *financial statements*.

**annuitant.**   One who receives an *annuity*.

**annuity.**   A series of payments, usually made at equally spaced time intervals.

**annuity certain.**   An *annuity* payable for a definite number of periods. Contrast with *contingent annuity*.

**annuity due.**   An *annuity* whose first payment is made at the start of period one (or at the end of period zero). Contrast with *annuity in arrears*.

**annuity in advance.**   An *annuity due*.

**annuity in arrears.**   An *ordinary annuity* whose first payment occurs at the end of the first period.

**annuity method of depreciation.**   See *compound interest depreciation*.

**anti-dilutive.**   Said of a *potentially dilutive security* which will increase *earnings per share* if it is *exercised* or *converted* into common stock. In computing *primary* and *fully diluted earnings per share*, anti-dilutive securities may not be assumed to be exercised or converted and hence do not affect reported earnings per share in a given period.

**APB.**   Accounting Principles Board of the *AICPA*. It set *accounting principles* from 1959 through 1973, issuing thirty-one *APB Opinions*. It was superseded by the *FASB*.

**APB Opinion.**   The name given to pronouncements of the APB that make up much of *generally accepted accounting principles;* there are thirty-one APB Opinions, issued from 1962 through 1973.

**APB's.**   An abbreviation used for *APB Opinions*.

**APB Statement.**   The *APB* issued four Statements between 1962 and 1970. The Statements were approved by at least two-thirds of the Board, but they are recommendations, not requirements. For example, Statement No. 3 (1969) suggested the publication of *general price level adjusted statements* but did not require them.

**application of funds.**   Any transaction that reduces *funds* (however funds is defined). A *use of funds*.

**applied cost.**   A *cost* that has been *allocated* to a department, product, or activity; need not be based on actual costs incurred.

**applied overhead.**   *Overhead costs* charged to departments, products, or activities.

**appraisal.**   The process of obtaining a valuation for an *asset* or *liability* that involves expert opinion rather than explicit market transactions.

**appraisal method of depreciation.**   The periodic *depreciation* charge is the difference between the beginning and end-of-period appraised value of the *asset* if that difference is positive. If negative, there is no charge. Not generally accepted.

**appreciation.**   An increase in economic worth caused by rising market prices for an *asset*. Contrast with *accretion*.

**appropriated retained earnings.**   See *retained earnings, appropriated*.

**appropriation.** In governmental accounting, an *expenditure* authorized for a specified amount, purpose, and time.

**appropriation account.** In governmental accounting, an account set up to record specific authorizations to spend; it is credited with appropriation amounts. *Expenditures* during the period and *encumbrances* outstanding at the end of the period are closed (debited) to this account at the end of the period.

**ARB.** *Accounting Research Bulletin.*

**arbitrage.** Strictly speaking, the simultaneous purchase in one market and sale in another of a *security* or commodity in hope of making a *profit* on price differences in the different markets. Often this term is loosely used when the item sold is somewhat different from the item purchased; for example, the sale of shares of *common stock* and the simultaneous purchase of a *convertible bond* which is convertible into identical common shares.

**arm's length.** Said of a transaction negotiated by unrelated parties, each acting in his or her own self interest; the basis for a *fair market value* determination.

**arrears.** Said of *cumulative preferred stock dividends* that have not been declared up to the current date. See *annuity in arrears* for another context.

**ARS.** *Accounting Research Study.*

**articles of incorporation.** Document filed with state authorities by persons forming a corporation. When the document is returned with a certificate of incorporation, it becomes the corporation's *charter.*

**articulate.** Said of the relationship between any operating statement (for example, *income statement* or *statement of changes in financial position*) and *comparative balance sheets,* where the operating statement explains (or reconciles) the change in some major balance sheet category (for example, *retained earnings or working capital*).

**ASR.** *Accounting Series Release.*

**assess.** To value property for the purpose of property taxation; the assessment is determined by the taxing authority. To levy a charge on the owner of property for improvements thereto, such as for sewers or sidewalks.

**asset.** A future benefit or service potential, recognized in accounting only when a transaction has occurred. May be *tangible* or *intangible, short-term* (current) or *long-term* (noncurrent).

**asset depreciation range. ADR.** The range of *depreciable lives* allowed by the *Internal Revenue Service* for a specific depreciable *asset.*

**asset turnover.** Ratio of net sales to average assets. See *ratio.*

**at par.** Said of a *bond* or *preferred stock* issued or selling at its *face amount.*

**attachment.** The laying claim to the *assets* of a borrower or debtor by a lender or creditor when the borrower has failed to pay debts on time.

**attest.** Rendering of an *opinion* by an auditor that the *financial statements* are fair. This procedure is called the "attest function" of the CPA. See *fair presentation.*

**audit.** Systematic inspection of accounting records involving analyses, tests, and *confirmations.* See *internal audit.*

**audit committee.** A committee of the board of directors of a *corporation* usually consisting of outside directors who nominate the independent auditors and discuss the auditors' work with them. If the auditors believe certain matters should be brought to the attention of stockholders, the auditors first bring these matters to the attention of the audit committee.

**Audit Guides.** See *Industry Audit Guides.*

**auditing standards.** A set of ten standards promulgated by the *AICPA,* including three general standards, three standards of field work, and four standards of reporting. According to the AICPA, these standards "deal with the measures of the quality of the performance and the objectives to be attained," rather than with specific auditing procedures.

**auditor.** One who checks the accuracy, fairness, and general acceptability of accounting records and statements and then *attests* to them.

**audit program.** The procedures followed by the *auditor* in carrying out the *audit.*

**auditor's opinion.** *Auditor's report.*

**auditor's report.** The auditor's statement of the work done and an opinion of the *financial statements.* Opinions are usually unqualified ("clean"), but may be *qualified,* or the auditor may disclaim an opinion in the report. Often called the "accountant's report." See *adverse opinion.*

**audit trail.** A reference accompanying an *entry,* or *posting,* to an underlying source record or document. A good audit trail is essential for efficiently checking the accuracy of accounting entries. See *cross-reference.*

**authorized capital stock.** The number of *shares* of stock that can be issued by a corporation; specified by the *articles of incorporation.*

**average.** The arithmetic mean of a set of numbers; obtained by summing the items and dividing by the number of items.

**average collection period of receivables.** See *ratio.*

**average-cost flow assumption.** An *inventory flow assumption* where the cost of units is the *weighted average* cost of the *beginning inventory* and purchases. See *inventory equation.*

**average tax rate.** The rate found by dividing *income tax expense* by *net income* before taxes. Contrast with *marginal tax rate, statutory tax rate.*

**avoidable cost.** An *incremental* or *variable cost.* See *programmed cost.*

## B

**bad debt.** An *uncollectible account receivable;* see *sales, uncollectible accounts adjustment.*

**bad debt expense.** See *sales, uncollectible accounts adjustment.*

**bad debt recovery.** Collection, perhaps partial, of a specific account receivable previously written off as uncollectible. If the *allowance method* is used, the *credit* is usually to the *allowance* account. If the direct write-off method is used, the credit is to a *revenue account.*

**bailout period.** In a *capital budgeting* context, the total time that must elapse before net accumulated cash inflows from a project including potential *salvage value* of assets at various times equal or exceed the accumulated cash outflows. Contrast with *payback period,* which assumes completion of the project and uses terminal salvage value. Bailout is superior to payback because bailout takes into account, at least to some degree, the *present value* of the cash flows after the termination date being considered. The potential salvage value at any time includes some estimate of the flows that can occur after that time.

**balance.**   The difference between the sum of *debit* entries minus the sum of *credit* entries in an *account.* If positive, the difference is called a debit balance; if negative, a credit balance.

**balance sheet.**   Statement of financial position which shows *total assets = total liabilities + owners' equity.*

**balance sheet account.**   An account that can appear on a balance sheet. A *permanent account;* contrast with *temporary account.*

**bank balance.**   The amount of the balance in a checking account shown on the *bank statement.* Compare with *adjusted bank balance* and see *bank reconciliation schedule.*

**bank prime rate.**   See *prime rate.*

**bank reconciliation schedule.**   A schedule that shows how the difference between the book balance of the cash in bank account and the bank's statement can be explained. Takes into account the amount of such items as checks issued that have not cleared or deposits that have not been recorded by the bank as well as errors made by the bank or the firm.

**bankrupt.**   Said of a company whose *liabilities* exceed its *assets* where a legal petition has been filed and accepted under the bankruptcy law. A bankrupt firm is usually, but need not be, *insolvent.*

**bank statement.**   A statement sent by the bank to a checking account customer showing deposits, checks cleared, and service charges for a period, usually one month.

**base stock method.**   A method of inventory valuation that assumes that there is a minimum normal or base stock of goods that must be kept on hand at all times for effective continuity of operations. This base quantity is valued at *acquisition cost* of the earliest period. The method is not allowable for income tax purposes and is no longer used, but is generally considered to be the forerunner of the *LIFO* method.

**basis.**   *Acquisition cost,* or some substitute therefor, of an asset used in computing gain or loss on disposition or retirement.

**basket purchase.**   Purchase of a group of assets for a single price; *costs* must be assigned to each of the assets so that the individual items can be recorded in the *accounts.*

**bear.**   One who believes that security prices will fall. A "bear market" refers to a time when stock prices are generally declining. Contrast with *bull.*

**bearer bond.**   See *registered bond* for contrast and definition.

**beginning inventory.**   Valuation of *inventory* on hand at the beginning of the accounting period.

**betterment.**   An *improvement,* usually *capitalized.*

**bid.**   An offer to purchase, or the amount of the offer.

**big bath.**   A *write off* of a substantial amount of costs previously treated as *assets.* Usually caused when a corporation drops a line of business that required a large investment but that proved to be unprofitable. Sometimes used to describe a situation where a cor-

poration takes a large write off in one period in order to free later periods of gradual write offs of those amounts. In this sense it frequently occurs when there is a change in top management.

**Big Eight.**   The eight largest *public accounting (CPA)* partnerships; in alphabetical order: Arthur Andersen & Co.; Coopers & Lybrand; Ernst & Ernst; Haskins & Sells; Peat, Marwick, Mitchell & Co.; Price Waterhouse & Co.; Touche Ross & Co.; and Arthur Young & Company.

**bill.**   An *invoice* of charges and *terms of sale* for *goods and services.* Also, a piece of currency.

**bill of materials.**   A specification of the quantities of *direct materials* expected to be used to produce a given job or quantity of output.

**board of directors.**   The governing body of a corporation elected by the stockholders.

**bond.**   A certificate to show evidence of debt. The *par value* is the *principal* or face amount of the bond payable at maturity. The *coupon rate* is the amount of interest payable in one year divided by the principal amount. Coupon bonds have attached to them coupons which can be redeemed at stated dates for interest payments. Normally, bonds are issued in $1,000 units and carry semiannual coupons.

**bond conversion.**   The act of exchanging *convertible bonds* for *preferred* or *common stock.*

**bond discount.**   From the standpoint of the issuer of a *bond* at the issue date, the excess of the *par value* of a bond over its initial sales price; at later dates the excess of par over the sum of (initial issue price plus the portion of discount already amortized). From the standpoint of a bondholder, the difference between par value and selling price when the bond sells below par.

**bond indenture.**   The contract between an issuer of *bonds* and the bondholders.

**bond premium.**   Exactly parallel to *bond discount* except that the issue price (or current selling price) is higher than *par value.*

**bond ratings.**   Ratings of corporate and *municipal bond* issues by Moody's Investors Service and by Standard & Poor's Corporation, based on the issuer's existing *debt* level, its previous record of payment, the *coupon rate* on the bonds, and the safety of the *assets* or *revenues* that are committed to paying off *principal* and *interest.* Moody's top rating is Aaa; Standard & Poor's is AAA.

**bond redemption.**   Retirement of *bonds.*

**bond refunding.**   To incur *debt,* usually through the issue of new *bonds,* intending to use the proceeds to retire an *outstanding* bond *issue.*

**bond sinking fund.**   See *sinking fund.*

**bond table.**   A table showing the current price of a *bond* as a function of the *coupon rate,* years to *maturity* and effective *yield to maturity* (or *effective rate*).

**bonus.**   Premium over normal *wage* or *salary,* paid usually for meritorious performance.

**bonus method.**   When a new partner is admitted to a *partnership* and the new partner is to be credited with *capital* in excess proportion to the amount of *tangible* assets he or she contributes, two methods may be used to recognize this excess, say $10,000. First, $10,000 may be transferred from the old partners to the new one. This is the bonus method. Second, goodwill in the amount of $10,000 may be recognized as an asset with the credit to the new partner's capital account. This is the *goodwill method*. (Notice that the new partner's percentage of total ownership is *not* the same under the two methods.) If the new partner is to be credited with capital in smaller proportion than the amount of contribution, then there will be bonus or goodwill for the old partners.

**book.** As a verb, to record a transaction. As a noun, usually plural, the *journals* and *ledgers*. As an adjective, see *book value*.

**book inventory.** An *inventory* amount that results, not from physical count, but from amount of initial inventory plus *invoice* amounts of purchases less invoice amounts of *requisitions* or withdrawals; implies a *perpetual method*.

**bookkeeping.** The process of analyzing and recording transactions in the accounting records.

**book of original entry.** A *journal*.

**book value.** The amount shown in the books or in the *accounts* for any *asset, liability,* or *owners' equity* item. Generally used to refer to the net amount of an *asset* or group of assets shown in the accounts which record the asset and reductions, such as for *amortization,* in its cost. Of a firm, the excess of total assets over total liabilities.

**book value per share of common stock.** Common *stockholders' equity* divided by the number of shares of *common stock outstanding*. See *ratio*.

**boot.** The additional money paid or received along with a used item in a trade-in or exchange transaction for another item. See *trade-in transaction*.

**borrower.** See *loan*.

**branch.** A sales office or other unit of an enterprise physically separated from the home office of the enterprise but not organized as a legally separate *subsidiary*. The term is rarely used to refer to manufacturing units.

**branch accounting.** An accounting procedure which enables the financial position and operations of each *branch* to be reported separately but later combined for published statements.

**breakeven analysis.** See *breakeven chart*.

**breakeven chart.** Two kinds of breakeven charts are shown on this page. The charts are based on the information for a month shown below. Revenue is $30 per unit.

| Cost Classification | Variable Cost, Per Unit | Fixed Cost, Per Month |
|---|---|---|
| Manufacturing costs: | | |
| Direct material ............... | $ 4 | — |
| Direct labor .................. | 9 | — |
| Overhead .................... | 4 | $3,060 |
| Total manufacturing costs... | $17 | $3,060 |
| Selling, general, and administrative costs ...... | 5 | 1,740 |
| Total costs................. | $22 | $4,800 |

The cost-volume-profit graph presents the relationship of changes in volume to the amount of *profit*, or *income*. On such a graph, total-*revenue* and total *costs* for each volume level are indicated and profit or loss at any volume can be read directly from the chart. The profit volume graph does not show

revenues and costs but more readily indicates profit (or loss) at various output levels.

Two caveats should be kept in mind about these graphs. Although the curve depicting *variable cost* and total cost is shown as being a straight line for its entire length, it is likely that at very low or very high levels of output, variable cost would probably be different from $22 per unit. The variable-cost figure was probably established by studies of operations at some broad central area of production, called the *relevant range*. For very low (or very high) levels of activity, the chart may not be applicable. For this reason, the total-cost and profit-loss curves are sometimes shown as dotted lines at lower (or higher) volume levels. Second, this chart is simplified because it assumes a single-product firm. For a multi-product firm, the horizontal axis would have to be stated in dollars rather than in physical units of output. Breakeven charts for multi-product firms necessarily assume that constant proportions of the several products are sold and changes in this mixture as well as in costs or selling prices would invalidate such a chart.

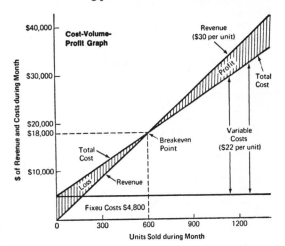

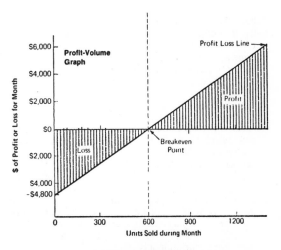

**BREAKEVEN CHARTS**
**Cost-Volume-Profit and Profit-Volume Graphs**

**breakeven point.** The volume of sales required so that total *revenues* and total *costs* are equal. May be expressed in units (*fixed costs/contribution per unit*) or in sales dollars [selling price per unit × (fixed costs/contribution per unit)]. See example at *breakeven chart*.

**budget.** A financial plan that is used to estimate the results of future operations. Frequently used to help control future operations.

**budgetary accounts.** In governmental accounting, the accounts that reflect estimated operations and financial condition, as affected by estimated *revenues, appropriations,* and *encumbrances. Proprietary accounts* record the transactions.

**budgetary control.** Management of governmental (nongovernmental) unit in accordance with an official (approved) *budget* in order to keep total expenditures within authorized (planned) limits.

**budgeted statements.** *Pro forma* statements prepared before the event or period occurs.

**bull.** One who believes that security prices will rise. A "bull market" refers to a time when stock prices are generally rising. Contrast with *bear*.

**burden.** See *overhead costs*.

**business combination.** As defined by the *APB* in Opinion No. 16, the bringing together into a single accounting *entity* of two or more incorporated or unincorporated businesses. The *merger* will be accounted for either with the *purchase method* or the *pooling of interests method*. See *conglomerate*.

**business entity.** *Entity. Accounting entity*.

**bylaws.** The rules adopted by the stockholders of a corporation that specify the general methods for carrying out the functions of the corporation.

**byproduct.** A *joint product* whose value is so small relative to the value of the other joint product(s) that it does not receive normal accounting treatment. The costs assigned to byproducts reduce the costs of the main product(s). Byproducts are allocated a share of joint costs such that the expected gain or loss upon their sale is zero. Thus, byproducts are shown in the *accounts* at *net realizable value*.

## C

**CA.** *Chartered Accountant*.

**callable bond.** A *bond* for which the issuer reserves the right to pay a specific amount, the call price, to retire the obligation before *maturity* date. If the issuer agrees to pay more than the *face amount* of the bond when called, the excess of the payment over the face amount is the call premium.

**call premium.** See *callable bond*.

**call price.** See *callable bond*.

**Canadian Institute of Chartered Accountants.** The national organization that represents *Chartered Accountants* in Canada.

**cancelable lease.** See *lease*.

**capacity.** Stated in units of product, the amount that can be produced per unit of time. Stated in units of input, such as *direct labor* hours, the amount of input that can be used in production per unit of time. This measure of output or input is used in allocating *fixed costs* if the amounts producible are normal, rather than maximum, amounts.

**capacity costs.** A *fixed cost* incurred to provide a firm with the capability to produce or to sell. Consists of *standby costs* and *enabling costs*. Contrast with *programmed costs*.

**capacity variance.** Standard fixed *overhead* rate per unit of normal *capacity* (or base activity) times (units of base activity budgeted or planned for a period minus actual units of base activity worked during the period). Often called a "volume variance."

**capital.** *Owners' equity* in a business. Often used, equally correctly, to mean the total assets of a business. Sometimes used to mean *capital assets*.

**capital asset.** Properly used, a designation for income tax purposes which describes property held by a taxpayer, except *cash*, inventoriable *assets*, goods held primarily for sale, most depreciable property, *real estate, receivables,* certain *intangibles,* and a few other items. Sometimes this term is imprecisely used to describe *plant* and *equipment*, which are clearly not capital assets under the income tax definition. Often the term is used to refer to an *investment* in *securities*.

**capital budget.** Plan of proposed outlays for acquiring long-term *assets* and the means of *financing* the acquisition.

**capital budgeting.** The process of choosing *investment* projects for an enterprise by considering the *present value* of cash flows and deciding how to raise the funds required by the investment.

**capital consumption allowance.** The term used for *depreciation expense* in national income accounting and the reporting of flows of funds in the economy.

**capital contributed in excess of par (or stated) value.** A preferred title for the account that shows the amount received by the issuer for *capital stock* in excess of *par* (or *stated*) *value*.

**capital expenditure (outlay).** An *expenditure* to acquire long-term *assets*.

**capital gain.** The excess of proceeds over *cost*, or other *basis*, from the sale of a *capital asset* as defined by the Internal Revenue Code. If the capital asset is held more than nine months before sale, then the tax on the gain is computed at a rate lower than is used for other gains and ordinary income.

**capitalization of a corporation.** A term used by investment analysts to indicate *stockholders' equity* plus *bonds outstanding*.

**capitalization of earnings.** The process of estimating the economic worth of a firm by computing the *net present value* of the predicted *net income* (not *cash flows*) of the firm for the future.

**capitalization rate.** An *interest rate* used to convert a series of payments or receipts or earnings into a single *present value*.

**capitalize.** To record an *expenditure* that may benefit a future period as an *asset* rather than to treat the expenditure as an *expense* of the period of its occurrence. Whether or not expenditures for advertising or for research and development should be capitalized is controversial, but *FASB Statement* No. 2 requires expensing of *R & D* costs. We believe expenditures should be capitalized if they lead to future benefits and thus meet the criterion to be an asset.

**capital lease.** See *financing lease*.

**capital loss.** A negative capital gain; see *capital gain*.

**capital rationing.** In a *capital budgeting* context, the imposing of constraints on the amounts of total capital expenditures in each period.

**capital stock.** The ownership shares of a corporation.

Consists of all classes of *common* and *preferred stock.*

**capital structure.** The composition of a corporation's equities; the relative proportions of *short-term debt, long-term debt,* and *owners' equity.*

**capital surplus.** An inferior term for *capital contributed in excess of par (or stated) value.*

**carryback, carryforward, carryover.** The use of losses or tax credits in one period to reduce income taxes payable in other periods. There are three common kinds of carrybacks: for net operating losses, for *capital losses,* and for the *investment tax credit.* The first two are applied against taxable income and the third against the actual tax. In general, carrybacks are for three years with the earliest year first. Operating losses, the investment tax credit, and the capital loss for corporations, can generally be carried forward for five years. The capital loss for individuals can be carried forward indefinitely.

**carrying cost.** Costs (such as property taxes and insurance) of holding, or storing, *inventory* from the time of purchase until the time of sale.

**carrying value (amount).** *Book value.*

**CASB.** Cost Accounting Standards Board. A board of five members authorized by the U.S. Congress to "promulgate cost-accounting standards designed to achieve uniformity and consistency in the cost-accounting principles followed by defense contractors and subcontractors under federal contracts." The *principles* promulgated by the CASB are likely to have considerable weight in practice where the *FASB* has not established a standard.

**cash.** Currency and coins, negotiable checks, and balances in bank accounts.

**cash basis of accounting.** In contrast to the *accrual basis of accounting,* a system of accounting in which *revenues* are recognized when *cash* is received and *expenses* are recognized as *disbursements* are made. No attempt is made to *match revenues* and *expenses* in determining *income.* See *modified cash basis.*

**cash budget.** A schedule of expected cash *receipts* and *disbursements.*

**cash collection basis.** The *installment method* for recognizing *revenue.* Not to be confused with the *cash basis of accounting.*

**cash cycle.** The period of time that elapses during which *cash* is converted into *inventories,* inventories are converted into *accounts receivable,* and receivables are converted back into cash. *Earnings cycle.*

**cash disbursements journal.** A specialized *journal* used to record *expenditures* by *cash* and by *check.* If a *check register* is also used, a cash disbursements journal records only expenditures of currency and coins.

**cash discount.** A reduction in sales or purchase price allowed for prompt payment.

**cash dividend.** See *dividend.*

**cash equivalent value.** A term used to describe the amount for which an *asset* could be sold. *Market value. Fair market price (value).*

**cash flow.** Cash *receipts* minus *disbursements* from a given *asset,* or group of assets, for a given period.

**cash flow statement.** A statement similar to the typical *statement of changes in financial position* where the flows of cash, rather than of *working capital,* are explained.

**cashier's check.** A bank's own *check* drawn on itself and signed by the cashier or other authorized official. It is a direct obligation of the bank. Compare with *certified check.*

**cash receipts journal.** A specialized *journal* used to record all *receipts* of *cash.*

**cash (surrender) value of life insurance.** An amount equal, not to the face value of the policy to be paid in event of death, but to the amount that could be realized if the policy were immediately canceled and traded with the insurance company for cash.

**cash yield.** See *yield.*

**central corporate expenses.** General *overhead expenses* incurred in running the corporate headquarters and related supporting activities of a corporation. These expenses are treated as *period expenses.* Contrast with *manufacturing overhead.* A major problem in *line-of-business reporting* is the treatment of these expenses.

**certificate.** The document that is the physical embodiment of a *bond* or a *share of stock.* A term sometimes used for the *auditor's report.*

**certificate of deposit.** Federal law constrains the *rate of interest* that banks can pay. Under current law banks are allowed to pay a higher rate than the one allowed on a *time deposit* if the depositor promises to leave funds on deposit for several months or more. When the bank receives such funds, it issues a certificate of deposit. The depositor can withdraw the funds before maturity if a penalty is paid.

**certified check.** The *check* of a depositor drawn on a bank on the face of which the bank has inserted the words "accepted" or "certified" with the date and signature of a bank official. The check then becomes an obligation of the bank. Compare with *cashier's check.*

**certified financial statement.** A financial statement attested to by an independent *auditor* who is a *CPA.*

**certified internal auditor.** See *CIA.*

**certified public accountant (CPA).** An accountant who has satisfied the statutory and administrative requirements of his or her jurisdiction to be registered or licensed as a public accountant. In addition to passing the Uniform CPA Examination administered by the *AICPA,* the CPA must meet certain educational, experience, and moral requirements that differ from jurisdiction to jurisdiction. The jurisdictions are the fifty states, the District of Columbia, Guam, Puerto Rico, and the Virgin Islands.

**chain discount.** A series of *discount* percentages; for example, if a chain discount of 10 and 5 percent is quoted, then the actual, or *invoice,* price is the nominal, or list, price times .90 times .95, or 85.5% of invoice price.

**change fund.** Coins and currency issued to cashiers, delivery drivers, and so on.

**changes, accounting.** See *accounting changes.*

**changes in financial position.** See *statement of changes in financial position.*

**charge.** As a noun, a *debit* to an account; as a verb, to debit.

**charge off.** To treat as a *loss* or *expense* an amount originally recorded as an *asset;* usually the term is used when the charge is not in accord with original expectations.

**charter.** Document issued by a state government authorizing the creation of a corporation.

**chartered accountant (CA).** The title used in Australia, Canada, and the United Kingdom for an accountant who has satisfied the requirements of the institute of his or her jurisdiction to be qualified to serve as a *public accountant*. In Canada, each provincial institute or order has the right to administer the examination and set the standards of performance and ethics for Chartered Accountants in its province. For a number of years, however, the provincial organizations have pooled their rights to qualify new members through the Inter-provincial Education Committee and the result is that there are nationally-set and graded examinations given in English and French. The pass/fail grade awarded by the Board of Examiners (a subcommittee of the Inter-provincial Education Committee) is rarely deviated from.

**chart of accounts.** A list of names and numbers of *accounts* systematically organized.

**check.** You know what a check is. The Federal Reserve Board defines a check as "a *draft* or order upon a bank or banking house purporting to be drawn upon a deposit of funds for the payment at all events of a certain sum of money to a certain person therein named or to him or his order or to bearer and payable instantly on demand." It must contain the phrase "pay to the order of." The amount shown on the check's face must be clearly readable and it must have the signature of the drawer. Checks need not be dated, although they usually are. The *balance* in the *cash account* is usually reduced when a check is issued, not later when it clears the bank and reduces cash in bank.

**check register.** A *journal* to record *checks* issued.

**CIA.** Certified Internal Auditor. One who has satisfied certain requirements of the *Institute of Internal Auditors* including experience, ethics, education, and examinations.

**CICA.** *Canadian Institute of Chartered Accountants*.

**CIF.** A term used in contracts along with the name of a given port to indicate that the quoted price includes insurance, handling, and freight charges up to delivery by the seller at the given port.

**circulating capital.** *Working capital*.

**clean opinion.** See *auditor's report*.

**clean surplus concept.** The notion that the only entries to the *retained earnings* account are to record net earnings and dividends. Contrast with *current operating performance concept*. This concept, with minor exceptions, is now controlling in *GAAP*. (See *APB Opinions* Nos. 9 and 30.)

**clearing account.** An account containing amounts to be transferred to another account(s) before the end of the *accounting period*. Examples are the *income summary* account (whose balance is transferred to retained earnings) and the purchases account (whose balance is transferred to *inventory* or to *cost of goods sold*).

**close.** As a verb, to transfer the *balance* of a *temporary* or *contra* or *adjunct* account to the main account to which it relates; for example, to transfer *revenue* and *expense* accounts directly, or through the *income summary* account, to an *owner's equity* account, or to transfer *purchase discounts* to purchases.

**closed account.** An account with equal debits and credits, usually as a result of a closing entry. See *ruling an account*.

**closing entries.** The entries that accomplish the transfer of balances in temporary accounts to the related balance sheet accounts. See *worksheet*.

**closing inventory.** *Ending inventory*.

**CMA.** Certificate in Management Accounting. Awarded by the Institute of Management Accounting of the *National Association of Accountants* to those who pass a set of examinations and meet certain experience and continuing education requirements.

**coding of accounts.** The numbering of *accounts*, as for a *chart of accounts*, which is particularly necessary for computerized accounting.

**coinsurance.** Insurance policies that protect against hazards such as fire or water damage often specify that the owner of the property may not collect the full amount of insurance for a loss unless the insurance policy covers at least some specified percentage, usually about 80 percent, of the *replacement cost* of the property. Coinsurance clauses induce the owner to carry full, or nearly-full, coverage.

**collateral.** Assets pledged by a *borrower* that will be given up if the *loan* is not paid.

**collectible.** Capable of being converted into cash; now, if due; later, otherwise.

**commercial paper.** *Short-term notes* issued by corporate borrowers.

**commission.** Remuneration, usually expressed as a percentage, to employees based upon an activity rate, such as sales.

**Committee on Accounting Procedure.** Predecessor of the *APB*. The *AICPA's* principle-promulgating body from 1939 through 1959. Its fifty-one pronouncements are called *Accounting Research Bulletins*.

**common cost.** *Cost* resulting from use of *raw materials*, a facility (for example, plant or machines) or a service (for example, fire insurance) that benefits several products or departments and must be allocated to those products or departments. Common costs result when multiple products are produced together although they could be produced separately; joint costs occur when multiple products are of necessity produced together. Many writers use common costs and *joint costs* synonymously. See *joint costs*, *indirect costs*, and *overhead*.

**common-dollar accounting.** General *price level adjusted* accounting.

**common monetary measuring unit.** For U.S. corporations, the dollar. See also *stable monetary unit assumption*.

**common-size statement.** A *percentage statement* usually based on total *assets* or *net sales* or *revenues*.

**common stock.** *Stock* representing the class of owners who have residual claims on the assets and earnings of a corporation after all debt and preferred stockholders' claims have been met.

**common stock equivalent.** A *security* whose primary value arises from its ability to be exchanged for *common shares;* includes *stock options, warrants*, and also *convertible bonds* or *convertible preferred stock* whose cash *yield* for any year within five years of issue is less than two-thirds the *prime rate* at the time of issue.

**company-wide control.** See *control system*.

**comparative (financial) statements.** Financial statements showing information for the same company for different times, usually two successive years. Nearly all published financial statements are in this form. See the General Electric annual report. Contrast with *historial summary*.

**compensating balance.** When a bank lends funds to a customer, it often requires that the customer keep on deposit in his or her checking account an amount equal to some percentage, say 20 percent, of the loan. The amount required to be left on deposit is the compensating balance. Such amounts effectively increase the *interest rate*. The amounts of such balances must be disclosed in *notes* to the *financial statements*.

**completed contract method.** Recognizing *revenues* and *expenses* for a job or order only when it is finished, except that when a loss on the contract is expected, revenues and expenses are recognized in the period when the loss is first forecast.

**completed sales basis.** See *sales basis of revenue recognition*.

**composite depreciation.** *Group depreciation* of dissimilar items.

**composite life method.** *Group depreciation*, which see, for items of unlike kind. The term may be used when a single item, such as a crane, which consists of separate units with differing service lives, such as the chassis, the motor, the lifting mechanism, and so on, is depreciated as a whole rather than treating each of the components separately.

**compound entry.** A *journal entry* with more than one *debit* or more than one *credit*, or both. See *trade-in transaction* for an example.

**compounding period.** The time period for which *interest* is calculated. At the end of the period, the interest may be paid to the lender or added (that is, converted) to principal for the next interest-earning period, which is usually a year or some portion of a year.

**compound interest.** *Interest* calculated on *principal* plus previously undistributed interest.

**compound interest depreciation.** A method designed to hold the *rate of return* on an asset constant. First find the *internal rate of return* on the cash inflows and outflows of the asset. The periodic depreciation charge is the cash flow for the period less the internal rate of return multiplied by the asset's book value at the beginning of the period. When the cash flows from the asset are constant over time, the method is sometimes called the "annuity method" of depreciation.

**comprehensive budget.** *Master budget.*

**comptroller.** Same meaning and pronunciation as *controller*.

**confirmation.** A formal memorandum delivered by the customers or suppliers of a company to its independent *auditor* verifying the amounts shown as receivable or payable. The confirmation document is originally sent by the auditor to the customer. If the auditor asks that the document be returned whether the *balance* is correct or incorrect, then it is called a "positive confirmation." If the auditor asks that the document be returned only if there is an error, it is called a "negative confirmation."

**conglomerate.** *Holding company.* This term is used when the owned companies are in dissimilar lines of business.

**conservatism.** A *reporting objective* that calls for anticipation of all *losses* and *expenses* but defers recognition of *gains* or *profits* until they are *realized*. In the absence of certainty, events are to be reported in a way that tends to minimize current income.

**consignee.** See *on consignment*.

**consignment.** See *on consignment*.

**consignor.** See *on consignment*.

**consistency.** Treatment of like *transactions* in the same way in consecutive periods so that financial statements will be more comparable than otherwise. The reporting policy implying that procedures, once adopted, should be followed from period to period by a reporting *entity*. See *accounting changes* for the treatment of inconsistencies.

**consol.** A *bond* that never matures; a *perpetuity* in the form of a bond. Originally issued by Britain after the Napoleonic wars to consolidate debt issues of that period. The term arose as an abbreviation for "consolidated annuities."

**consolidated financial statements.** Statements issued by legally separate companies that show financial position and income as they would appear if the companies were one legal *entity*. Such statements reflect an economic, rather than a legal, concept of the *entity*.

**constructive receipt.** An item is included in taxable income when the taxpayer can control funds whether or not cash has been received. For example, *interest* added to *principal* in a savings account is deemed to be constructively received.

**consumer price index (CPI).** A *price index* computed and issued monthly by the Bureau of Labor Statistics of the U.S. Department of Labor. The index attempts to track the price level of a group of goods and services purchased by the average consumer. Contrast with *GNP Implicit Price Deflator*.

**contingent annuity.** An *annuity* whose number of payments depends upon the outcome of an event whose timing is uncertain at the time the annuity is set up; for example, an annuity payable for the life of the *annuitant*. Contrast with *annuity certain*.

**contingent issue (securities).** Securities issuable to specific individuals upon the occurrence of some event, such as the firm's attaining a specified level of earnings.

**contingent liability.** A potential *liability;* if a specified event were to occur, such as losing a lawsuit, a liability would be recognized. Until the outcome is known, the contingency is merely disclosed in notes rather than shown in the balance sheet accounts. A *material* contingency may lead to a qualified, "*subject to,*" auditor's opinion.

**continuing appropriation.** A governmental *appropriation* automatically renewed without further legislative action until it is altered or revoked or expended.

**continuing operations.** See *income from continuing operations*.

**continuity of operations.** The assumption in accounting that the business *entity* will continue to operate long enough for current plans to be carried out. The *going-concern assumption*.

**continuous compounding.** *Compound interest* where the *compounding period* is every instant of time. See *e* for the computation of the equivalent annual or periodic rate.

**continuous inventory method.** The *perpetual inventory* method.

**contra account.** An *account*, such as *accumulated depreciation*, that accumulates subtractions from another account, such as machinery. Contrast with *adjunct account*.

**contributed capital.** The sum of the balances in *capi-*

*tal stock* accounts plus *capital contributed in excess of par (or stated) value* accounts. Contrast with *donated capital*.

**contributed surplus.** An inferior term for *capital contributed in excess of par value*.

**contribution margin.** *Revenue* from *sales* less all variable *expenses*. See *gross margin*.

**contribution per unit.** Selling price less *variable costs* per unit.

**contributory.** Said of a *pension plan* where employees, as well as employers, make payments to a pension *fund*. Note that the provisions for *vesting* are applicable to the employer's payments. Whatever the degree of vesting of the employer's payments, the employee typically gets back his or her payments, with interest, in case of death, or other cessation of employment, before retirement.

**control (controlling) account.** A summary *account* with totals equal to those of entries and balances that appear in individual accounts in a *subsidiary ledger*. Accounts Receivable is a control account backed up with accounts for each customer. The balance in a control account should not be changed unless a corresponding change is made in the subsidiary accounts.

**control system.** A device for ensuring that actions are carried out according to plan or for safeguarding *assets*. A system for ensuring that actions are carried out according to plan can be designed for a single function with the firm, called "operational control," for autonomous segments within the firm which generally have responsibility for both revenues and costs, called "divisional control," or for activities of the firm as a whole, is called "company-wide control." Systems designed for safeguarding *assets* are called "internal control" systems.

**controllable cost.** A *cost* whose amount can be influenced by the way in which operations are carried out, such as advertising costs. These costs can be *fixed* or *variable*.

**controlled company.** A company, a majority of whose voting stock is held by an individual or corporation. Effective control can sometimes be exercised when less than 50 percent of the stock is owned.

**controller.** The title often used for the chief accountant of an organization. Often spelled *comptroller*.

**conversion.** The act of exchanging a convertible security for another security.

**conversion cost.** *Direct labor* costs plus factory *overhead* costs incurred in producing a product. That is, the cost to convert raw materials to finished products. *Manufacturing cost*.

**conversion period.** *Compounding period*. Period during which a *convertible bond* or *preferred stock* can be converted into *common stock*.

**convertible bond.** A *bond* that may be converted into a specified number of shares of *capital stock* during the *conversion period*.

**convertible preferred stock.** *Preferred stock* that may be converted into a specified number of shares of *common stock*.

**copyright.** Exclusive right granted by the government to an individual author, composer, playright and the like for twenty-eight years (renewable for another twenty-eight years) to enjoy the benefit of a piece of written work. Commencing January 1, 1978, copyrights extend for the life of the individual plus 50

years. If the copyright is granted to a firm, then the right extends 75 years after the original publication. The *economic life* of a copyright may be considerably less than the legal life as, for example, the copyright of this book.

**corporation.** A legal entity authorized by a state to operate under the rules of the entity's *charter*.

**correction of errors.** See *accounting errors*.

**cost.** The sacrifice, measured by the *price* paid or required to be paid, to acquire *goods* or *services*. See *acquisition cost* and *replacement cost*. The term "cost" is often used when referring to the valuation of a good or service acquired. When "cost" is used in this sense, a cost is an *asset*. When the benefits of the acquisition (the goods or services acquired) expire, the cost becomes an expense or *loss*. Some writers, however, use cost and expense as synonyms. Contrast with *expense*.

**cost accounting.** Classifying, summarizing, recording, reporting, and allocating current or predicted *costs*. A subset of *managerial accounting*.

**Cost Accounting Standards Board.** See *CASB*.

**cost center.** A unit of activity for which *expenditures* and *expenses* are accumulated.

**cost effective.** Among alternatives, the one whose benefit, or payoff, divided by cost is highest. Sometimes said of an action whose expected benefits exceed expected costs whether or not there are other alternatives with larger benefit/cost ratios.

**cost flow assumption.** See *flow assumption*.

**cost flows.** Costs passing through various classifications within an entry. See *flow of costs* for a diagram.

**costing.** The process of determining the cost of activities, products, or services. The British word for *cost accounting*.

**cost method (for investments).** Accounting for an investment in the *capital stock* of another company where the investment is shown at *acquisition cost*, and only *dividends* declared are treated as *revenue*. Used if less than twenty percent of the voting stock is held by the investor.

**cost method (for treasury stock).** The method of showing *treasury stock* as a *contra* to all other items of *stockholders' equity* in an amount equal to that paid to reacquire the stock.

**cost of capital.** The average rate per year a company must pay for its *equities*. In efficient capital markets, the *discount rate* that equates the expected *present value* of all future cash flows to common stockholders with the market value of common stock at a given time.

**cost of goods manufactured.** The sum of all costs allocated to products completed during a period; includes materials, labor, and *overhead*.

**cost of goods purchased.** Net purchase price of goods acquired plus costs of storage and delivery to the place where the items can be productively used.

**cost of goods sold.** Inventoriable *costs* that are expensed because the units are sold; equals beginning inventory plus cost of goods purchased or manufactured minus ending inventory.

**cost of sales.** Generally refers to *cost of goods sold;* occasionally, to *selling expenses*.

**cost or market, whichever is lower.** See *lower of cost or market*.

**cost principle.** The *principle* that requires reporting

*assets* at *historical* or *acquisition cost,* less accumulated *amortization.* This principle is based on the assumption that cost is equal to *fair market value* at the date of acquisition and subsequent changes are not likely to be significant.

**cost-recovery method.** A method of *revenue* recognition that *credits cost* as collections are received until all costs are recovered. Only after costs are completely recovered is *income* recognized. To be used only when the total amount of collections is highly uncertain. Contrast with the *installment method* where *pro rata* portions of all collections are credited both to cost and to income.

**cost sheet.** Statement that shows all the elements comprising the total cost of an item.

**cost-to-cost.** The *percentage of completion method* where the estimate of completion is the ratio of costs incurred to date divided by total costs expected to be incurred for the entire project.

**cost-volume-profit graph (chart).** A graph that shows the relation between *fixed costs, contribution per unit, breakeven point* and *sales.* See *breakeven chart.*

**coupon.** That portion of a *bond* document redeemable at a specified date for *interest* payments. Its physical form is much like a ticket; each coupon is dated and is deposited at a bank, just like a check, for collection or is mailed to the issuer's agent for collection.

**coupon rate.** Of a *bond,* the amount of annual coupons divided by par value. Contrast with *effective rate.*

**covenant.** A promise with legal validity.

**CPA.** See *certified public accountant.* The *AICPA* suggests no periods be shown in the abbreviation.

**CPI.** *Consumer price index.*

**cr.** Abbreviation for *credit.*

**credit.** As a noun, an entry on the right-hand side of an *account.* As a verb, to make an entry on the right-hand side of an account. Records increases in *liabilities, owners' equity, revenues* and *gains;* records decreases in *assets* and *expenses.* See *debit and credit conventions.* Also the ability or right to buy or borrow in return for a promise to pay later.

**credit loss.** The amount of *accounts receivable* that is, or is expected to become, *uncollectible.*

**credit memorandum.** A document used by a seller to inform a buyer that the buyer's *account receivable* is being credited (reduced) because of *errors, returns,* or *allowances.* Also, the document provided by a bank to a depositor to indicate that the depositor's balance is being increased because of some event other than a deposit, such as the collection by the bank of the depositor's *note receivable.*

**creditor.** One who lends.

**cross-reference (index).** A number placed by each *account* in a *journal entry* indicating the *ledger* account to which the entry is posted and placing in the ledger the page number of the journal where the entry was made. Used to link the *debit* and *credit* parts of an entry in the ledger accounts back to the original entry in the journal. See *audit trail.*

**cross section analysis.** Analysis of *financial statements* of various firms for a single period of time, as opposed to time series analysis where statements of a given firm are analyzed over several periods of time.

**cumulative dividend.** Preferred stock *dividends* that if not paid, accrue as a commitment which must be paid before dividends to common stockholders can be declared.

**cumulative preferred stock.** *Preferred* stock with *cumulative dividend* rights.

**current asset.** *Cash* and other *assets* that are expected to be turned into cash, sold, or exchanged within the normal operating cycle of the firm, usually one year. Current assets include *cash, marketable securities, receivables, inventory,* and *current prepayments.*

**current cost.** *Cost* stated in terms of current market prices rather than in terms of *acquisition cost. Current replacement cost.* See *net realizable value, current selling price.*

**current fund.** In governmental accounting, a synonym for *general fund.*

**current funds.** *Cash* and other assets readily convertible into cash. In governmental accounting, funds spent for operating purposes during the current period. Includes *general, special revenue, debt service,* and enterprise funds.

**current (gross) margin.** See *operating margin (based on replacement costs).*

**current liability.** A debt or other obligation that must be discharged within a short time, usually the *earnings cycle* or one year, normally by expending *current assets.*

**current operating performance concept.** The notion that reported *income* for a period ought to reflect only ordinary, normal, and recurring operations of that period. A consequence is that *extraordinary* and nonrecurring items are entered directly in the Retained Earnings account. Contrast with *clean surplus concept.* This concept is no longer acceptable. (See *APB Opinions* Nos. 9 and 30.)

**current ratio.** Sum of *current assets* divided by sum of *current liabilities.* See *ratio.*

**current replacement cost.** Of an *asset,* the amount currently required to acquire an identical asset (in the same condition and with the same service potential) or an asset capable of rendering the same service at a current *fair market price.* If these two amounts differ, the lower is usually used. See *reproduction cost.*

**current selling price.** The amount for which an *asset* could be sold as of a given time in an *arm's length* transaction, rather than in a forced sale.

**current value accounting.** The form of accounting where all assets are shown at *current replacement cost (entry value)* or *current selling price* or *net realizable value (exit value)* and all *liabilities* are shown at *present value.* Entry and exit values may be quite different from each other so there is no general agreement on the precise meaning of current value accounting.

**currently attainable standard cost.** *Normal standard cost.*

**customers' ledger.** The *ledger* that shows accounts receivable of individual customers. It is the *subsidiary ledger* for the *controlling account,* Accounts Receivable.

# D

**days of average inventory on hand.** See *ratio.*

**DDB.** *Double-declining-balance depreciation.*

**debenture bond.** A *bond* not secured with *collateral.*

**debit.** As a noun, an entry on the left-hand side of an *account.* As a verb, to make an entry on the left-hand side of an account. Records increases in *assets* and *expenses;* records decreases in *liabilities, owners' equity,* and *revenues.* See *debit and credit conventions.*

**debit and credit conventions.** The equality of the two sides of the *accounting equation* is maintained by recording equal amounts of *debits* and *credits* for each *transaction.* The conventional use of the *T-account* form and the rules for debit and credit in *balance sheet accounts* are summarized as follows.

### Any Asset Account

| Opening Balance Increase | Decrease |
|---|---|
| + | - |
| Dr. | Cr. |
| Ending Balance | |

### Any Liability Account

| | Opening Balance Increase |
|---|---|
| Decrease | + |
| - | Cr. |
| Dr. | Ending Balance |

### Any Owners' Equity Account

| | Opening Balance Increase |
|---|---|
| Decrease | + |
| - | Cr. |
| Dr. | Ending Balance |

Revenue and expense accounts belong to the owners' equity group. The relationship and the rules for debit and credit in these accounts can be expressed as follows.

### Owners' Equity

| Decrease | | Increase | |
|---|---|---|---|
| - | | + | |
| Dr. | | Cr. | |
| **Expenses** | | **Revenues** | |
| Dr. | Cr. | Dr. | Cr. |
| + | - | - | + |
| * | | | * |

*Normal balance prior to closing.

**debit memorandum.** A document used by a seller to inform a buyer that the seller is debiting (increasing) the amount of the buyer's *account receivable* because of an error. Also, the document provided by a bank to a depositor to indicate that the depositor's *balance* is being decreased because of some event other than

payment for a *check,* such as monthly service charges or the printing of checks.

**debt.** An amount owed. The general name for *notes, bonds, mortgages,* and the like which are evidence of amounts owed and have definite payment dates.

**debt-equity ratio.** Total *liabilities* divided by total *equities.* See *ratio.* Sometimes the denominator is merely total *stockholders' equity.* Sometimes the numerator is restricted to long-term *debt.*

**debt financing.** Raising *funds* by issuing *bonds, mortgages,* or *notes.* Contrast with *equity financing. Leverage.*

**debtor.** One who borrows.

**debt ratio.** *Debt-equity ratio.*

**debt service fund.** In governmental accounting, a *fund* established to account for payment of *interest* and *principal* on all general obligation *debt* other than that payable from special *assessments.*

**debt service requirement.** The amount of cash required for payments of *interest,* current maturities of *principal* on outstanding *debt,* and payments to *sinking funds* (corporations) or to the *debt service fund* (governmental).

**declaration date.** Time when a *dividend* is declared by the *board of directors.*

**declining-balance depreciation.** The method of calculating the periodic *depreciation* charge by multiplying the *book value* at the start of the period by a constant percentage. In pure declining balance depreciation the constant percentage is $1 - \sqrt[n]{s/c}$ where n is the *depreciable life,* s is *salvage value,* and c is *acquisition cost.* See *double-declining-balance depreciation.*

**deep discount bonds.** Said of *bonds* selling much below (exactly how much is not clear) *par value.* A term sometimes used when there is a presumption that the *face amount* will not be paid at *maturity.*

**defalcation.** Embezzlement.

**default.** Failure to pay *interest* or *principal* on a *debt* when due.

**deferral method.** See *flow-through method* (of accounting for the *investment tax credit*) for definition and contrast.

**deferred annuity.** An *annuity* whose first payment is made sometime after the end of the first period.

**deferred asset.** *Deferred charge.*

**deferred charge.** *Expenditure* not recognized as an *expense* of the period when made but carried forward as an *asset* to be *written off* in future periods, such as for advance rent payments or insurance premiums.

**deferred cost.** *Deferred charge.*

**deferred credit.** Sometimes used to indicate *advances from customers.* Also sometimes used to describe the *deferred income tax liability.*

**deferred debit.** *Deferred charge.*

**deferred expense.** *Deferred charge.*

**deferred gross margin.** *Unrealized gross margin.*

**deferred income.** *Advances from customers.*

**deferred income tax (liability).** An *indeterminate-term liability* that arises when the pre-tax income shown on the tax return is less than what it would have been had the same *accounting principles* been used in tax returns as used for financial reporting. *APB Opinion* No. 11 requires that the firm debit income tax *expense* and credit deferred income tax with the amount of the taxes delayed by using different accounting principles in tax returns from those used in financial reports. See *timing difference* and *permanent difference*. See *installment sales*. If, as a result of timing differences, cumulative taxable income exceeds cumulative reported income before taxes, the deferred income tax account will have a *debit* balance and will be reported as a *deferred charge*. See the *Accounting Magic* section of this book for an example calculation.

**deferred revenue.** Sometimes used to indicate *advances from customers*.

**deferred tax.** See *deferred income tax*.

**deficit.** A *debit balance* in the Retained Earnings account; presented on the balance sheet as a *contra* to stockholders' equity.

**defined benefit plan.** A *pension plan* where the employer promises specific benefits to each employee. The employer's cash contributions and pension expense are adjusted in relation to investment performance of the pension *fund*. Sometimes called a "fixed-benefit" pension plan. Contrast with *money-purchase plan*.

**defined contribution plan.** A *money-purchase (pension) plan*.

**deflation.** A period of declining general prices.

**demand deposit.** *Funds* in a *checking account* at a bank.

**demand loan.** See *term loan* for definition and contrast.

**denominator volume.** Capacity measured in expected number of units to be produced this period; divided into *budgeted fixed costs* to obtain fixed costs applied per unit of product.

**depletion.** Exhaustion or *amortization* of a *wasting asset*, or natural resource. Also see *percentage depletion*.

**depletion allowance.** See *percentage depletion*.

**deposit, sinking fund.** Payments made to a *sinking fund*.

**deposits in transit.** Deposits made by a firm but not yet reflected on the *bank statement*.

**depreciable cost.** That part of the *cost* of an asset, usually *acquisition cost* less *salvage value*, that is to be charged off over the life of the asset through the process of *depreciation*.

**depreciable life.** For an *asset*, the time period or units of activity (such as miles driven for a truck) over which *depreciable cost* is to be allocated. For tax returns, depreciable life may be shorter than estimated *service life*.

**depreciation.** *Amortization* of *plant assets;* the process of allocating the cost of an asset to the periods of benefit—the *depreciable life*. Classified as a *production cost* or a *period expense*, depending upon the asset and whether *absorption* or *direct costing* is used. Depreciation methods described in this glossary include the *annuity method, appraisal method, composite method, compound interest method, declining-balance method, double-declining-balance method, production method, replacement method, retirement method, straight-line method, sinking-fund method* and *sum-of-the-years'-digits method*.

**depreciation reserve.** An inferior term for *accumu-lated depreciation*. See *reserve*. Do not confuse with a replacement *fund*.

**Descartes' rule of signs.** In a *capital-budgeting* context, the rule says that a series of cash flows will have a non-negative number of *internal rates of return*. The number is equal to the number of variations in the sign of the cash flow series or is less than that number by an even integer. Consider the following series of cash flows, the first occurring now and the others at subsequent yearly intervals: $-100$, $-100$, $+50$, $+175$, $-50$, $+100$. The internal rates of return are the numbers for r that satisfy the equation

$$-100 - 100/(1 + r) + 50/(1 + r)^2 + 175/(1 + r)^3 \\ -50/(1 + r)^4 + 100/(1 + r)^5 = 0.$$

The series of cash flows has three variations in sign: a change from minus to plus, a change from plus to minus, and a change from minus to plus. The rule says that this series must have either three or one internal rates of return; in fact, it has only one, about 12 percent. But also see *reinvestment rate*.

**differential analysis.** Analysis of *incremental costs*.

**differential cost.** *Incremental cost*.

**dilution.** A potential reduction in *earnings per share* or *book value* per share by the potential *conversion* of securities or by the potential exercise of *warrants* or *options*.

**dilutive.** Said of a *security* that would reduce *earnings per share* if it were exchanged for *common stock*.

**dipping into LIFO layers.** See *LIFO inventory layer*.

**direct cost.** Cost of *direct material, direct labor,* and *variable overhead* incurred in producing a product. See *prime cost*.

**direct costing.** The method of allocating costs that assigns only *variable manufacturing costs* to product and treats *fixed manufacturing costs* as *period* expenses. Sometimes called "variable costing."

**direct labor (material) cost.** Cost of labor (material) applied and assigned directly to a product; contrast with *indirect labor (material)*.

**direct posting.** A method of bookkeeping where *entries* are made directly in *ledger accounts*, without the use of a *journal*.

**disbursement.** Payment by *cash* or by a *check*. See *expenditure*.

**DISC.** Domestic International Sales Corporation. A U.S. *corporation*, usually a *subsidiary*, whose *income* is primarily attributable to exports. *Income tax* on 50 percent of a DISC's income is usually deferred for a long period. Generally, this results in a lower overall corporate tax for the *parent* than would otherwise be incurred.

**disclosure.** The showing of facts in *financial statements, notes* thereto, or the *auditor's report*.

**discontinued operations.** See *income from discontinued operations*.

**discount.** In the context of *compound interest, bonds,* and *notes*, the difference between *face* or *future value* and *present value* of a payment. In the context of *sales* and *purchases*, a reduction in price granted for prompt payment. See also *chain discount, quantity discount,* and *trade discount*.

**discounted bailout period.** In a *capital budgeting*

context, the total time that must elapse before discounted value of net accumulated cash flows from a project, including potential *salvage value* at various times of assets, equal or exceed the *present value* of net accumulated cash outflows. Contrast with *discounted payback period*.

**discounted payback period.** Amount of time over which the discounted present value of cash inflows from a project equal the discounted *present value* of the cash outflows.

**discount factor.** The reciprocal of one plus the *discount rate*. If the discount rate is 10 percent per period, the discount factor for three periods is $(1.10)^{-3} = 0.75131$.

**discounting a note.** See *note receivable discounted* and *factoring*.

**discount rate.** *Interest rate* used to convert future payments to *present values*.

**discounts lapsed (lost).** The sum of *discounts* offered for prompt payment that were not taken (or allowed) because of expiration of the discount period. See *terms of sale*.

**discovery value accounting.** In exploration for natural resources, there is the problem of what to do with the expenditures for exploration. Suppose $10 million is spent to drill ten holes ($1 million each) and that nine of them are dry while one is a gusher containing oil with a *net realizable value* of $40 million. Dry-hole, or successful-efforts, accounting would *expense* $9 million and *capitalize* $1 million to be *depleted* as the oil was lifted from the ground. Full costing would expense nothing but capitalize the $10 million of drilling costs to be depleted as the oil is lifted from the single productive well. Discovery value accounting would capitalize $40 million to be depleted as the oil is lifted, with a $30 million *credit* to *income* or *contributed capital*.

**Discussion Memorandum.** A neutral discussion of all the issues concerning an accounting problem of current concern to the *FASB*. The publication of such a document usually implies that the FASB is considering issuing a *Statement of Financial Accounting Standards* on this particular problem. The discussion memorandum brings together material about the particular problem to facilitate interaction and comment by those interested in the matter. It may lead to an *Exposure Draft*.

**dishonored note.** A *promissory note* whose maker does not repay the loan at *maturity* for a *term loan*, or on demand, for a *demand loan*.

**disintermediation.** Federal law regulates the maximum *interest rate* that both banks and savings and loan associations can pay for *time deposits*. When free market interest rates exceed the regulated interest ceiling for such time deposits, some depositors withdraw their funds and invest them elsewhere at a higher interest rate. This process is known as "disintermediation."

**distributable income.** The portion of conventional accounting net income that can be distributed to owners (usually in the form of *dividends*) without impairing the physical capacity of the firm to continue operations at current levels. Pretax distributable income is conventional pretax income less the excess of *replacement cost* of goods sold and *depreciation* charges based on the replacement cost of *productive*

*capacity* over cost of goods sold and depreciation on an *acquisition cost basis*. Since *SEC Accounting Series Release* No. 190 became effective, annual reports of large manufacturing and retailing companies disclose information sufficient for calculation of distributable income. Contrast with *sustainable income*. See *inventory profit*.

**distribution expense.** *Expense* of selling, advertising, and delivery activities.

**dividend.** A distribution of *earnings* to owners of a corporation; it may be paid in cash (cash dividend), with stock (stock dividend), with property, or with other securities (dividend in kind). Dividends, except stock dividends, become a legal liability of the corporation when they are declared. Hence, the owner of stock ordinarily recognizes *revenue* when a dividend, other than a stock dividend, is declared. See also *liquidating dividend* and *stock dividend*.

**dividends in arrears.** Dividends on *cumulative preferred stock* that have not been declared in accordance with the preferred stock contract. Such arrearages must usually be cleared before dividends on *common stock* can be declared.

**dividends in kind.** See *dividend*.

**dividend yield.** *Dividends* declared for the year divided by market price of the stock as of a given time of the year.

**divisional control.** See *control system*.

**divisional reporting.** *Line of business reporting*.

**dollar sign rules.** In presenting accounting statements or schedules, place a dollar sign beside the first figure in each column and beside any figure below a horizontal line drawn under the preceding figure. See the statements in the Accounting Magic or U.S. Government annual report sections of this book for examples. The General Electric statements use a modification of this general rule.

**dollar value LIFO method.** A form of *LIFO* inventory accounting with inventory quantities (*layers*) measured in dollar, rather than physical, terms. Adjustments to account for changing prices are made by use of a specific price index appropriate for the kinds of items in the inventory.

**Domestic International Sales Corporation.** See *DISC*.

**donated capital.** A *stockholders' equity* account credited when contributions, such as land or buildings, are freely given to the company. Do not confuse with *contributed capital*.

**double-declining-balance depreciation (DDB).** *Declining-balance depreciation*, which see, where the constant percentage used to multiply by book value in determining the depreciation charge for the year is $2/n$ and $n$ is the *depreciable life* in periods. Maximum declining-balance rate permitted in the *income tax* laws. *Salvage value* is omitted from the depreciable amount. Thus if the asset cost $100 and has a depreciable life of 5 years, the depreciation in the first year would be $40 = 2/5 \times $100$, in the second would be $24 = 2/5 \times ($100 - $40)$, and in the third year would be $14.40 = 2/5 \times ($100 - $40 - $24)$. By the fourth year, the remaining undepreciated cost could be depreciated under the straight-line method at $10.80 = 1/2 \times ($100 - $40 - $24 - $14.40)$ per year for tax purposes.

**double entry.** The system of recording transactions

that maintains the equality of the accounting equation; each entry results in recording equal amounts of *debits* and *credits*.

**double T-account.** *T-account* with an extra horizontal line showing a change in the account balance to be explained by the subsequent entries into the account, such as:

**Trucks**

|  |  |
|---|---|
| 42,000 |  |

This account shows an increase in the asset account, Trucks, of $42,000 to be explained. Such accounts are useful in preparing the *statement of changes in financial position;* they are not a part of the formal record keeping process.

**double taxation.** Corporate income is subject to the corporate income tax and the after-tax income, when distributed to owners, is subject to the personal income tax.

**doubtful accounts.** *Accounts receivable* estimated to be *uncollectible.*

**dr.** The abbreviation for *debit.*

**draft.** A written order by the first party, called the drawer, instructing a second party, called the drawee (such as a bank), to pay a third party, called the payee. See also *check, cashier's check, certified check, sight draft,* and *trade acceptance.*

**drawee.** See *draft.*

**drawer.** See *draft.*

**drawing account.** A *temporary account* used in *sole proprietorships* and *partnerships* to record payments to owners or partners during a period. At the end of the period, the drawing account is closed by crediting it and debiting the owner's or partner's share of income or, perhaps, his or her capital account.

**drawings.** Payments made to a *sole proprietor* or to a *partner* during a period. See *drawing account.*

**dry-hole accounting.** See *discovery value accounting* for definition and contrast.

**duality.** The axiom of *double-entry* record keeping that every *transaction* is broken down into equal *debit* and *credit* amounts.

**dual transactions assumption (fiction).** In presenting the *statement of changes in financial position,* some transactions not involving *working capital* accounts are reported as though working capital was generated and then used. For example, the issue of *capital stock* in return for the *asset,* land, is reported in the statement of changes in financial position as though stock were issued for *cash* and cash were used to acquire land. Other examples of transactions that require the dual transaction fiction are the issue of a *mortgage* in return for a noncurrent asset and the issue of stock to bondholders in return for their *bonds.*

**E**

**e.** The base of natural logarithms; 2.718281828459045.... If *interest* is compounded continuously during a period at stated rate of *r* per period, then the effective *interest rate* is equivalent to interest compounded once per period at rate *i* where *i* = $e^r - 1$. Tables of $e^r$ are widely available. If 12 percent annual interest is compounded continuously, the effective rate is $e^{.12} - 1 = 12.75$ percent.

**earned surplus.** A term once used, but no longer considered proper, for *retained earnings.*

**earnings.** *Income,* or sometimes *profit.*

**earnings cycle.** The period of time that elapses for a given firm, or the series of transactions, during which *cash* is converted into *goods* and *services,* goods and services are sold to customers, and customers pay for their purchases with cash. *Cash cycle.*

**earnings per share (of common stock).** *Net income* to common stockholders (net income minus *preferred dividends*) divided by the average number of *common shares* outstanding; see also *primary earnings per share* and *fully diluted earnings per share.* See *ratio.*

**earnings per share (of preferred stock).** *Net income* divided by the average number of *preferred shares* outstanding during the period. This ratio indicates how well the preferred dividends are covered or protected; it does not indicate a legal share of *earnings.* See *ratio.*

**earnings, retained.** See *retained earnings.*

**easement.** The acquired right or privilege of one person to use, or have access to, certain property of another. For example, a public utility's right to lay pipes or lines under property of another and to service those facilities.

**economic entity.** See *entity.*

**economic life.** The time span over which the benefits of an *asset* are expected to be received. The economic life of a *patent, copyright,* or *franchise* may be less than the legal life. *Service life.*

**economic order quantity.** In mathematical *inventory* analysis, the optimal amount of stock to order when inventory is reduced to a level called the "re-order point." If *A* represents the *incremental cost* of placing a single order, *D* represents the total demand for a period of time in units, and *H* represents the incremental holding cost during the period per unit of inventory, then the economic order quantity $Q = \sqrt{2AD/H}$. *Q* is sometimes called the "optimal lot size."

**effective interest method.** A systematic method for amortizing *bond discount* or *premium* that makes the *interest expense* for each period divided by the amount of the net *liability* (face amount minus *discount* or plus *premium*) at the beginning of the period equal to the *yield rate* on the bond at the time of issue. Interest expense for a period is yield rate (at time of issue) multiplied by the net liability at the start of the period. The *amortization* of discount or premium is the *plug* to give equal *debits* and *credits.* (Interest expense is a debit and the amount of coupon payments is a credit.) The bond holder makes a similar calculation.

**effective (interest) rate.** Of a bond, the *internal rate of return* or *yield to maturity* at the time of issue. Contrast with *coupon rate.* If the bond is issued for a price below *par,* the effective rate is higher than the coupon rate; if it is issued for a price greater than par, then the effective rate is lower than the coupon rate. In the context of *compound interest,* when the *compounding period* on a *loan* is different from one year, such as a nominal interest rate of 12 percent compounded monthly, then the single payment that could be made at the end of a year that is economically equivalent to the series of interest payments is larger than an amount equal to the quoted nominal rate multiplied by the *principal*. If 12 percent per year is compounded monthly, the effective interest rate is 12.683 percent. In general, if the nominal rate is *r* percent per year and is compounded *m* times per year, then the effective rate is $(1 + r/m)^m - 1$.

**efficiency variance.** A term used for the *quantity variance* for labor or *variable overhead* in a *standard cost system*.

**efficient market hypothesis.** The supposition in finance that securities prices reflect all available information and react nearly instantaneously and in an unbiased fashion to new information.

**eliminations.** *Work sheet* entries to prepare *consolidated statements* that are made to avoid duplicating the amounts of *assets, liabilities, owners' equity, revenues,* and *expenses* of the consolidated *entity* when the accounts of the *parent* and *subsidiaries* are summed.

**employee stock option.** See *stock option*.

**Employee Stock Ownership Trust (or Plan).** See *ESOT*.

**employer, employee payroll taxes.** See *payroll taxes*.

**enabling costs.** A type of *capacity cost* that will stop being incurred if operations are shut down completely but must be incurred in full if operations are carried out at any level. Costs of a security force or of a quality control inspector for an assembly line might be examples. Contrast with *standby costs*.

**encumbrance.** In governmental accounting, an anticipated *expenditure,* or *funds* restricted for anticipated expenditure, such as for outstanding purchase orders. *Appropriations* less expenditures less outstanding encumbrances yields unencumbered balance.

**ending inventory.** The *cost* of *inventory* on hand at the end of the *accounting period,* often called "closing inventory." The dollar amount of inventory to be carried to the subsequent period.

**endorsee.** See *endorser*.

**endorsement.** See *draft*. The *payee* signs the draft and transfers it to a fourth party, such as the payee's bank.

**endorser.** The *payee* of a *note* or *draft* signs it, after writing "Pay to the order of X," transfers the note to person X, and presumably receives some benefit, such as cash, in return. The payee who signs over the note is called the endorser and person X is called the endorsee. The endorsee then has the rights of the payee and may in turn become an endorser by endorsing the note to another endorsee.

**enterprise.** Any business organization, usually defining the accounting *entity*.

**enterprise fund.** A *fund* established by a governmental unit to account for acquisition, operation, and maintenance of governmental services that are supposed to be self-supporting from user charges, such as for water or airports.

**entity.** A person, *partnership, corporation,* or other organization. The *accounting entity* for which accounting statements are prepared may not be the same as the entity defined by law. For example, a *sole*

*proprietorship* is an accounting entity but the individual's combined business and personal assets are the legal entity in most jurisdictions. Several affiliated corporations may be separate legal entities while *consolidated financial statements* are prepared for the group of companies operating as a single economic entity.

**entity theory.** The view of the corporation that emphasizes the form of the *accounting equation* that says *assets = equities*. Contrast with *proprietorship theory*. The entity theory is less concerned with a distinct line between *liabilities* and *stockholders' equity* than is the proprietorship theory. Rather, all equities are provided to the corporation by outsiders who merely have claims of differing legal standings. The entity theory implies using a *multiple-step* income statement.

**entry value.** The current *cost* of acquiring an asset or service at a *fair-market price. Replacement cost.*

**EOQ.** *Economic order quantity*.

**EPS.** *Earnings per share*.

**EPVI.** *Excess present value index*.

**equalization reserve.** An inferior title for the allowance account when the *allowance method* is used for such things as maintenance expenses. Periodically, maintenance *expense* is debited and the allowance is credited. As maintenance *expenditures* are actually incurred, the allowance is debited and cash or the other asset expended is credited.

**equities.** *Liabilities* plus *owners' equity*.

**equity.** A claim to *assets;* a source of assets.

**equity financing.** Raising *funds* by issuance of *capital stock*. Contrast with *debt financing*.

**equity method.** A method of accounting for an *investment* in the stock of another company in which the proportionate share of the earnings of the other company is debited to the investment account and credited to a *revenue* account as earned. When *dividends* are received, *cash* is debited and the investment account is credited. Used in reporting when the investor owns twenty percent or more of the stock of an unconsolidated company. One of the few instances where revenue is recognized without a change in *working capital*.

**equity ratio.** *Stockholders' equity* divided by total *assets*. See *ratio*.

**equivalent production.** *Equivalent units*.

**equivalent units (of work).** The number of units of completed output that would require the same costs as were actually incurred for production during a period. Used primarily in *process costing* calculations to measure in uniform terms the output of a continuous process.

**ERISA.** Employee Retirement Income Security Act of 1974. The federal law that sets *pension plan* requirements.

**error accounting.** See *accounting errors*.

**ESOP.** Employee Stock Ownership Plan. See *ESOT*.

**ESOT.** Employee Stock Ownership Trust. A trust *fund* created by a corporate employer that can provide certain tax benefits to the corporation while providing for employee stock ownership. The corporate employer can contribute up to 25 percent of its payroll per year to the trust. The contributions are *deductions* from otherwise taxable income for federal *income tax* purposes. The assets of the trust must be used for the benefit of employees—for example, to fund death or retirement benefits. The assets of the trust are usually the *common stock*, sometimes nonvoting, of the corporate employer. As an example of the potential *tax shelter*, consider the case of a corporation with $1 million of *debt* outstanding, which it wishes to retire, and an annual payroll of $2 million. The corporation sells $1 million of common stock to the ESOT. The ESOT borrows $1 million with the loan guaranteed by, and therefore a *contingent liability* of, the corporation. The corporation uses the $1 million proceeds of the stock issue to retire its outstanding debt. (The debt of the corporation has been replaced with the debt of the ESOT.) The corporation can contribute $500,000 (= .25 × $2 million payroll) to the ESOT each year and treat the contribution as a deduction for tax purposes. After a little more than two years, the ESOT has received sufficient funds to retire its loan. The corporation has effectively repaid its original $1 million debt with pre-tax dollars. Assuming an income tax rate of 40 percent, it has saved $400,000 (= .40 × $1 million) of after-tax dollars *if* the $500,000 expense for the contribution to the ESOT for the pension benefits of employees would have been made, in one form or another, anyway. Observe that the corporation could use the proceeds ($1 million in the example) of the stock issue to the ESOT for any of several different purposes: financing expansion, replacing plant assets, or acquiring another company.

Basically this same form of pretax dollar financing through pensions is "almost" available with any corporate pension plan, but with one important exception. The trustees of an ordinary pension trust must invest the assets "prudently" and if they do not, they are personally liable to employees. Current judgment about "prudent" investment requires diversification—pension trust assets should be invested in a wide variety of investment opportunities. (Not more than 10 percent of a pension trust's assets can ordinarily be invested in the parent's common stock.) Thus the ordinary pension trust cannot, in practice, invest all, or even most, of its assets in the parent corporation's stock. This constraint does not apply to the investments of an ESOT. All ESOT assets may be invested in the parent company's stock.

The ESOT also provides a means for closely-held corporations to achieve wider ownership of shares without *going public*. The laws enabling ESOT's provide for independent professional appraisal of shares not traded in public markets and for transactions between the corporation and the ESOT or between the ESOT and the employees to be based on the appraised values of the shares.

**estimated expenses.** See *after cost*.

**estimated liability.** The preferred terminology for estimated costs to be incurred for such uncertain things as repairs under *warranty*. An estimated liability is shown in the *balance sheet*. Contrast with *contingent liability*.

**estimated revenue.** A term used in governmental accounting to designate revenue expected to accrue during a period whether or not it will be collected during the period. A *budgetary account* usually established at the beginning of the budget period.

**estimated salvage value.** Synonymous with *salvage value* of an *asset* before its retirement.

**estimates, changes in.** See *accounting changes*.

**excess present value.** In a *capital budgeting* context, *present value* of (anticipated net cash inflows minus cash outflows including initial cash outflow) for a project.

**excess present value index.** *Excess present value* divided by initial cash outlay.

**except for.** Qualification in *auditor's report*, usually caused by a change, approved by the auditor, from one acceptable accounting principle or procedure to another.

**exchange.** The generic term for a transaction (or more technically, a reciprocal transfer) between one entity and another. In another context, the name for a market, such as the New York Stock Exchange.

**exchange gain or loss.** The phrase used by the *FASB* for *foreign exchange gain or loss*.

**exchange rate.** The *price* of one country's currency in terms of another country's currency. For example, the British pound might be worth $1.80 at a given time. The exchange rate would be stated as "one pound is worth one dollar and eighty cents" or "one dollar is worth .5556 (= £1/$1.80) pounds."

**excise tax.** Tax on the manufacture, sale, or consumption of a commodity.

**ex-dividend.** Said of a stock at the time when the declared *dividend* becomes the property of the person who owned the stock on the *record date*. The payment date follows the ex-dividend date.

**exemption.** A term used for various amounts subtracted from gross income to determine taxable income. Not all such subtractions are called "exemptions". See *tax deduction*.

**exercise.** When the owner of an *option* or *warrant* purchases the security that the option entitles him or her to purchase, he or she has exercised the option or warrant.

**exercise price.** See *option*.

**exit value.** The proceeds that would be received if assets were disposed of in an *arm's-length transaction*. *Current selling price*. *Net realizable value*.

**expected value.** The mean or arithmetic *average* of a statistical distribution or series of numbers.

**expendable fund.** In governmental accounting, a *fund* whose resources, *principal*, and earnings may be distributed.

**expenditure.** Payment of *cash*. Virtually synonymous with *disbursement*, except that some use expenditure as a narrower term and exclude from its definition all payments to discharge liabilities.

**expense.** As a noun, the *cost* of *assets* used up in producing *revenue*. A "gone" asset; an expired cost. Do not confuse with *expenditure* or *disbursement*, which may occur before, when, or after the related expense is recognized. Use the word cost to refer to an item that still has service potential and is an asset. Use the word expense after the asset's service potential has been used. As a verb, to designate a past or current expenditure as a current expense.

**expense account.** An *account* to accumulate *expenses;* such accounts are closed at the end of the accounting period. A *temporary owners' equity* account. Also used to describe a listing of expenses by an employee submitted to the employer for reimbursement.

**experience rating.** A term used in insurance, particularly unemployment insurance, to denote changes from ordinary rates to reflect extraordinarily large or small amounts of claims over time by the insured.

**expired cost.**   An *expense* or a *loss.*

**Exposure Draft.**   A preliminary statement of the *FASB* (or *APB* between 1962 and 1973) which shows the contents of a pronouncement the Board is considering making effective.

**external reporting.**   Reporting to stockholders and the public, as opposed to internal reporting for management's benefit. See *financial accounting* and contrast with *managerial accounting.*

**extraordinary item.**   A *material expense* or *revenue* item characterized both by its unusual nature and infrequency of occurrence that is shown along with its income tax effects separately from ordinary income and *income from discontinued operations* on the *income statement.* A *loss* from an earthquake would probably be classified as an extraordinary item. Gain (or loss) on retirement of *bonds* is treated as an extraordinary item under the terms of *FASB Statement* No. 4.


**F**


**face amount (value).**   The nominal amount due at *maturity* from a *bond* or *note* not including contractual interest that may also be due on the same date. The corresponding amount of a stock certificate is best called the *par* or *stated value,* whichever is applicable.

**factoring.**   The process of buying *notes* or *accounts receivable* at a *discount* from the holder to whom the debt is owed; from the holder's point of view, the selling of such notes or accounts. When a single note is involved, the process is called "discounting a note."

**factory.**   Used synonymously with *manufacturing* as an adjective.

**factory burden.**   Manufacturing *overhead.*

**factory cost.**   *Manufacturing cost.*

**factory expense.**   Manufacturing *overhead. Expense* is a poor term in this context because the item is a *product cost.*

**factory overhead.**   Usually an item of *manufacturing cost* other than *direct labor* or *direct materials.*

**fair market price (value).**   Price (value) determined at *arm's length* between a willing buyer and a willing seller, each acting rationally in their own self-interest. May be estimated in the absence of a monetary transaction.

**fair presentation (fairness).**   When the *auditor's report* says that the *financial statements* "present fairly...," the auditor means that the accounting alternatives used by the entity are all in accordance with *GAAP.* In recent years, however, courts are finding that conformity with *generally acceptable accounting principles* may be insufficient grounds for an opinion that the statements are fair. *SAS* No. 5 requires that the auditor judge the accounting principles used "appropriate in the circumstances" before attesting to fair presentation.

**FASB.**   Financial Accounting Standards Board. An independent board responsible, since 1973, for establishing *generally accepted accounting principles.* Its official pronouncements are called "Statements of Financial Accounting Standards" and "Interpreta-

tions of Financial Accounting Standards." See *Discussion Memorandum.*

**FASB Interpretation.**   An official statement of the *FASB* interpreting the meaning of *Accounting Research Bulletins, APB Opinions,* and *Statements of Financial Accounting Standards.*

**favorable variance.**   An excess of *standard cost* over actual cost.

**federal income tax.**   *Income tax* levied by the U.S. government on individuals and corporations.

**Federal Unemployment Tax Act.**   See *FUTA.*

**feedback.**   The process of informing employees about how their actual performance compares with the expected or desired level of performance in the hope that the information will reinforce desired behavior and reduce unproductive behavior.

**FEI.**   *Financial Executives Institute.*

**FICA.**   Federal Insurance Contributions Act. The law that sets "*Social Security*" *taxes* and benefits.

**fiduciary.**   Someone responsible for the custody or administration of property belonging to another, such as an executor (of an estate), agent, receiver (in *bankruptcy*), or trustee (of a trust).

**FIFO.**   First-in, first-out; an *inventory flow assumption* by which *ending inventory* cost is determined from most recent purchases and *cost of goods sold* is determined from oldest purchases including beginning inventory. See *LISH.* Contrast with *LIFO.*

**finance.**   As a verb, to supply with *funds* through the *issue* of stocks, bonds, notes, or mortgages, or through the retention of earnings.

**financial accounting.**   The accounting for *assets, equities, revenues,* and *expenses* of a business. Primarily concerned with the historical reporting of the *financial position* and operations of an *entity* to external users on a regular, periodic basis. Contrast with *managerial accounting.*

**Financial Accounting Standards Board.**   *FASB.*

**Financial Executives Institute.**   An organization of financial executives, such as chief accountants, *controllers,* and treasurers, of large businesses.

**financial expense.**   An *expense* incurred in raising or managing *funds.*

**financial position (condition).**   Statement of the *assets* and *equities* of a firm displayed on the *balance sheet* statement.

**financial ratio.**   See *ratio.*

**financial statements.**   The *balance sheet, income statement, statement of retained earnings, statement of changes in financial position,* statement of changes in *owners' equity accounts,* and *notes* thereto.

**financial structure.**   *Capital structure.*

**financing lease.**   A *lease* treated by the lessee as both the borrowing of funds and the acquisition of an *asset* to be *amortized.* Both the *liability* and the asset are recognized on the balance sheet. Expenses consist of *interest* on the *debt* and *amortization* of the asset. The lessor treats the lease as the sale of the asset in return for a series of future cash receipts. Contrast with *operating lease.* Called a "capital lease" by the *FASB* in *Statement No. 13.*

**finished goods.**   Manufactured product ready for sale; a *current asset (inventory) account.*

**firm.**   Informally, any business entity. (Strictly speaking, a firm is a *partnership.*)

**first-in, first-out.**   See *FIFO.*

**fiscal year.** A period of twelve consecutive months chosen by a business as the *accounting period* for annual reports. May or may not be a *natural business year* or a calendar year.

**FISH.** An acronym, conceived by George H. Sorter, for *first-in, still-here*. FISH is the same cost flow assumption as *LIFO*. Many readers of accounting statements find it easier to think about inventory questions in terms of items still on hand. Think of LIFO in connection with *cost of goods sold* but of FISH in connection with *ending inventory*. See *LISH*.

**fixed assets.** *Plant assets*.

**fixed-benefit plan.** A *defined benefit (pension) plan*.

**fixed budget.** A plan that provides for specified amounts of *expenditures* and *receipts* that do not vary with activity levels. Sometimes called a "static budget." Contrast with *flexible budget*.

**fixed cost (expense).** An *expenditure* or *expense* that does not vary with volume of activity, at least in the short run. See *capacity costs*, which include *enabling costs* and *standby costs*, and *programmed costs* for various subdivisions of fixed costs.

**fixed liability.** *Long-term* liability.

**fixed manufacturing overhead applied.** The portion of *fixed manufacturing overhead cost* allocated to units produced during a period.

**flexible budget.** *Budget* that projects receipts and expenditures as a function of activity levels. Contrast with *fixed budget*.

**flexible budget allowance.** With respect to manufacturing overhead, the total cost that should have been incurred at the level of activity actually experienced during the period.

**float.** *Checks* that have been *credited* to the depositor's bank account, but not yet *debited* to the *drawer's* bank account.

**flow.** The change in the amount of an item over time. Contrast with *stock*.

**flow assumption.** When a *withdrawal* is made from *inventory*, the cost of the withdrawal must be determined by a flow assumption if *specific identification* of units is not used. The usual flow assumptions are *FIFO*, *LIFO*, and *weighted-average*.

**flow of costs.** *Costs* passing through various classifications within an *entity*. See the diagram below for a summary of *product* and *period cost* flows.

**flow-through method.** Accounting for the *investment tax credit* to show all income statement benefits of the credit in the year of acquisition, rather than spreading them over the life of the asset acquired, called the "deferral method." The *APB* preferred the deferral method in Opinion No. 2 (1962) but accepted the flow-through method in Opinion No. 4 (1964). See the Accounting Magic section for examples of both methods. Sometimes also used in connection with *depreciation* accounting where *straight-line method* is used for financial reporting and an *accelerated* method for tax reporting. Followers of the flow-through method would not recognize a *deferred tax liability*. APB Opinion No. 11 prohibited the use of the flow-through approach in this connection.

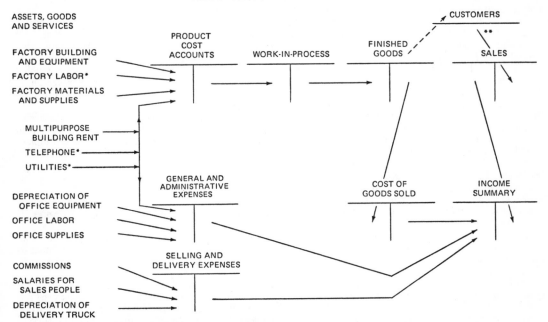

FLOW OF COSTS (AND SALES REVENUE)

*The credit in the entry to record these items is usually to a payable; for all others, the credit is usually to an asset, or to an asset contra account.
**When sales to customers are recorded, the Sales account is credited. The debit is usually to Cash or Accounts Receivable.

**FOB.** Free on board some location (for example, FOB shipping point; FOB destination); the *invoice* price includes delivery at seller's expense to that location. Title to goods usually passes from seller to buyer at the FOB location.

**footing.** Adding a column of figures.

**footnotes.** More detailed information than that provided in the *income statement, balance sheet, statement of retained earnings,* and *statement of changes in financial position;* these are considered an integral part of the statements and are covered by the *auditor's report.* Sometimes called "notes."

**forecast.** An estimate or projection of costs or revenues or both.

**foreign exchange gain or loss.** Gain or loss from holding *net* foreign *monetary items* during a period when the *exchange rate* changes. See the General Electric annual report at note 43.2.

**Form 10-K.** See *10-K.*

**franchise.** A privilege granted or sold, such as to use a name or to sell products or services.

**free on board.** *FOB.*

**freight-in.** The *cost* of freight or shipping in acquiring *inventory*, preferably treated as a part of the cost of *inventory*. Often shown temporarily in an *adjunct account* which is closed at the end of the period with other purchase accounts to inventory account by the acquirer.

**freight-out.** The *cost* of freight or shipping in selling *inventory*, treated by seller as a selling *expense* in the period of sale.

**full costing.** *Absorption costing.* See *discovery value accounting* for another definition in the context of accounting for natural resources.

**full disclosure.** The reporting policy requiring that all significant or *material* information is to be presented in the financial statements. See *fair presentation.*

**fully diluted earnings per share.** Smallest *earnings per share* figure on *common stock* that can be obtained by computing an earnings per share for all possible combinations of assumed *exercise* or *conversion* of *potentially dilutive securities*. Must be reported on the *income statement* if it is less than 97 percent of earnings available to common stockholders divided by the average number of common shares outstanding during the period.

**fully vested.** Said of a *pension plan* when an employee (or his or her estate) has rights to all the benefits purchased with the employer's contributions to the plan even if the employee is not employed by this employer at the time of retirement.

**function.** In governmental accounting, said of a group of related activities for accomplishing a service or regulatory program for which the governmental unit is responsible. In mathematics, a rule for associating a number, called the dependent variable, with another number or numbers, called independent variable(s).

**functional classification.** *Income statement* reporting form in which *expenses* are reported by functions, that is, cost of goods sold, administrative expenses, financing expenses, selling expenses; contrast with *natural classification.*

**fund.** An *asset* or group of assets set aside for a specific purpose. See also *fund accounting.*

**fund accounting.** The accounting for resources, ob-

ligations, and *capital* balances, usually of a not-for-profit or governmental *entity*, which have been segregated into *accounts* representing logical groupings based on legal, donor, or administrative restrictions or requirements. The groupings are described as "funds." The accounts of each fund are *self-balancing* and from them a *balance sheet* and an operating statement for each fund can be prepared. See *fund* and *fund balance.*

**fund balance.** In governmental accounting context, the excess of assets of a *fund* over its liabilities and reserves; the not-for-profit equivalent of *owners' equity.*

**funded.** Said of a *pension plan* or other obligation when *funds* have been set aside for meeting the obligation when it becomes due. The federal law for pension plans requires that all *normal costs* be funded as recognized. In addition, *past and prior service costs* of pension plans must be funded over 30 or over 40 years, depending upon the circumstances.

**funding.** Replacing *short-term* liabilities with *long-term* debt.

**funds.** Generally *working capital;* current assets less current liabilities. Sometimes used to refer to *cash* or to cash and *marketable securities.*

**funds provided by operations.** An important subtotal in the *statement of changes in financial position.* This amount is the total of revenues producing *funds* less *expenses* requiring funds. Often, the amount is shown as *net income* plus expenses not requiring funds (such as depreciation charges) minus revenues not producing funds (such as revenues recognized under the *equity method* of accounting for a long-term investment). The statement of changes in financial position maintains the same distinctions between *continuing operations, discontinued operations,* and *income* or *loss* from *extraordinary items* as in the *income statement.*

**funds statement.** An informal name often used for the *statement of changes in financial position.*

**funny money.** Said of securities such as *convertible preferred stock, convertible bonds, options,* and *warrants* which have aspects of *common stock* equity but which did not reduce reported *earnings per share* prior to the issuance of *APB Opinions* No. 9 in 1967 and No. 15 in 1969.

**FUTA.** Federal Unemployment Tax Act which provides for taxes to be collected at the federal level, to help subsidize the individual states' administration of their unemployment compensation programs.

## G

**GAAP.** *Generally accepted accounting principles.* A plural noun.

**gain.** Excess of *revenues* over *expenses* from a specific transaction. Frequently used in the context of describing a transaction not part of a firm's typical, day-to-day operations.

**general debt.** Debt of a governmental unit legally payable from general revenues and backed by the full faith and credit of the governmental unit.

**General Electric Annual Report.** Another section of this book.

**general expenses.** *Operating expenses* other than

those specifically assigned to cost of goods sold, selling, and administration.

**general fixed asset (group of accounts).** Accounts showing those long-term assets of a governmental unit not accounted for in *enterprise, trust,* or intra-governmental service funds.

**general fund.** Assets and liabilities of a nonprofit entity not specifically earmarked for other purposes; the primary operating fund of a governmental unit.

**general journal.** The formal record where transactions, or summaries of similar transactions, are recorded in *journal entry* form as they occur. Use of the adjective "general" usually implies only two columns for cash amounts or that there are also various *special journals,* such as a *check register* or *sales journal,* in use.

**general ledger.** The name for the formal *ledger* containing all of the financial statement accounts. It has equal debits and credits as evidenced by the *trial balance.* Some of the accounts in the general ledger may be *controlling accounts,* supported by details contained in *subsidiary ledgers.*

**generally accepted accounting principles (GAAP).** As previously defined by the *APB* and now by the *FASB,* the conventions, rules, and procedures necessary to define accepted accounting practice at a particular time; includes both broad guidelines and relatively detailed practices and procedures.

**generally accepted auditing standards.** The standards, as opposed to particular procedures, promulgated by the *AICPA* (in *Statements on Auditing Standards*) which concern "the auditor's professional qualities" and "the judgment exercised by him in the performance of his examination and in his report." Currently, there are ten such standards, three general ones (concerned with proficiency, independence, and degree of care to be exercised), three standards of field work, and four standards of reporting. The first standard of reporting requires that the *auditor's report* state whether or not the *financial statements* are prepared in accordance with *generally accepted accounting principles.* Thus the typical auditor's report says that the examination was conducted in accordance with generally accepted auditing standards and that the statements are prepared in accordance with generally accepted accounting principles. See *auditor's report.*

**general partner.** Member of *partnership* personally liable for all debts of the partnership; contrast with *limited partner.*

**general price index.** A measure of the aggregate prices of a wide range of goods and services in the economy at one time relative to the prices during a base period. See *consumer price index* and *GNP Implicit Price Deflator.* Contrast with *specific price index.*

**general price level adjusted statements.** See *price level adjusted statements.*

**general price level changes.** Changes in the aggregate prices of a wide range of goods and services in the economy. These price changes are measured using a *general price index.* Contrast with *specific price changes.*

**general purchasing power of the dollar.** The command of the dollar over a wide range of goods and

services in the economy. The general purchasing power of the dollar is inversely related to changes in a general price index. See *general price index.*

**GNP Implicit Price Deflator (Index).** A *price index* issued quarterly by the Office of Business Economics of the U.S. Department of Commerce. This index attempts to trace the price level of all *goods and services* comprising the *gross national product.* Contrast with *consumer price index.*

**going-concern assumption.** For accounting purposes a business is assumed to remain in operation long enough for all its current plans to be carried out. This assumption is part of the justification for the *acquisition cost* basis, rather than a *liquidation* or *exit value* basis, of accounting.

**going public.** Said of a business when its *shares* become widely traded, rather than being closely held by relatively few *stockholders.* Issuing shares to the general investing public.

**goods.** Items of merchandise, supplies, raw materials, or finished goods. Sometimes the meaning of "goods" is extended to include all *tangible* items, as in the phrase "goods and services."

**goods available for sale.** The sum of *beginning inventory* plus all acquisitions, or purchases, of merchandise or finished goods during an *accounting period.*

**goods in process.** *Work in process.*

**goodwill.** The excess of cost of an acquired firm or operating unit over the current or *fair market value* of *net assets* of the acquired unit. Informally used to indicate the value of good customer relations, high employee morale, a well-respected business name, and so on, which are expected to result in greater than normal earning power.

**goodwill method.** A method of accounting for the *admission* of a new partner to a *partnership* when the new partner is to be credited with a portion of capital different from the value of the *tangible* assets contributed as a fraction of tangible assets of the partnership. See *bonus method* for a description and contrast.

**graded vesting.** Said of a *pension plan* where not all employee benefits are currently *vested.* By law, the benefits must become vested according to one of several formulas as time passes.

**gross.** Not adjusted or reduced by deductions or subtractions. Contrast with *net.*

**gross margin.** *Net sales* minus *cost of goods sold.*

**gross margin percentage.** $100 \times (1 - cost\ of\ goods\ sold/net\ sales) = 100 \times (gross\ margin/net\ sales).$

**gross national product (GNP).** The market value within a nation for a year of all goods and services produced as measured by final sales of goods and services to individuals, corporations, and governments plus the excess of exports over imports.

**gross price method (of recording purchase or sales discounts).** The *purchase* (or *sale*) is recorded at its *invoice price,* not deducting the amounts of *discounts* available. Discounts taken are recorded in a *contra* account to purchases (or sales). Information on discounts lapsed is not made available, and for this reason, most firms prefer the *net-price method* of recording purchase discounts.

**gross profit.** *Gross margin.*

**gross profit method.** A method of estimating *ending*

*inventory* amounts. *Cost of goods sold* is measured as some fraction of sales; the *inventory equation* is then used to value *ending inventory*.

**gross profit ratio.** *Gross margin* divided by *net sales*.

**gross sales.** All *sales* at *invoice* prices, not reduced by *discounts, allowances, returns,* or other adjustments.

**group depreciation.** A method of calculating *depreciation* charges where similar assets are combined, rather than depreciated separately. No gain or loss is recognized on retirement of items from the group until the last item in the group is sold or retired. See *composite life method.*

## H

**hidden reserve.** The term refers to an amount by which *owners' equity* has been understated, perhaps deliberately. The understatement arises from an undervaluation of *assets* or overvaluation of *liabilities.* By undervaluing assets on this period's *balance sheet, net income* in some future period can be made to look artificially high by disposing of the asset: actual *revenues* less artificially-low cost of assets sold yields artificially-high net income. There is no *account* that has this title.

**historical cost.** *Acquisition cost; original cost;* a *sunk cost.*

**historical summary.** A part of the *annual report* to stockholders that shows important items, such as *net income, revenues, expenses, asset* and *equity* totals, *earnings per share,* and the like, for five or ten periods including the current one. Usually not as much detail is shown in the historical summary as in *comparative statements,* which typically report as much detail for the immediately preceding year as for the current year. Annual reports may contain both comparative statements and a historical summary. See pages 82–83 of this book.

**holding company.** A company that confines its activities to owning *stock* in, and supervising management of, other companies. A holding company usually owns a controlling interest in, that is more than 50 percent of the voting stock of, the companies whose stock it holds. Contrast with *mutual fund.* See *conglomerate.*

**holding gain or loss.** Difference between end-of-period price and beginning-of-period price of an asset held during the period. Ordinarily, realized holding gains and losses are not separately reported in financial statements. Unrealized gains are not usually reflected in income at all. Some unrealized losses, such as on inventory or marketable securities, are reflected in income or *owners' equity* as the losses occur. See *inventory profit* for further refinement, including *gains* on *assets* sold during the period.

**horizontal analysis.** *Time series analysis.*

**human resource accounting.** A term used to describe a variety of proposals that seek to report and emphasize the importance of human resources—knowledgeable, trained, and loyal employees—in a company's earning process and total assets.

**hypothecation.** The *pledging* of property, without transfer of title or possession, to secure a loan.

## I

**I.** *Identity matrix.*

**ideal standard costs.** *Standard costs* set equal to those that would be incurred under the best possible conditions.

**identity matrix.** A square *matrix* with ones on the main diagonal and zeros elsewhere; a matrix **I** such that for any other matrix **A, IA = AI = A.** The matrix equivalent to the number one.

**IIA.** *Institute of Internal Auditors.*

**IMA.** Institute of Management Accounting. See *CMA* and *National Association of Accountants.*

**imprest fund.** *Petty cash fund.*

**improvement.** An *expenditure* to extend the useful life of an *asset* or to improve its performance (rate of output, cost) over that of the original asset. Such expenditures are *capitalized* as part of the asset's cost. Contrast with *maintenance* and *repair.*

**imputed cost.** A cost that does not appear in accounting records, such as the *interest* that could be earned on cash spent to acquire inventories rather than, say, government bonds. Or, consider a firm that owns the buildings it occupies. This firm has an imputed cost for rent in an amount equal to what it would have to pay to use similar buildings owned by another.

**imputed interest.** See *interest imputed.*

**income.** *Excess of revenues* and *gains* over *expenses* and *losses* for a period; *net income.* Sometimes used with an appropriate modifier to refer to the various intermediate amounts shown in a *multiple-step income statement.* Sometimes used to refer to revenues, as in "rental income."

**income accounts.** *Revenue* and *expense accounts.*

**income distribution account.** *Temporary account* sometimes debited when *dividends* are declared; closed to *retained earnings.*

**income from continuing operations.** As defined by *APB Option* No. 30, all *revenues* less all *expenses* except for the following: results of operations, including income tax effects, that have been or will be discontinued; *gains* or *losses,* including income tax effects, on disposal of segments of the business; gains or losses, including income tax effects, from *extraordinary items;* and the cumulative effect of *accounting changes.*

**income from discontinued operations.** *Income,* net of tax effects, from parts of the business that have been discontinued during the period or are to be discontinued in the near future. Such items are reported on a separate line of the *income statement* after *income from continuing operations* but before *extraordinary items.*

**income (revenue) bond.** See *special revenue debt.*

**income statement.** The statement of *revenues, expenses, gains,* and *losses* for the period ending with *net income* for the period. The *earnings per share* amount is usually shown on the income statement; the *reconciliation* of beginning and ending balances of *retained earnings* may also be shown in a combined statement of income and retained earnings. See *income from continuing operations, income from discontinued operations, extraordinary items, multiple-step, single-step.*

**income summary.** An *account* used in problem solving that serves as a surrogate for the *income statement.* All *revenues* are closed to the Income Summary as *credits* and all *expenses,* as *debits.* The *balance* in the account, after all other *closing entries* are made, is then closed to the retained earnings or other *owners' equity* account and represents *net income* for the period.

**income tax.** An annual tax levied by the federal and other governments on the income of an entity. An *expense;* if not yet paid, a *liability*.

**income tax allocation.** See *deferred tax liability* and *tax allocation: intrastatement*.

**incremental.** An adjective used to describe the change in *cost, expense, investment, cash flow, revenue, profit,* and the like if one more unit is produced or sold or if an activity is undertaken.

**indenture.** See *bond indenture*.

**independence.** The mental attitude required of the *CPA* in performing the *attest* function. It implies impartiality and that the members of the auditing CPA firm own no stock in the corporation being audited.

**independent accountant.** The *CPA* who performs the *attest* function for a firm.

**indeterminate-term liability.** A *liability* lacking the criterion of being due at a definite time. This term is our own coinage to encompass the *deferred income tax liability* and *minority interest*.

**indexation.** An attempt by lawmakers or parties to a contract, to cope with the effects of *inflation*. Amounts fixed in law or contracts are "indexed" when these amounts change as a given measure of price changes. For example, a so-called escalator clause in a labor contract might provide that hourly wages will be increased as the *consumer price index* increases. Many economists have suggested the indexation of numbers fixed in the *income tax* laws. If, for example, the personal *exemption* is $750 at the start of the period, prices rise by 10 percent during the period, and the personal exemption is indexed, then the personal exemption would automatically rise to $825 (= $750 + .10 × $750) at the end of the period.

**indirect costs.** Costs of production not easily associated with the production of specific goods and services; *overhead costs*. May be *allocated* on some arbitrary basis to specific products or departments.

**indirect labor (material) cost.** An *indirect cost* for labor (material) such as supervisors (supplies).

**individual proprietorship.** *Sole proprietorship*.

**Industry Audit Guide.** A series of publications by the AICPA providing specific *accounting* and *auditing principles* for specialized situations. Audit guides have been issued covering government contractors, state and local government units, investment companies, finance companies, colleges and universities, stock life insurance companies, brokers and dealers in securities, and many others.

**inflation.** A time of generally rising prices.

**information system.** A system, sometimes formal and sometimes informal, for collecting, processing, and communicating data that are useful for the managerial functions of decision making, planning, and control, and for financial reporting under the *attest* requirement.

**insolvent.** Unable to pay debts when due. Said of a company even though *assets* exceed *liabilities*.

**installment.** Partial payment of a debt or collection of a receivable, usually according to a contract.

**installment contracts receivable.** The name used for *accounts receivable* when the *installment method* of recognizing revenue is used. Its *contra, unrealized*

*gross margin,* is shown on the balance sheet as a subtraction from the amount receivable.

**installment (sales) method.** Recognizing *revenue* and *expense* (or *gross margin*) from a sales transaction in proportion to the fraction of the selling price collected during a period. Allowed by the *IRS* for income tax reporting, but acceptable in *GAAP* (*APB Opinion* No. 10) only when cash collections are reasonably uncertain. See *unrealized* (and *realized*) *gross margin*.

**installment sales.** Sales on account where the buyer promises to pay in several separate payments, called *installments*. Sometimes are, but need not be, accounted for on the *installment method*. If installment sales are accounted for with the sales *basis of revenue recognition* for financial reporting but with the installment method for income tax returns, then a *deferred income tax liability* arises.

**Institute of Internal Auditors.** The national association of accountants who are engaged in internal auditing and are employed by business firms. See *IIA*.

**Institute of Management Accounting.** See *CMA*.

**insurance.** A contract for reimbursement of specific losses; purchased with insurance premiums. Self-insurance is not insurance but merely the willingness to assume risk of incurring losses while saving the premium.

**intangible asset.** A nonphysical, *noncurrent* asset such as a *copyright, patent, trademark, goodwill, organization costs, capitalized* advertising cost, computer programs, licenses for any of the preceding, government licenses (e.g., broadcasting or the right to sell liquor), *leases, franchises,* mailing lists, exploration permits, import and export permits, construction permits, marketing quotas, and other rights which give a firm an exclusive or preferred position in the marketplace.

**intercompany elimination.** See *eliminations*.

**intercompany profit.** If one *affiliated company* sells to another, and the goods remain in the second company's *inventory* at the end of the period, then the first company's *profit* has not been realized by a sale to an outsider. That profit is called "intercompany profit" and is eliminated from net *income* in *consolidated income statements* or when the *equity method* is used.

**interest.** The charge or cost for using money; expressed as a rate of per period, usually one year, called the interest rate. See *effective interest rate* and *nominal interest rate*.

**interest factor.** One plus the *interest* rate.

**interest, imputed.** If a borrower merely promises to pay a single amount, sometime later than the present, then the present value (computed at a *fair market* interest rate, called the "imputed interest rate") of the promise is less than the *face amount* to be paid at *maturity*. The difference between the face amount and the present value of a promise is called imputed interest. See also *imputed cost*.

**interest method.** See *effective interest method*.

**interest rate.** See *interest*.

**inter-fund accounts.** In governmental accounting, the accounts that show transactions between funds, especially inter-fund receivables and payables.

**interim statements.** Statements issued for periods less than the regular, annual *accounting period*. Most corporations are required to issue interim statements on a quarterly basis. The basic issue in preparing interim reports is whether their purpose is to report on the interim period (1) as a self-contained accounting period, or (2) as an integral part of the year of which they are a part so that forecasts of annual performance can be made. *APB Opinion* No. 28 and the *SEC* require that interim reports be constructed largely to satisfy the second purpose.

**internal audit.**  An *audit* conducted by employees to ascertain whether or not *internal control* procedures are working, as opposed to an external audit conducted by a *CPA*.

**internal control.**  See *control system*.

**internal rate of return.**  The discount rate that equates the net *present value* of a stream of cash outflows and inflows to zero.

**Internal Revenue Service (IRS).**  Agency of the U.S. Treasury Department responsible for administering the Internal Revenue Code and collecting income, and certain other, taxes.

**internal reporting.**  Reporting for management's use in planning and control; contrast with *external reporting* for financial statement users.

**International Accounting Standards Committee.**  An organization that promotes the establishment of international accounting standards.

**interperiod tax allocation.**  See *deferred income tax liability*.

**interpolation.**  The estimation of an unknown number intermediate between two (or more) known numbers.

**Interpretations of Statements of Financial Accounting Standards.**  See *FASB Interpretations*.

**in the black (red).**  Operating at a profit (loss).

**intra-statement tax allocation.**  See *tax allocation: intra-statement*.

**inventoriable costs.**  *Costs* that "attach" to products. *Product costs (assets)* as opposed to *period expenses*.

**inventory.**  As a noun, the *balance* in an asset *account* such as raw materials, supplies, work in process, and finished goods. As a verb, to calculate the *cost* of goods on hand at a given time or to physically count items on hand.

**inventory equation.**  *Beginning inventory* + *net additions* − *withdrawals* = *ending inventory*. Ordinarily, additions are net purchases and withdrawals are *cost of goods sold*. Notice that ending inventory, to be shown on the balance sheet, and cost of goods sold, to be shown on the income statement, are not independent of each other. The larger is one, the smaller must be the other. In valuing inventories, beginning inventory and net purchases are usually known. In some inventory methods (for example, some applications of the *retail inventory method*), cost of goods sold is measured and the equation is used to find the cost of ending inventory. In most methods, cost of ending inventory is measured and the equation is used to find the cost of goods sold (withdrawals). In *replacement cost* (in contrast to *historical cost*) accounting, *additions* (in the equation) include holding gains, whether realized or not. Thus the replacement cost inventory equation is: Beginning Inventory (at Replacement Cost) + Purchases (where Replacement Cost is Historical Cost) + Holding Gains (whether Realized or not) − Ending Inventory (at Replacement Cost) = Cost of Goods Sold (Replacement Cost).

**inventory holding gains.**  See *inventory profit*.

**inventory layer.**  See LIFO *inventory layer*.

**inventory profit.**  This term has several possible meanings. Consider the data in the accompanying illustration. The *historical cost* data are derived in the conventional manner; the firm uses a *FIFO cost flow assumption*. The *replacement cost* data are assumed, but are of the kind that the *SEC* requires in *ASR* No. 190.

We use the term *distributable income* to refer to revenues less expenses based on replacement, rather than historical, costs. To that subtotal add realized holding gains to arrive at realized (conventional) income. To that, add unrealized holding gains to arrive at *economic income*. See page 31.

The SEC, in its *Accounting Series Releases,* uses the term "inventory profit" to refer to the realized holding gain, $110 in the illustration. The amount of inventory profit will usually be material when FIFO is used and prices are rising.

Others, including us, prefer to use the term "inventory profit" to refer to the total *holding gain*, $300 (= $110 + $190, both realized and unrealized), but this appears to be a lost cause.

In periods of rising prices and increasing inventories, the realized holding gains under a FIFO cost flow assumption will be substantially larger than under LIFO. In the illustration, for example, assume under a LIFO that the historical cost of goods sold is $4,800, that historical LIFO cost of beginning inventory is $600, and that historical LIFO cost of ending inventory is $800. Then distributable income, based on replacement costs, remains $350 (= $5,200 − $4,850), realized holding gains are $50 (= $4,850 − $4,800), realized income is $400 (= $350 + $50), the unrealized holding gain for the year is $250 (= ($1,550 − $800) − ($1,100 − $600)), and economic income is $650 (= $350 + $50 + $250). Since the only real effect of the cost flow assumption is to split the total holding gain into realized and unrealized portions, economic income is the same, independent of the cost flow assumption. The total of holding gains is $300 in the illustration. The choice of cost flow assumption governs how much holding gain is conventionally reported as realized (SEC "inventory profit") and how much is not.

**inventory turnover.**  Number of times the average *inventory* has been sold during a period; *cost of goods sold* for a period divided by average inventory for the period. See *ratio*.

**investee.**  A company whose *stock* is owned by another.

**invested capital.**  *Contributed capital*.

**investment.**  An *expenditure* to acquire property or other assets in order to produce *revenue*; the *asset* so acquired; hence a *current* expenditure made in anticipation of future income. Said of *securities* of other companies held for the long term and shown in a separate section of the *balance sheet*; in this context, contrast with *marketable securities*.

**investment tax credit.**  A reduction in income tax liability granted by the federal government to firms that buy new equipment. This item is a credit, in that it is deducted from the tax bill, not from pre-tax income. The tax credit has been a given percentage of the purchase price of certain assets purchased. The actual rules and rates have changed over the years. See *flow-through method* and *carry forward*.

## INVENTORY PROFIT ILLUSTRATION

| Assumed Data | (Historical) Acquisition Cost Assuming FIFO | Replacement Cost |
|---|---|---|
| Inventory, 1/1/XO ................ | $ 900 | $1,100 |
| Inventory, 12/13/XO .............. | 1,160 | 1,550 |
| Cost of Goods Sold for 19XO ........ | 4,740 | 4,850 |
| Sales for 19XO ............ $5,200 | | |
| | | |
| **Income Statement for 19XO** | | |
| | | |
| Sales ........................ | $5,200 | $5,200 |
| Cost of Goods Sold ................ | 4,740 | 4,850 |
| (1) **Distributable Income** ............ | | $ 350 |
| Realized Holding Gains .............. | | 110[a] |
| (2) **Realized Income** = Conventional | | |
| Net Income (under FIFO) ....... | $ 460 | $ 460 |
| Unrealized Holding Gain ......................... | | 190[b] |
| (3) **Economic Income** ......................... | | $ 650 |

[a]Realized holding gain during a period is replacement cost of goods sold less historical cost of goods sold; for 19XO the realized holding gain under FIFO is $110 = $4,850 − $4,740. The SEC refers to this as "inventory profit".

[b]The total unrealized holding gain at any time is replacement cost of inventory on hand at that time less historical cost of that inventory. The unrealized holding gain during a period is unrealized holding gain at the end of the period less the unrealized holding gain at the beginning of the period. Unrealized holding gain prior to 19XO is $200 = $1,100 − $900. Unrealized holding gain during 19XO = ($1,550 − $1,160) − ($1,100 − $900) = $390 − $200 = $190.

**invoice.** A document showing the details of a sale or purchase transaction.

**issue.** When a corporation exchanges its stock (or bonds) for cash or other assets, the corporation is said to issue, not sell, that stock (or bonds). Also used in the context of withdrawing supplies or materials from inventory for use in operations and drawing of a *check*.

**issued shares.** Those shares of *authorized capital stock* of a *corporation* that have been distributed to the stockholders. See *issue*. Shares of *treasury stock* are legally issued but are not considered to be *outstanding* for the purpose of voting, *dividend declarations*, and *earnings per share* calculations.

### J

**job cost sheet.** A schedule showing actual or budgeted inputs for a special order.

**job development credit.** The name used for the *investment tax credit* in the 1971 tax law on this subject.

**job-order costing.** Accumulation of *costs* for a particular identifiable batch of product, known as a *job*, as it moves through production.

**joint cost.** Cost of simultaneously producing or otherwise acquiring two or more products, called joint products, that must, by the nature of the process, be produced or acquired together, such as the cost of beef and hides of cattle. Other examples include central *corporate expenses*, *overhead* of a department when several products are manufactured, and *basket purchases*. See *common cost*.

**joint product.** One of two or more outputs from a process that must be produced or acquired simultaneously. See *by-product* and *joint cost*.

**journal.** The place where transactions are recorded as they occur. The book of original entry.

**journal entry.** A recording in a *journal*, of equal *debits* and *credits*, with an explanation of the *transaction*, if necessary.

**journalize.** To make an entry in a *journal*.

**Journal of Accountancy.** A monthly publication of the *AICPA*.

**Journal of Accounting Research.** Scholarly journal containing articles on theoretical and empirical aspects of accounting. Published three times a year by the Graduate School of Business of the University of Chicago.

**journal voucher.** A *voucher* documenting (and sometimes authorizing) a transaction, leading to an entry in the *journal*.

### K

**kiting.** This term means slightly different things in banking and auditing contexts. In both, however, it refers to the wrongful practice of taking advantage of the *float*, the time that elapses between the deposit of a *check* in one bank and its collection at another. In the banking context, an individual deposits in Bank A a check written on Bank B. He (or she) then writes checks against the deposit created in Bank A. Several days later, he deposits in Bank B a check written on Bank A, to cover the original check written in Bank B. Still later, he deposits in Bank A a check written on Bank B. The process of covering the deposit in Bank

A with a check written on Bank B and vice versa is continued until an actual deposit of cash can be arranged. In the auditing context, kiting refers to a form of *window dressing* where the amount of the account Cash in Bank is made to appear larger than it actually is by depositing in Bank A a check written on Bank B without recording the check written on Bank B in the *check register* until after the close of the *accounting period*.

# L

**labor variances.** The *price* (or *rate*) and *quantity* (or *usage*) *variances* for *direct labor* inputs in a *standard cost system*.

**land.** An *asset shown at acquisition cost* plus the *cost* of any nondepreciable *improvements*. In accounting, implies use as a plant or office site, rather than as a *natural resource*, such as timberland or farm land.

**lapping (accounts receivable).** The theft, by an employee, of cash sent in by a customer to discharge the latter's *payable*. The theft from the first customer is concealed by using cash received from a second customer. The theft from the second customer is concealed by using the cash received from a third customer, and so on. The process is continued until the thief returns the funds or can make the theft permanent by creating a fictitious *expense* or receivable write off, or until the fraud is discovered.

**lapse.** To expire; said of, for example, an insurance policy or discounts made available for prompt payment that are not taken.

**last-in, first-out.** See *LIFO*.

**layer.** See *LIFO inventory layer*.

**lead time.** The time that elapses between order-placing and receipt of the ordered *goods or services*.

**lease.** A contract calling for the lessee (user) to pay the lessor (owner) for the use of an asset. A cancelable lease is one the lessee can cancel at any time. A noncancelable lease requires payments from the lessee for the life of the lease and usually has many of the economic characteristics of *debt financing*. A noncancelable lease meets the usual criteria to be classified as a *liability* but some leases entered into before 1977 need not be shown as a liability. *FASB Statement No. 13* and the *SEC* require disclosure in notes to the financial statements of the commitments for noncancelable leases. See *financing lease* and *operating lease*.

**leasehold.** The *asset* representing the right of the *lessee* to use leased property. See *lease* and *leasehold improvement*.

**leasehold improvement.** An *improvement* to leased property. Should be *amortized* over *service life* or the life of the lease, whichever is shorter.

**least and latest rule.** Pay the least amount of taxes as late as possible within the law to minimize the *present value* of tax payments for a given set of operations.

**ledger.** A book of accounts. See *general ledger* and *subsidiary ledger;* contrast with *journal*.

**legal capital.** *Par* or *stated value* of issued *capital stock*. The amount of *contributed capital* that, according to state law, must remain permanently in the firm as protection for creditors.

**legal entity.** See *entity*.

**lender.** See *loan*.

**lessee.** See *lease*.

**lessor.** See *lease*.

**leverage.** Operating leverage refers to the tendency of *net income* to rise at a faster rate than sales when there are *fixed costs*. A doubling of sales, for example, usually implies a more-than-doubling of net income. This phenomenon can be studied at *breakeven chart*. Capital leverage refers to the increased rate of return on owners' equity (see *ratio*) when an investment earns a return larger than the *interest rate* paid for *debt* financing. Since the interest charges on debt are usually fixed, any *incremental* income benefits owners and none benefits debtors. When this term is used without a qualifying adjective, it usually refers to the capital leverage and means the use of *long-term* debt in securing *funds* for the *entity*.

**leveraged lease.** A special form of lease involving three parties—a *lender*, a *lessor*, and a *lessee*. The lender, such as a bank or insurance company, lends a portion, say 80 percent, of the cash required for acquiring the *asset*. The lessor puts up the remainder 20 percent, of the cash required. The lessor acquires the asset with the cash, using the asset as security for the loan and leases it to the lessee on a *noncancelable* basis. The lessee makes periodic lease payments to the lessor, who in turn makes payments on the loan to the lender. Typically, the lessor has no obligation for the debt to the lender other than transferring a portion of the receipts from the lessee. If the lessee should default on required lease payments, then the lender can repossess the leased asset. The lessor is usually entitled to deductions for tax purposes for depreciation on the asset, for interest expense on the loan from the lender, and for any investment tax credit. The lease is leveraged in the sense that the lessor, who enjoys most of the risks and rewards of ownership, usually borrows most of the funds needed to acquire the asset. See *leverage*.

**liability.** Usually, a legal obligation to pay a definite or reasonably certain amount at a definite or reasonably certain time in return for a current benefit. Some of the criteria are not met by items classified as liabilities where there are special circumstances. Examples are *pension* liabilities, estimates of future *warranty* expenditures, and *deferred tax liabilities*. See *indeterminate-term liability*. Other items meet the criteria to be a liability but are not shown as such. For example, noncancelable leases, which are sometimes disclosed only in footnotes; see *lease*.

**lien.** The right of person A to satisfy a claim against person B by holding B's property as security or by seizing B's property.

**life annuity.** A *contingent annuity* in which payments cease at death of a specified person(s), usually the *annuitant(s)*.

**LIFO.** An *inventory* flow assumption where the *cost of goods sold* is the cost of the most recently acquired units and the *ending inventory cost* is determined from costs of the oldest units; contrast with *FIFO*. In periods of rising prices and increasing inventories, LIFO leads to higher reported expenses and therefore lower reported income and lower balance sheet inventories than does FIFO. See the example in the Accounting Magic section of this book. See also *FISH* and *inventory profit*.

**LIFO, dollar value method.** See *dollar value LIFO method*.

**LIFO inventory layer.** The *ending inventory* for a

period is likely to be larger than the *beginning inventory*. Under a *LIFO cost flow assumption,* this increase in physical quantities is given a value determined by the prices of the earliest purchases during the year. The LIFO inventory then consists of layers, sometimes called "slices," which typically consist of relatively small amounts of physical quantities from each of the past several years. Each layer carries the prices from near the beginning of the period when it was acquired. The earliest layers will typically (in periods of rising prices) have prices very much less than current prices. If inventory quantities should decline in a subsequent period, the latest layers enter cost of goods sold first.

**limited liability.** Stockholders of corporations are not personally liable for debts of the company.

**limited partner.** Member of a *partnership* not personally liable for debts of the partnership; every partnership must have at least one *general partner* who is fully liable.

**line of business reporting.** See *segment reporting.*

**line of credit.** An agreement with a bank or set of banks for short-term borrowings on demand.

**liquid.** Said of a business with a substantial amount (the amount is unspecified) of *working capital,* especially *quick assets.*

**liquid assets.** *Cash, current marketable securities,* and, sometimes, *current receivables.*

**liquidating dividend.** *Dividend* declared in the winding up of a business to distribute the assets of the company to the stockholders. Usually treated by recipient as a return of *investment,* not as *revenue.*

**liquidation.** Payment of a debt. Sale of assets in closing down a business or a segment thereof.

**liquidation value per share.** The amount each *share* of stock will receive if the corporation is dissolved. For *preferred stock* with a *liquidation preference,* a stated amount per share.

**LISH.** An acronym, conceived by George H. Sorter, for *last-in, still-here.* LISH is the same cost flow assumption as *FIFO.* Many readers of accounting statements find it easier to think about inventory questions in terms of items still on hand. Think of FIFO in connection with *cost of goods sold* but of LISH in connection with *ending inventory.* See *FISH.*

**list price.** The published or nominally quoted price for goods.

**list-price method.** See *trade-in transaction.*

**loan.** An arrangement where the owner of property, called the lender, allows someone else, called the borrower, the use of the property for a period of time that is usually specified in the agreement setting up the loan. The borrower promises to return the property to the lender and, often, to make a payment for use of the property. Generally used when the property is *cash* and the payment for its use is *interest.*

**long-lived (term) asset.** An asset whose benefits are expected to be received over several years. A *noncurrent* asset, usually includes *investments, plant assets,* and *intangibles.*

**long-term (construction) contract accounting.** The *percentage of completion method* of *revenue* recognition.

**loss.** Excess of *cost* over net proceeds for a single transaction; negative *income* for a period. A cost expiration that produced no *revenue.*

**lower of cost or market.** A basis for *inventory* valuation where the inventory value is set at the lower of *acquisition cost* or *current replacement cost* (market), subject to the following constraints: First, the market value of an item used in the computation cannot exceed its *net realizable value*—an amount equal to selling price less reasonable costs to complete production and to sell the item. Second, the market value of an item used in the computation cannot be less than the net realizable value minus the normal *profit* ordinarily realized on disposition of completed items of this type. The lower of cost or market valuation is chosen as the lower of acquisition cost or replacement cost (market) subject to the upper and lower bounds on replacement cost established in the first two steps. The method for valuing by lower of cost or market is easier to remember and use when the method is translated into symbols as follows: Let: *AC* represent acquisition cost, *RC* represent replacement cost, *NRV* represent net realizable value, and *PROF* represent the normal profit. Then the lower of cost or market valuation is:

minimum [*AC, NRV,* maximum (*RC, NRV − PROF*)].

In words, find the maximum of replacement cost and net realizable value minus normal profit. Call that quantity *MAX.* Then choose the smallest of acquisition cost, net realizable value, and *MAX.* (The minimum of *NRV* and *MAX* is the "market" figure used in the computation.) The following example illustrates the application of the rule for lower of cost or market when the normal profit margin is nine cents ($.09) per unit.

| | Item | | | |
|---|---|---|---|---|
| | 1 | 2 | 3 | 4 |
| (a) Acquisition Cost | $ .90 | $ .97 | $ .96 | $ .90 |
| (b) Net Realizable Value | .95 | .95 | .95 | .95 |
| (c) Net Realizable Value Less Normal Profit Margin | .86 | .86 | .86 | .86 |
| (d) Replacement Cost | .92 | .96 | .92 | .85 |
| (e) Maximum [(d), (c)] = MAX | .92 | .96 | .92 | .86 |
| (f) Lower of Cost of Market = Minimum [(a), (b), (e)] | .90 | .95 | .92 | .86 |

Notice in this illustration that each of the four possible valuations is used once to determine lower of cost or market. Item 1 uses acquisition cost; Item 2 uses net realizable value; Item 3 uses replacement cost; and Item 4 uses net realizable value less normal profit.

Lower of cost or market cannot be used for tax returns in combination with a *LIFO* flow assumption.

**lump-sum acquisition.** *Basket purchase.*

## M

**maintenance.** *Expenditures* undertaken to preserve an *asset's* service potential for its originally-intended life; these expenditures are treated as *period expenses* or *product costs;* contrast with *improvement.* See *repair.*

**make-or-buy decision.** A managerial decision about whether the firm should produce a product internally or purchase it from others. Proper make-or-buy decisions in the short run result only when *opportunity* *costs* are the only costs considered in decision making.

**maker (of note) (of check).** One who signs a *note* to borrow. One who signs a *check*; in this context, synonymous with drawer; see *draft*.

**management.** Executive authority that operates a business.

**Management Accounting.** Monthly publication of the *NAA*.

**management (managerial) accounting.** Reporting designed to enhance the ability of management to do its job of decision making, planning, and control; contrast with *financial accounting*.

**management audit.** An audit conducted to determine whether the objectives, policies, and procedures for a firm or one of its operating units are properly carried out. Generally applies only to activities for which qualitative standards can be specified. See *audit* and *internal audit*.

**management by exception.** A principle of management where attention is focused only on performance that is significantly different from that expected.

**managerial accounting.** See *management accounting*.

**manufacturing cost.** Costs of producing goods, usually in a factory.

**manufacturing expense.** Another, less useful, title for *manufacturing overhead*.

**manufacturing overhead.** General manufacturing *costs* incurred in providing a capacity to carry on productive activities but which are not directly associated with identifiable units of product. *Fixed* manufacturing overhead costs are treated as a *product cost* under *absorption costing* but as an *expense* of the period under *direct costing*.

**margin.** *Revenue* less specified expenses. See *contribution margin, gross margin* and *current margin*.

**marginal cost.** *Incremental cost* per unit.

**marginal costing.** *Direct costing*.

**marginal revenue.** The increment in *revenue* from sale of one additional unit of product.

**marginal tax rate.** The tax imposed on the next dollar of taxable income generated; contrast with *statutory tax rate* and *average tax rate*.

**margin of safety.** Excess of actual, or budgeted, sales over *breakeven* sales. Usually expressed in dollars; may be expressed in units of product.

**markdown.** The reduction below an originally established retail price.

**marketable securities.** *Stocks* and *bonds* of other companies held that can be readily sold on stock exchanges or over-the-counter markets and that the company plans to sell as cash is needed. Classified as *current* assets and as part of *working capital*. The same securities held for *long-term* purposes would be classified as *noncurrent assets*. *FASB Statement* No. 12 requires the *lower-of-cost-or-market* valuation basis for all marketable equity securities but different accounting treatments (with differing effects on income) depending upon whether the security is a *current* or a *noncurrent asset*.

**market price.** See *fair market price*.

**market rate.** The rate of *interest* a company must pay to borrow *funds* currently. See *effective rate*.

**markon.** An amount originally added to *cost* to obtain *list price*. Usually expressed as a percentage of cost.

Further increases in list price are called *markups*; decreases are called *markdowns*.

**markup.** An amount originally added to cost. Usually expressed as a percentage of selling price. Also refers to an increase above an originally-established retail price. See *markon*.

**markup percentage.** *Markup* divided by (acquisition cost plus *markup*).

**master budget.** A *budget* projecting all *financial statements* and their components.

**matching convention.** The concept of recognizing cost expirations (*expenses*) in the same accounting period when the related *revenues* are recognized.

**material.** As an adjective, it means relatively important. See *materiality*. Currently, no operational definition exists. As a noun, *raw material*.

**materiality.** The concept that accounting should disclose separately only those events that are relatively important (no operable definition yet exists) for the business or for understanding its statements.

**material variances.** *Price* and *quantity variances* for *direct materials* in *standard cost systems*. Sometimes used to mean variances that are significant; see *materiality*.

**matrix.** A rectangular array of numbers or mathematical symbols.

**matrix inverse.** For a given square *matrix*, A, the square matrix inverse is the matrix, $A^{-1}$, such that $AA^{-1} = A^{-1}A = 1$, the *identity matrix*. Not all square matrices have inverses. Those that do not are called singular; those that do are nonsingular.

**maturity.** The date at which an obligation, such as the *principal* of a *bond* or a *note*, becomes due.

**maturity value.** The amount expected to be collected when a loan reaches *maturity*. Depending upon the context, the amount may be *principal* or principal and *interest*.

**merchandise.** *Finished goods* bought by a retailer or wholesaler for resale; contrast with finished goods of a manufacturing business.

**merchandise turnover.** *Inventory turnover* for merchandise; see *ratio*.

**merchandising business.** As opposed to a manufacturing or service business, one that purchases (rather than manufactures) *finished goods* for resale.

**merger.** The joining of two or more businesses into a single *economic entity*. See *holding company*.

**minority interest.** A *balance sheet account* on *consolidated statements* showing the *equity* in a *subsidiary* company allocable to those who are not part of the controlling (majority) interest. May be classified either as stockholders' equity or as a liability of *indeterminate term* on the consolidated balance sheet. On the *income statement*, the minority's interest in current income must be subtracted to arrive at consolidated *net income* for the period.

**minority investment.** A holding of less than 50 percent of the *voting stock* in another corporation. Accounted for with the *cost method* when less than 20 percent is held, and with the *equity method* otherwise. See *mutual fund*.

**minutes book.** A record of all actions authorized at corporate *board of directors'* or stockholders' meetings.

**mixed cost.** A *semifixed* or a *semivariable* cost.

**modified cash basis.** The *cash basis of accounting*

with long-term assets accounted for with the *accrual basis of accounting*.

**monetary assets, liabilities.** See *monetary items*.

**monetary gain or loss.** The *gain* or *loss* in general purchasing power as a result of holding *monetary assets* or liabilities during a period when the *general purchasing power of the dollar* changes. During periods of *inflation*, holders of net monetary assets lose, and holders of net monetary liabilities gain, general purchasing power. During periods of *deflation*, holders of net monetary assets gain, and holders of net monetary liabilities lose, general purchasing power.

**monetary items.** Amounts fixed in terms of dollars by statute or contract. *Cash, accounts receivable, accounts payable,* and *debt*. The distinction between monetary and nonmonetary items is important for general *price level adjusted statements* and for *foreign exchange gain or loss* computations. In the foreign exchange context, account amounts denominated in dollars are not monetary items while amounts denominated in any other currency are monetary.

**money.** A word seldom used with precision in accounting, at least in part because economists have not yet agreed on its definition. Economists use the term to refer to both a medium of exchange and a unit of value. See *cash* and *monetary items*.

**money-purchase plan.** A *pension plan* where the employer contributes a specified amount of cash each year to each employee's pension fund. Benefits ultimately received by the employee are not specifically defined but depend on the rate of return on the cash invested. Sometimes called a "defined-contribution" pension plan; contrast with *defined-benefit plan*. As of the mid-1970's, most corporate pension plans were defined benefit plans because both the law and *generally accepted accounting principles* for pensions made defined benefit plans more attractive than money purchase plans. The federal pension law of 1974 makes money purchase plans relatively more attractive than they had been. We expect the number of money-purchase plans to increase. See *ERISA*.

**mortality table.** Data on life expectancies or probabilities of death for persons of specified ages and sex.

**mortgage.** A claim given by the borrower (mortgagor) to the lender (mortgagee) against the borrower's property in return for a loan.

**moving average.** An *average* computed on observations over time. As a new observation becomes available, the oldest one is dropped so that the average is always computed for the same number of observations and only the most recent ones. Sometimes, however, this term is used synonymously with *weighted-average*.

**moving average method.** *Weighted-average method*.

**multiple-step.** Said of an *income* statement where various classes of *expenses* and *losses* are subtracted from *revenues* to show intermediate items such as *operating income*, income of the enterprise (operating income plus *interest* income), income to investors (income of the enterprise less *income taxes*), net income to shareholders (income to investors less interest charges), and income retained (income to stockholders less dividends). See *entity theory*.

**municipal bond.** A *bond* issued by a village, town, city, county, state, or other public body. *Interest* on such bonds is generally exempt from federal *income taxes* and from some state income taxes. Sometimes referred to as "tax exempts."

**mutual fund.** An investment company that issues its own stock to the public and uses the proceeds to invest in securities of other companies. A mutual fund usually owns less than five or ten percent of the stock of any one company and accounts for its investments using current *market values;* contrast with *holding company*.

**mutually exclusive projects.** Competing investment projects, where accepting one project eliminates the possibility of undertaking the remaining projects.

# N

**National Association of Accountants (NAA).** A national society generally open to all engaged in activities closely associated with *managerial accounting*. Oversees the administration of the *CMA* Examinations through the Institute of Management Accounting.

**natural business year.** A twelve-month period chosen as the reporting period so that the end of the period coincides with a low point in activity or inventories. See *ratio* for a discussion of analyses of financial statements of companies using a natural business year.

**natural classification.** *Income statement* reporting form in which *expenses* are classified by nature of items as acquired, that is materials, wages, salaries, insurance, and taxes, as well as depreciation; contrast with *functional classification*.

**natural resources.** Timberland, oil and gas wells, ore deposits, and other products of nature that have economic value. The cost of natural resources is subject to *depletion*. Often called "wasting assets." See also *discovery value accounting* and *percentage depletion*.

**negative confirmation.** See *confirmation*.

**negative goodwill.** Refer to *goodwill*. When the purchase of the company acquired is less than the sum of the *fair market value* of the *net assets* acquired, APB Opinion No. 16 requires that the valuation of noncurrent assets (except *investments* in *marketable securities*) acquired be reduced until the purchase price equals the adjusted valuation of the fair market value of net assets acquired. If after the adjusted valuation of noncurrent assets is reduced to zero and the purchase price is still less than the net assets acquired, then the difference is shown as a credit balance in the balance sheet as negative goodwill and is amortized to income over a period not to exceed forty years. For negative goodwill to exist, someone must be willing to sell a company for less than the fair market value of net current assets and marketable securities. Since such a bargain purchase is rare, negative goodwill is rarely found in the financial statements.

**negotiable.** Legally capable of being transferred by endorsement. Usually said of *checks* and *notes* and sometimes of *stocks* and *bearer bonds*.

**net.** Reduced by all relevant deductions.

**net assets.** *Owners' equity;* total *assets* minus total *liabilities*.

**net current assets.** *Working capital = current assets − current liabilities.*

**net current asset value (per share).** *Working capital* divided by the number of common shares outstanding. Many security analysts think that when a common share trades in the market for an amount less than net current asset value, then the shares are undervalued and should be purchased.

**net income.** The excess of all *revenues* and *gains* for a period over all *expenses* and *losses* of the period.

**net loss.** The excess of all *expenses* and *losses* for a period over all *revenues* and *gains* of the period. Negative *net income*.

**net markup.** In the context of *retail inventory methods, markups* less markup cancellations; a figure which usually ignores *markdowns* and markdown cancellations.

**net of tax method.** A nonsanctioned method for dealing with the problem of income tax allocation; described in *APB* Opinion No. 11. Deferred tax credit items are subtracted from specific asset amounts rather than being shown as a deferred credit or liability.

**net of tax reporting.** Reporting, such as for *income from discontinued operations, extraordinary items,* and *prior-period adjustments,* where the amounts presented in *financial statements* have been adjusted for all income tax effects. For example, if an extraordinary loss amounted to $10,000 and the average tax rate were 40 percent, then the extraordinary item would be reported "net of taxes" as a $6,000 loss. Hence, all income taxes may not be reported on one line of the income statement. The taxes will be allocated to *income from continuing operations,* income from discontinued operations, extraordinary items, and prior-period adjustments.

**net present value.** Discounted or *present value* of all cash inflows and outflows of a project or from an *investment* at a given *discount rate.*

**net price method (of recording purchase or sales discounts).** The *purchase* (or *sale*) is recorded at its *invoice* price less all *discounts* made available under the assumption that nearly all discounts will be taken. Discounts lapsed through failure to pay promptly are recorded in an *adjunct account* to purchases (or sales) or in the purchasing context, to an *expense* account. In the context of purchases, management usually prefers to know about the amount of discounts lost because of inefficient operations, not the amounts taken, so that most managers prefer the net price method to the *gross price method.*

**net realizable value.** Selling price of an item less reasonable further costs to make the item ready for sale and to sell it. See *lower of cost or market.*

**net sales.** Sales (at gross invoice amount) less *returns, allowances,* freight paid for customers, and *discounts* taken.

**net working capital.** *Working capital*; the "net" is redundant in accounting. Financial analysts sometimes mean *current* assets when they speak of working capital, so for them the "net" is not redundant.

**net worth.** A misleading term, to be avoided, that means the same as *owners' equity.* See the Penn Central annual report.

**New York Stock Exchange (NYSE).** A public market where various corporate *securities* are traded.

**next-in, first-out.** See *NIFO.*

**NIFO.** *Next-in, first-out.* In making decisions, many managers consider *replacement costs* (rather than *historical costs*) and refer to them as NIFO costs.

**nominal accounts.** *Temporary accounts* as opposed to *balance sheet accounts.* All nominal accounts are *closed* at the end of each *accounting period.*

**nominal interest rate.** A rate specified on a *debt* instrument, which usually differs from the market or *effective rate.* Also, a rate of *interest* quoted for a year. If the interest is compounded more often than annually, then the *effective interest rate* is higher than the nominal rate.

**noncancelable.** See *lease.*

**noncontributory.** Said of a *pension plan* where only the employer makes payments to a pension *fund;* contrast with *contributory.*

**noncurrent.** Due more than one year (or more than one *operating cycle*) hence.

**nonexpendable fund.** A governmental fund, whose *principal,* and sometimes earnings, may not be spent.

**noninterest-bearing note.** A *note* which bears no explicit interest. The *present value* of such a note at any time before *maturity* is less than the *face value* so long as *interest rates* are positive. *APB Opinion* No. 21 requires that the present value, not face value, of long-term noninterest-bearing notes be reported as the *asset* or *liability* amount in financial statements.

**nonmonetary items.** All items that are not monetary; see *monetary items.*

**nonoperating.** In the *income statement* context, said of revenues and expenses arising from transactions incidental to the company's main line(s) of business. In the *statement of changes in financial position* context, said of all sources or uses of *working capital* other than working capital provided by operations.

**nonprofit corporation.** An incorporated *entity,* such as a hospital, with no owners who share in the earnings. It usually emphasizes providing services rather than maximizing income.

**nonrecurring.** Said of an event that is not expected to happen often for a given firm. Under *APB* Opinion No. 30, the effects of such events should be disclosed separately, but as part of *ordinary* items unless the event is also unusual. See *extraordinary* item.

**no par.** Said of *stock* without a *par value.*

**normal cost.** *Pension plan expenses* incurred during an *accounting period* for employment services performed during that period; contrast with *past* and *prior service cost* and see *funded.*

**normal spoilage.** Costs incurred because of ordinary amounts of spoilage; such costs should be prorated to units produced as *product costs;* contrast with *abnormal spoilage.*

**normal standard cost.** The *cost* expected to be incurred under reasonably efficient operating conditions with adequate provision for an average amount of rework, spoilage, and the like.

**normal volume.** The level of production over a time span, usually one year, that will satisfy demand by purchasers.

**note.** An unconditional written promise by the maker (borrower) to pay a certain amount on demand or at a certain future time. See *footnotes* for another context.

**note receivable discounted.** A *note* assigned by the holder to another. If the note is assigned with recourse, it is the *contingent liability* of the assignor until the debt is paid. See *factoring.*

**number of days sales in inventory (or receivables).** Days of average inventory on hand (or average collection period for receivables). See *ratio*.

**NYSE.** *New York Stock Exchange*.

# O

**OASD(H)I.** *Old Age, Survivors, Disability, and (Hospital) Insurance*.

**objective.** See *reporting objective* and *objectivity*.

**objectivity.** The reporting policy implying that formal recognition will not be given to an event in financial statements until the magnitude of the events can be measured with reasonable accuracy and is subject to independent verification.

**obsolescence.** A decline in *market value* of an *asset* caused by improved alternatives becoming available that will be more *cost-effective;* the decline in market value is unrelated to physical changes in the asset itself. See *partial obsolescence*.

**Occupational Safety and Health Act.** *OSHA*.

**off balance sheet financing.** A description often used for a *long-term, noncancelable lease* accounted for as an *operating lease*.

**Old Age, Survivors, Disability and (Hospital) Insurance.** The technical name for Social Security under the Federal Insurance Contribution Act (FICA).

**on (open) account.** Said of a *purchase* or *sale* when payment is expected sometime after delivery and no *note* evidencing the *debt* is given or received. When a sale (purchase) is made on open account, *accounts receivable (payable)* is *debited (credited)*.

**on consignment.** Said of goods delivered by the owner (the consignor) to another (the consignee) to be sold by the consignee; the owner is entitled to the return of the property or payment of an amount agreed upon in advance. The goods are assets of the consignor.

**open account.** Any *account* with a nonzero debit or credit *balance*. See *on (open) account*.

**operating.** An adjective used to refer to *revenue* and *expense* items relating to the company's main line(s) of business.

**operating accounts.** *Revenue, expense,* and *production cost accounts;* contrast with *balance sheet accounts*.

**operating cycle.** *Earnings cycle*.

**operating expenses.** *Expenses* incurred in the course of *ordinary* activities of an *entity*. Frequently, a narrower classification including only *selling, general,* and *administrative expenses,* thereby excluding *cost of goods sold, interest,* and *income tax* expenses.

**operating lease.** A *lease* accounted for by the *lessee* without showing an *asset* for the lease rights (*leasehold*) or a *liability* for the lease payment obligations. Rental payments of the lessee are merely shown as *expenses* of the period. The lessor keeps the asset on his or her *books* and shows the rental payments as *revenues;* contrast with *financing lease*.

**operating margin (based on replacement costs).** *Revenues* from *sales* minus current *replacement cost* of goods sold. A measure of operating efficiency that is independent of the *cost flow assumption* for *inventory*. Sometimes called "current (gross)

margin." See *inventory profit* for example computations.

**operating ratio.** See *ratio*.

**operational control.** See *control system*.

**opinion.** The *auditor's report* containing an attestation or lack thereof. Also, *APB Opinion*.

**opportunity cost.** The *present value* of the *income* (or *costs*) that could be earned (or saved) from using an *asset* in its best alternative use to the one being considered.

**option.** The legal right to buy something during a specified period at a specified price, called the *exercise* price. Employee stock options should not be confused with put and call options traded in various public markets.

**ordinary annuity.** An *annuity in arrears*.

**ordinary income.** For income tax purposes, reportable *income* not qualifying as *capital gains*.

**organization costs.** The *costs* incurred in planning and establishing an *entity;* example of an *intangible* asset. Often, since the amounts are not *material,* the costs are treated as *expenses* in the period incurred even though the *expenditures* clearly provide future benefits and should be treated as *assets*.

**original cost.** *Acquisition cost*. In public-utility accounting, the acquisition cost to the *entity* first devoting the asset to public use.

**original entry.** Entry in a *journal*.

**OSHA.** Occupational Safety and Health Act. The federal law that governs working conditions in commerce and industry.

**outlay.** The amount of an *expenditure*.

**out-of-pocket.** Said of an *expenditure* usually paid for with cash. An *incremental* cost.

**out-of-stock cost.** The estimated decrease in future *profit* as a result of losing customers because insufficient quantities of *inventory* are currently on hand to meet customers' demands.

**output.** Physical quantity or monetary measurement of *goods* and *services* produced.

**outside director.** A member of a corporate board of directors who is not a company officer and does not participate in the corporation's day-to-day management.

**outstanding.** Unpaid or uncollected. When said of *stock,* the shares issued less *treasury stock*. When said of checks, it means a check issued that did not clear the *drawer's* bank prior to the *bank statement* date.

**over-and-short.** Title for an *expense account* used to account for small differences between book balances of cash and actual cash and vouchers or receipts in *petty cash* or *change funds*.

**overapplied (overabsorbed) overhead.** An excess of costs applied, or *charged,* to product for a period over actual *overhead* costs during the period. A *credit balance* in an overhead account after overhead is assigned to product.

**overdraft.** A check written on a checking account which contains less funds than the amount of the check.

**overhead costs.** Any *cost* not specifically or directly associated with the production or sale of identifiable goods and services. Sometimes called "burden" or "indirect costs" and, in Britain, "oncosts." Frequently limited to manufacturing overhead. See *cen-*

*tral corporate expenses* and *manufacturing overhead.*

**overhead rate.** Standard, or other predetermined, rate at which *overhead costs* are applied to products or to services.

**over-the-counter.** Said of a *security* traded in a negotiated transaction, rather than in an auctioned one on an organized stock exchange, such as the *New York Stock Exchange.*

**owners' equity.** *Proprietorship; assets* minus *liabilities; paid-in capital* plus *retained earnings* of a corporation; partners' capital accounts in a *partnership;* owner's capital account in a *sole proprietorship.*

# P

**paid-in capital.** Sum of balances in *capital stock* and *capital contributed in excess of par (or stated) value* accounts. Same as *contributed capital* (minus *donated capital*).

**paper profit.** A *gain* not yet realized through a *transaction.* An *unrealized holding gain.*

**par.** See *at par* and *face amount.*

**parent company.** Company owning more than 50 percent of the voting shares of another company, called the *subsidiary.*

**partially funded.** Said of a *pension plan* where not all earned benefits have been funded. See *funded* for funding requirements.

**partially vested.** Said of a *pension plan* where not all employee benefits are *vested.* See *graded vesting.*

**partial obsolescence.** As technology improves, the economic value of existing *assets* declines. In many cases, however, it will not pay a firm to replace the existing asset with a new one even though the new type, rather than the old, would be acquired if the acquisition were to be made currently. In these cases, the accountant should theoretically recognize a loss from partial obsolescence from the firm's owning an old, out-of-date asset, but *GAAP* does not permit recognition of partial obsolescence. The old asset will be carried at *cost* less *accumulated depreciation* until it is retired from service. See *obsolescence.*

**participating dividend.** *Dividend* paid to preferred stockholders in addition to the minimum preferred dividends when the *preferred stock* contract allows such sharing in earnings. Usually applies after dividends on *common stock* have reached a certain level.

**participating preferred stock.** *Preferred stock* with rights to *participating dividends.*

**partner's drawing.** A payment to a partner to be charged against his or her share of income or capital. The name of a *temporary account* to record such payments.

**partnership.** Contractual arrangement between individuals to share resources and operations in a jointly run business. See *general* and *limited partner* and *Uniform Partnership Act.*

**par value.** *Face amount* of a *security.*

**par value method.** The method of accounting for *treasury stock* that *debits* a common stock account with the *par value* of the shares reacquired and allocates the remaining debits between the *additional paid-in capital* and *retained earnings* accounts; contrast with *cost method.*

**past service cost.** *Present value* at a given time of a *pension plan's* unrecognized, and usually unfunded, benefits assigned to employees for their service before the inception of the plan. A part of *prior service cost.* See *prior service cost* for disclosure rules. See *funded;* contrast with *normal cost.*

**patent.** A right granted for up to 17 years by the federal government to exclude others from manufacturing, using or selling a claimed design, product or plan (e.g. a new breed of rose) or from using a claimed process or method of manufacture. An asset if acquired by purchase. If developed internally, the development costs are *expensed* when incurred under current *GAAP.*

**payable.** Unpaid but not necessarily due or past due.

**pay as you go.** Said of an *income tax* scheme where periodic payments of income taxes are made during the period when the income to be taxed is being earned; in contrast to a scheme where no payments are due until the end of, or after, the period whose income is being taxed. (Called PAYE—pay as you earn—in Britain.) Sometimes this phrase is used to describe an *unfunded pension plan,* where payments to pension plan beneficiaries are made from general corporate funds, not from cash previously contributed to a pension fund. Not acceptable as a method of accounting for pension plans.

**payback period.** Amount of time that must elapse before the cash inflows from a project equal the cash outflows.

**payback reciprocal.** One divided by the *payback period.* This number approximates the *internal rate of return* on a project when the project life is more than twice the payback period and the cash inflows are identical in every period after the initial investment.

**PAYE.** See *pay as you go.*

**payee.** The person or entity to whom a cash payment is made or who will receive the stated amount of money on a check. See *draft.*

**payout ratio.** *Common stock dividends* declared for a year divided by net *income* to common stock for the year. A term used by financial analysts; contrast with *dividend yield.*

**payroll taxes.** Taxes levied because salaries or wages are paid; for example, *FICA* and unemployment compensation insurance taxes. Typically, the employer pays a portion and withholds part of the employee's wages for the other portion.

**pension fund.** *Fund,* the assets of which are to be paid to retired ex-employees, usually as a *life annuity.* Usually held by an independent trustee and then is not an *asset* of the firm.

**pension plan.** Details or provisions of employer's contract with employees for paying retirement *annuities* or other benefits. See *funded, vested, normal cost, past service cost, prior service cost, money-purchase plan,* and *defined-benefit plan.*

**per books.** An expression used to refer to the *book value* of an item at a specific time.

**percent.** Any number, expressed as a decimal, multiplied by 100.

**percentage depletion (allowance).** Deductible *expense* allowed in some cases by the federal *income tax* regulations; computed as a percentage of gross income from a *natural resource* independent of the unamortized cost of the asset. Since the amount of the total deductions for tax purposes is usually greater than the cost of the asset being *depleted,* many people think the deduction is an unfair tax advantage or "loophole."

**percentage of completion method.** Recognizing *revenues* and *expenses* on a job, order, or contract (a) in proportion to the *costs* incurred for the period divided by total costs expected to be incurred for the job or order, or (b) in proportion to engineers' estimates of the incremental degree of completion of the job, order, or contract during the period. Contrast with *completed contract method.*

**percentage statement.** A statement containing, in addition to dollar amounts, ratios of dollar amounts to some base. In a percentage *income statement,* the base is usually either *net sales* or total *revenues* and in a percentage *balance sheet,* the base is usually total *assets.*

**period.** *Accounting period.*

**period cost.** An inferior term for *period expense.*

**period expense (charge).** *Expenditure,* usually based upon the passage of time, charged to operations of the accounting period rather than *capitalized* as an asset; contrast with *product cost.*

**periodic inventory.** A method of recording *inventory* that uses data on beginning inventory, additions to inventories, and ending inventory in order to find the cost of withdrawals from inventory.

**periodic procedures.** The process of making *adjusting entries, closing entries,* and preparing the *financial statements,* usually by use of *trial balances* and *work sheets.*

**permanent account.** An account which appears on the *balance sheet;* contrast with *temporary account.*

**permanent difference.** Difference between reported income and taxable income that will never be reversed and, hence, requires no entry in the *deferred income tax (liability)* account. An example is the difference between taxable and reportable income from interest earned on state and municipal bonds; contrast with *timing difference* and see *deferred income tax liability.*

**perpetual annuity.** *Perpetuity.*

**perpetual inventory.** Records on quantities and amounts of *inventory* that are changed or made current with each physical addition to or withdrawal from the stock of goods; an inventory so recorded. The records will show the physical quantities and, frequently, the dollar valuations that should be on hand at any time. A perpetual inventory facilitates *control*; contrast with *periodic inventory.*

**perpetuity.** An *annuity* whose payments continue forever. The *present value* of a perpetuity in *arrears* is p/r where p is the periodic payment and r is the *interest rate* per period.

**personal account.** *Drawing account.*

**petty cash fund.** Currency maintained for expenditures that are conveniently made with Cash on hand.

**physical verification.** *Verification,* by an *auditor,* performed by actually inspecting items in *inventory, plant assets,* and the like; may be based on statistical sampling procedures; contrasted with mere checking of written records.

**plant.** *Plant assets.*

**plant assets.** Buildings, machinery, equipment, land, and natural resources. The phrase "property, plant, and equipment" is, therefore, a redundancy. In this context, "plant" means buildings.

**pledging.** The borrower assigns *assets* as security or *collateral* for repayment of a loan.

**pledging of receivables.** The process of using expected collections on amounts receivable as *collateral* for a loan. The borrower remains responsible for collecting the receivable but promises to use the proceeds for repaying the debt.

**plow back.** To retain earnings for continued investment in the business.

**plug.** For any *account,* beginning balance + additions − deductions = ending balance; if any three of the four items are known, the fourth can be found by plugging. In making a *journal entry,* often all *debits* are known, as are all but one of the *credits* (or vice versa). Since *double-entry* bookkeeping requires equal debits and credits, the unknown quantity can be determined by subtracting the sum of the known credits from the sum of all the debits (or vice versa). This process is also known as plugging. The unknown found is called the plug. For example, if a *discount* on *bonds payable* is being *amortized* with the *straight-line method,* then *interest expense* is a plug: interest expense = interest payable + discount amortization. See *trade-in transaction* for an example.

**pooling of interests method.** Accounting for a *business combination* by merely adding together the *book value* of the *assets* and *equities* of the combined firms. Contrast with *purchase method.* Generally leads to a higher reported *net income* for the combined firms than would be reported had the business combination been accounted for as a purchase. See *APB Opinion* No. 16 for the conditions that must be met before the pooling of interests treatment is acceptable.

**positive confirmation.** See *confirmation.*

**post.** To record entries in an *account* in a *ledger;* usually the entries are transferred from a *journal.*

**post-closing trial balance.** *Trial balance* taken after all *temporary accounts* have been closed.

**post-statement events.** Events with *material* impact that occur between the end of the *accounting period* and the formal publication of the *financial statements.* Such events must be disclosed in notes for the auditor to give a *clean opinion,* even though the events are subsequent to the period being reported on.

**potentially dilutive.** A *security* which may be converted into, or exchanged for, common stock and thereby reduce reported *earnings per share: options, warrants, convertible bonds,* and *convertible preferred stock.*

**pre-closing trial balance.** *Trial balance* taken at the end of the period before *closing entries.* In this sense, an *adjusted trial balance.* Sometimes taken before *adjusting entries* and then is synonymous with *unadjusted trial balance.* The hyphen is often omitted in spelling.

**predetermined (factory) overhead rate.** Rate used in applying *overhead* to products or departments developed at the start of a period by dividing estimated overhead cost by the estimated number of units of the overhead allocation base (or *denominator volume*) activity.

**pre-emptive right.** The privilege of a stockholder to maintain a proportionate share of ownership by purchasing a proportionate share of any new stock issues.

**preference as to assets.** The rights of *preferred stockholders* to receive certain payments in case of dissolution before common stockholders receive payments.

**preferred stock.** *Capital stock* with a claim to income or assets after bondholders but before *common stock*. *Dividends* on preferred stock are income distributions, not expenses. See *cumulative preferred stock*.

**premium.** The excess of issue (or market) price over *par value*. For a different context, see *insurance*.

**premium on capital stock.** Alternative but inferior title for *capital contributed in excess of par (or stated) value*.

**prepaid expense.** An *expenditure* that leads to a *deferred charge* or *prepayment;* strictly speaking, a contradiction in terms for an *expense* is a gone asset and this title refers to past *expenditures*, such as for rent or insurance premiums, that still have future benefits and thus are *assets*.

**prepaid income.** An inferior alternative title for *advances from customers*. An item should not be called *revenue* or *income* until earned, when goods are delivered or services are rendered.

**prepayments.** *Deferred charges*. *Assets* representing *expenditures* for future benefits. Rent and insurance premiums paid in advance are usually classified as *current* prepayments.

**present value.** Value today of an amount or amounts to be paid or received later, discounted at some *interest* or *discount rate*.

**price.** The quantity of one *good* or *service*, usually *cash*, asked in return for a unit of another good or service. See *fair market price*.

**price-earnings ratio.** At a given time, the market value of a company's *common stock*, per share, divided by the *earnings per* common *share* for the past year. See *ratio*.

**price index.** A series of numbers, one for each period, that purports to represent some *average* of prices for a series of periods, relative to a base period.

**price level.** The number from a *price index* series for a given period or date.

**price level adjusted statements.** *Financial statements* expressed in terms of dollars of uniform purchasing power. *Nonmonetary* items are restated to reflect changes in general *price levels* since the time specific *assets* were acquired and *liabilities* were incurred. A *gain* or *loss* is recognized on *monetary items* as they are held over time periods when the general *price level* changes. Conventional financial statements show *historical costs* and ignore differences in purchasing power in different periods.

**price variance.** In accounting for *standard costs*, (actual cost per unit − standard cost per unit) times quantity purchased.

**primary earnings per share.** Net *income* to *common stockholders* plus *interest (net of tax* effects) and *dividends* paid on *common stock equivalents* divided by (weighted-average of common shares outstanding plus the net increase in the number of common shares that would become *outstanding* if all common stock equivalents were exchanged for common shares with cash proceeds, if any, used to retire common shares).

**prime cost.** Sum of *direct materials* plus *direct labor* costs assigned to product.

**prime rate.** The rate for loans charged by commercial banks to their most preferred risks. For the *earnings-per-share* purpose of deciding whether a security is or is not a *common stock equivalent*, the corporation should use the rate in effect at the bank at which it does business or an average of such rates if the corporation does business with more than one bank. The *Federal Reserve Bulletin* is considered the authoritative source of information about historical prime rates.

**principal.** An amount on which *interest* is charged or earned.

**principle.** See *generally accepted accounting principles*.

**prior-period adjustment.** A *debit* or *credit* made directly to *retained earnings* (that does not affect *income* for the period) to adjust retained earnings for such things as lawsuit settlements and changes in *income tax expense* of prior periods. Theory would suggest that corrections of errors in accounting estimates (such as the *depreciable life* or *salvage value* of an asset) should be treated as adjustments to retained earnings. But *GAAP* require that corrections of such estimates flow through current, and perhaps future, *income statements*. See *accounting changes* and *accounting errors*.

**prior service cost.** *Present value* at a given time of a *pension plan's* unrecognized benefits assigned to employees for their service before that given time. Includes *past service cost*. Such obligations are not recognized as liabilities in the accounting records, but must be disclosed in the notes to the financial statements; contrast with *normal cost*. See *funded*. See the General Electric annual report at notes 37.6 and 37.7 for examples.

**proceeds.** The *funds* received from disposition of assets or from the issue of securities.

**process costing.** A method of *cost accounting* based on average costs (total cost divided by the *equivalent units* of work done in a period). Typically used for assembly lines or for products that are produced in a series of steps that are more continuous than discrete.

**product.** *Goods* or *services* produced.

**product cost.** Any *manufacturing cost* that can be inventoried. See *flow of costs* for example and contrast with *period expenses*.

**production cost.** *Manufacturing cost*.

**production cost account.** A *temporary account* for collecting *manufacturing costs* during a period.

**production department.** A department producing salable *goods* or *services;* contrast with *service department*.

**production method (depreciation).** The depreciable asset is given a *depreciable life* measured, not in elapsed time, but in units of output or perhaps in units of time of actual use. Then the *depreciation* charge for a period is a portion of depreciable cost equal to a fraction determined by dividing the actual output produced during the period by the expected total output to be produced over the life of the asset.

Sometimes called the "units of production (or output) method."

**production method (revenue recognition).** *Percentage of completion method* for recognizing *revenue.*

**productive capacity.** In computing *replacement costs* of *long-term assets,* we are interested in the cost of reproducing the productive capacity (for example, the ability to manufacture one million units a year), not the cost of reproducing the actual physical assets currently used (see *reproduction cost*). Replacement cost of productive capacity will be the same as reproduction cost of assets only in the unusual case when there has been no technological improvement in production processes and the relative prices of goods and services used in production have remained approximately the same as when the currently-used ones were acquired.

**profit.** Excess of *revenues* over *expenses* for a *transaction;* sometimes used synonymously with *net income* for the period.

**profitability accounting.** *Responsibility accounting.*

**profit and loss sharing ratio.** The fraction of *net income* or loss allocable to a partner in a *partnership.* Need not be the same fraction as the partner's share of capital.

**profit and loss statement.** *Income statement.*

**profit center.** A unit of activity for which both *revenue* and *expenses* are accumulated; contrast with *cost center.*

**profit margin.** Sales minus all expenses as a single amount. Frequently used to mean the ratio of sales minus all *operating* expenses divided by sales.

**profit maximization.** The doctrine that a given set of operations should be accounted for so as to make reported *net income* as large as possible; contrast with *conservatism.* This concept in accounting is slightly different from the profit maximizing concept in economics where the doctrine states that businesses should be run to maximize the present value of the firm's wealth, generally by equating *marginal costs* and *marginal revenues.*

**profit-volume graph.** See *breakeven chart.*

**profit-volume ratio.** Net *income* divided by net sales in dollars.

**pro forma statements.** Hypothetical statements. Financial statements as they would appear if some event, such as a *merger* or increased production and sales, had occurred or were to occur. Pro forma is often spelled as one word.

**programmed costs.** A *fixed cost* not essential for carrying out operations. Research and development and advertising designed to generate new business are controllable, but once a commitment is made to incur them, they become fixed costs. Sometimes called *managed costs* or *discretionary costs;* contrast with *capacity costs.*

**progressive tax.** Tax for which the rate increases as the taxed base, such as income, increases; contrast with *regressive tax.*

**projected financial statement.** *Pro forma* financial statement.

**promissory note.** An unconditional written promise to pay a specified sum of money on demand or at a specified date.

**proof of journal.** The process of checking arithmetic accuracy of *journal entries* by testing for the equality of all *debits* with all *credits* since the last previous proof.

**property dividend.** A *dividend in kind.*

**proprietary accounts.** See *budgetary accounts* for contrast in context of governmental accounting.

**proprietorship.** *Assets* minus *liabilities* of an *entity;* equals *contributed capital* plus *retained earnings.*

**proprietorship theory.** The view of the corporation that emphasizes the form of the *accounting equation* that says *assets – liabilities = owners' equity;* contrast with *entity theory.* The major implication of a choice between these theories deals with the treatment of *subsidiaries.* For example, the view that *minority interest* is an *indeterminate-term liability* is based on the proprietorship theory. The proprietorship theory implies using a *single-step income statement.*

**prorate.** To *allocate* in proportion to some base; for example, to allocate *service department* costs in proportion to hours of service used by the benefited departments.

**prospectus.** Formal written document describing *securities* to be issued. See *proxy.*

**protest fee.** Fee charged by banks or other financial agencies when items (such as checks) presented for collection cannot be collected.

**provision.** Often the exact amount of an *expense* is uncertain, but must be recognized currently anyway. The entry for the estimated expense, such as for *income taxes* or expected costs under *warranty,* is:

```
Expense (Estimated) .......................... X
    Liability (Estimated) .......................... X
```

In American usage, the term "provision" is often used in the expense account title of the above entry. Thus, Provision for Income Taxes is used to mean the estimate of income tax expense. (In British usage, the term "provision" is used in the title for the estimated liability of the above entry, so that Provision for Income Taxes is a balance sheet account.)

**proxy.** Written authorization given by one person to another so that the second person can act for the first, such as to vote shares of stock. Of particular significance to accountants because the *SEC* presumes that financial information is distributed by management along with its proxy solicitations.

**public accountant.** Generally, this term is synonymous with *certified public accountant.* In some jurisdictions individuals have been licensed as public accountants without being CPA's.

**public accounting.** That portion of accounting primarily involving the *attest* function, culminating in the *auditor's report.*

**PuPU.** An acronym for *p*urchasing *p*ower *u*nit. Some, including the Chief Accountant of the *SEC,* who think *general price level adjusted* accounting is not particularly useful, poke fun at it by calling it "PuPU accounting."

**purchase allowance.** A reduction in sales *invoice price* usually granted because the *goods* received by the purchaser were not exactly as ordered. The goods are not returned to the seller, but are purchased at a price lower than originally agreed upon.

**purchase discount.** A reduction in purchase *invoice price* granted for prompt payment. See *sales discount* and *terms of sale*.

**purchase method.** Accounting for a *business combination* by adding the acquired company's assets at the price paid for them to the acquiring company's assets. Contrast with *pooling of interests method*. Since the acquired assets are put on the books at current, rather than original costs, the *amortization expenses* are usually larger (and reported income, smaller) than for the same business combination accounted for as a pooling of interests. The purchase method is required unless all criteria to be a pooling are met.

**purchase order.** Document authorizing a seller to deliver goods with payment to be made later.

## Q

**qualified report (opinion).** *Auditor's* report containing a statement that the auditor was unable to complete a satisfactory examination of all things considered relevant or that the auditor has doubts about the financial impact of some material item reported in the financial statements. See *except for* and *subject to*.

**qualified (stock) option (plan).** Said of a compensation scheme in which *options* to purchase *stock* are granted to employees and in which the implicit compensation is neither tax deductible as an *expense* by the employer nor taxable *income* to the employee.

**quantity discount.** A reduction in purchase price as quantity purchased increases; amount of the discount is constrained by law (Robinson-Patman Act). Not to be confused with *purchase discount*.

**quantity variance.** In *standard cost* systems, the standard price per unit times (actual quantity used minus standard quantity that should be used).

**quasi-reorganization.** A *reorganization* where no new company is formed or no court has intervened, as would happen in *bankruptcy*. The primary purpose is to absorb a *deficit* and get a "fresh start."

**quick assets.** *Assets* readily convertible into *cash*; includes cash, *current marketable securities* and *current receivables*.

**quick ratio.** *Acid test* ratio. See *ratio*.

## R

**R & D.** See *research and development*.

**rate of return on common stock equity.** See *ratio*.

**rate of return on stockholders' equity.** See *ratio*.

**rate of return (on total capital).** See *ratio* and *all capital earnings rate*.

**rate variance.** *Price variance*, usually for *direct labor costs*.

**ratio.** The number resulting when one number is divided by another. Ratios are generally used to assess aspects of profitability, solvency, and liquidity. The commonly used financial ratios are of essentially two kinds:

(1) those that summarize some aspect of operations for a period, usually a year, and

(2) those that summarize some aspect of *financial position* at a given moment—the moment for which a balance sheet has been prepared.

The table on the next page lists the most common financial ratios and shows separately both the numerator and denominator used to calculate the ratio.

For all ratios that require an average balance during the period, the average is most often derived as one-half the sum of the beginning and ending balances. Sophisticated analysts recognize, however, that when companies use a fiscal year different from the calendar year, this averaging of beginning and ending balances may be misleading. Consider, for example, the *all capital earnings rate* of Sears, Roebuck & Company whose fiscal year ends on January 31. Sears chooses a January 31 closing date at least in part because inventories are at a low level and are therefore easy to count—the Christmas merchandise has been sold and the Easter merchandise has not yet all been received. Furthermore, by January 31, most Christmas sales have been collected or returned. so receivable amounts are not unusually large. Thus at January 31, the amount of total assets is lower than at many other times during the year. Consequently, the denominator of the all capital earnings rate, total assets, for Sears is more likely to represent the smallest amount of total assets on hand during the year than the average amount. The all capital earnings rate for Sears and other companies who choose a fiscal year-end to coincide with low points in the inventory cycle is likely to be larger than if a more accurate estimate of the average amounts of total assets were used.

**raw material.** Goods purchased for use in manufacturing a product.

**reacquired stock.** *Treasury stock*.

**real accounts.** *Balance sheet accounts;* as opposed to *nominal accounts*. See *permanent accounts*.

**real estate.** *Land* and its *improvements,* such as landscaping and roads but not buildings.

**realizable value.** *Market value* or, sometimes, *net realizable value*.

**realization convention.** The accounting practice of delaying the recognition of *gains* and *losses* from changes in the market price of *assets* until the assets are sold. However, unrealized losses on *inventory* and *marketable securities* classified as *current assets* are recognized prior to sale when the *lower-of-cost-or-market* valuation basis is used.

**realize.** To convert into *funds*. See *recognize*.

**realized holding gain.** See *inventory profit* for definition and an example.

**rearrangement costs.** *Costs* of re-installing an asset, perhaps in a different location. May be *capitalized* as part of the asset's cost, just as is original installation cost.

**recapitalization.** *Reorganization*.

**receipt.** Acquisition of *cash*.

**receivable.** Any *collectible* whether or not it is currently due.

**receivables turnover.** See *ratio*.

**reciprocal holdings.** Company A owns stock of Company B and Company B owns stock of Company A.

**recognize.** To enter a transaction in the books. Some writers use "recognize" to indicate that an event has been *journalized* and use "realize" only for those events that affect the *income s..tement*.

**reconciliation.** A calculation that shows how one balance or figure is derived systematically from

## FINANCIAL RATIOS DEFINED

| Ratio | Numerator | Denominator |
|---|---|---|
| *Ratios Summarizing Operations of a Period* | | |
| All Capital Earnings Rate | Net Income + Minority Share of After-tax Income + Interest Charges Net of Tax Effects[1] | Average of Total Assets during the Period. |
| Rate of Return on Stockholders' Equity | Net Income | Average Stockholders' Equity during the Period |
| Rate of Return on Common-Stock Equity | Net Income — Preferred Stock Dividends | Average Common Stockholders' Equity during the Period |
| Earnings per Share on Common Stock[2] | Net Income — Preferred Stock Dividends | Average Number of Common Shares Outstanding during the Period |
| Operating Ratio Based Upon Revenues | Total Expenses | Total Revenues |
| Operating Ratio Based Upon Net Sales | Total Expenses | Net Sales |
| Inventory Turnover | Cost of Goods Sold | Average Inventory during the Period |
| Days of Average Inventory on Hand | 365 | Inventory Turnover |
| Receivables Turnover | Net Sales on Account | Average Net Accounts Receivable during the Period |
| Average Collection Period of Receivables | 365 | Receivables Turnover |
| Asset Turnover | Net Sales | Average Assets during the Period |
| Turnover of Plant and Equipment | Net Sales | Average of Land, Buildings, and Equipment (Net) Accounts during the Period |
| Times Interest Earned | Income before Interest and Income Tax Charges[3] | Interest Charges |
| *Ratios Summarizing Financial Position at a Moment in Time* | | |
| Current Ratio | Total Current Assets | Total Current Liabilities |
| Acid-Test or Quick Ratio | Quick Assets (Ordinarily: Cash, Marketable Securities, and Receivables[4]) | Total Current Liabilities |
| Equity Ratio[5] | Total Stockholders' Equity | Total Equities (=Total Assets) |
| Debt-Equity Ratio[6] | Total Liabilities[7] | Total Equities |
| Book Value per Share of Common Stock | Total Stockholders' Equity — Preferred Stockholders' Equity | Number of Common Shares Outstanding |
| Price-Earnings Ratio | Market Price per Share of Common Stock | Earnings per Share of Common Stock for the Last Year |

[1] Interest charges net of tax effects = $(1 - t) \times$ interest charges where $t$ is the average tax rate.
[2] See *primary earnings per share* and *fully diluted earnings per share* for complications when there are residual securities outstanding.
[3] May be merely income before interest charges.
[4] Receivables should be excluded for some businesses and inventories should be included for others. In practice, however, neither of these realistic adjustments is made.
[5] Sometimes called the *worth-debt ratio.*
[6] We include minority interest in total liability
[7] Often only long-term debt.

another, such as a *reconciliation of retained earnings* or a *bank reconciliation schedule*. See *articulate*.

**record date.** *Dividends* are paid on payment date to those who own the stock on the record date.

**recourse.** See *note receivable discounted*.

**redemption.** Retirement by the issuer, usually by a purchase or *call*, of *stocks* or *bonds*.

**redemption premium.** *Call premium*.

**redemption value.** The price to be paid by a corporation to retire *bonds* or *preferred stock* if called before *maturity*.

**refunding bond issue.** Said of a *bond* issue whose proceeds are used to retire bonds already *outstanding*.

**register.** Collection of consecutive entries, or other information, in chronological order, such as a check register or an insurance register, which lists all insurance policies owned. If entries are recorded, it may serve as a *journal*.

**registered bond.** *Principal* of such a *bond* and *interest*, if registered as to interest, is paid to the owner listed on the books of the issuer. As opposed to a bearer bond where the possessor of the bond is entitled to interest and principal.

**registrar.** An *agent*, usually a bank or trust company, appointed by a corporation to keep track of the names of stockholders and distributions of earnings.

**registration statement.** Statement required by the Securities Act of 1933 of most companies wishing to *issue securities* to the public or by the Securities Exchange Act of 1934 of a company wishing to have its securities traded in public markets. The statement discloses financial data and other items of interest to potential investors.

**regressive tax.** Tax for which the rate decreases as the taxed base, such as income, increases. Contrast with *progressive tax*.

**Regulation S-X.** The *SEC*'s regulation specifying the form and content of financial reports to the SEC.

**reinvestment rate.** In a *capital budgeting* context, the rate at which cash inflows from a project occurring before the project's completion are invested. Once such a rate is assumed, there will never be multiple *internal rates of return*. See *Descartes' rule of signs*.

**relative sales value method.** A method for *allocating joint costs* in proportion to *net realizable values* of the joint products. For example, joint products A and B together cost $100 and A sells for $60 while B sells for $90. Then A would be allocated ($60/$150) × $100 = .40 × $100 = $40 of cost while B would be allocated ($90/$150) × $100 = $60 of cost.

**relevant cost.** *Incremental cost. Opportunity cost.*

**relevant range.** Activity levels over which costs are linear or for which *flexible budget* estimates and *breakeven charts* will remain valid.

**remittance advice.** Information on a *check* stub, or on a document attached to a check by the *drawer*, which tells the *payee* why a payment is being made.

**rent.** A charge for the use of land, buildings, or other assets.

**re-order point.** See *economic order quantity*.

**reorganization.** A major change in the *capital structure* of a corporation that leads to changes in the rights, interests, and implied ownership of the various security owners. Usually results from a *merger* or

another, such as a *reconciliation of retained earnings* agreement by senior security holders to take action to forestall *bankruptcy*.

**repair.** An *expenditure* to restore an *asset's* service potential after damage or after prolonged use. In the second sense, after prolonged use, the difference between repairs and maintenance is one of degree and not of kind. Treated as an *expense* of the period when incurred. Because repairs and maintenance are treated similarly in this regard, the distinction is not important. A repair helps to maintain capacity intact at levels planned when the *asset* was acquired; contrast with *improvement*.

**replacement cost.** For an asset, the current fair market price to purchase another, similar asset (with the same future benefit or service potential). *Current cost*. SEC ASR No. 190 requires certain large firms to disclose replacement cost data. See *reproduction cost* and *productive capacity*. See also *distributable income* and *inventory profit*.

**replacement cost method of depreciation.** The original-cost *depreciation* charge is augmented by an amount based upon a portion of the difference between the *current replacement cost* of the asset and its *original cost*.

**replacement system of depreciation.** See *retirement method of depreciation* for definition and contrast.

**report.** *Financial statement; auditor's report.*

**report form.** This form of *balance sheet* typically shows *assets* minus *liabilities* as one total. Then, below that it shows the components of *owners' equity* summing to the same total. Often, the top section shows *current* assets less current liabilities before *noncurrent* assets less noncurrent liabilities. Contrast with *account form*.

**reporting objectives (policies).** The general doctrines underlying accounting. These include *full disclosure, objectivity, consistency, conservatism*, the assumption of *continuity of operations*, and *materiality*.

**reproduction cost.** The *cost* necessary to acquire an *asset* similar in all physical respects to another asset for which a *current value* is wanted. See *replacement cost* and *productive capacity* for further contrast.

**requisition.** A formal written order or request, such as for withdrawal of supplies from the storeroom.

**resale value.** *Exit value. Net realizable value.*

**research and development.** Research is activity aimed at discovering new knowledge in hopes that such activity will be useful in creating a new product, process, or service or improving a present product, process, or service. Development is the translation of research findings or other knowledge into a new or improved product, process, or service. The *FASB* requires that costs of such activities be *expensed* as incurred on the grounds that the future benefits are too uncertain to warrant *capitalization* as an *asset*. This treatment seems questionable to us because we wonder why firms would continue to undertake R & D if there were no expectation of future benefit; if future benefits exist, then the *costs* should be assets.

**reserve.** When properly used in accounting, the term refers to an account that appropriates *retained earnings* and restricts dividend declarations. Appropriating retained earnings is itself a poor and slowly vanishing practice, so the word should seldom be used in accounting. In addition, used in the past to indicate an asset *contra* (for example, "reserve for depreciation") or an *estimated liability* (for example, "reserve for warranty costs"). In any case, reserve accounts have credit balances and are not pools of *funds* as the unwary reader might infer. If a company has set aside a pool of *cash (or marketable securities)*, then that cash will be called a *fund*.

No other word in accounting is so misunderstood and misused by laymen and "experts" who should know better. A leading unabridged dictionary defines *reserve* as "Cash, or assets readily convertible into cash, held aside, as by a corporation, bank, state or national government, etc. to meet expected or unexpected demands." This definition is absolutely wrong in accounting. Reserves are not funds. For example, a contingency fund of $10,000 is created by depositing cash in a fund and this entry is made:

```
Dr. Contingency Fund ................... 10,000
    Cr. Cash ............................        10,000
```

The following entry may accompany this entry, if retained earnings are to be appropriated:

```
Dr. Retained Earnings ................... 10,000
    Cr. Reserve for Contingencies.........        10,000
```

The transaction leading to the first entry is an event of economic significance. The second entry has little economic impact for most firms. The problem with the word *reserves* arises because the second entry can be made without the first—a company can create a reserve, that is appropriate retained earnings, without creating a fund. The problem is at least in part caused by the fact that in common usage, "reserve" means a pool of assets, as in the phrase "oil reserves." The *Internal Revenue Service* does not help in dispelling confusion about the term *reserves*. The federal *income tax* return for corporations uses the title "Reserve for Bad Debts" to mean the "Allowance for Uncollectible Accounts" and speaks of the "Reserve Method" in referring to the *allowance method* for estimating *revenue* or *income* reductions from estimated *uncollectibles*.

**residual income.** *Net income* to *common stock* = net income less *preferred stock dividends*.

**residual security.** A *potentially dilutive security*. Options, warrants, convertible bonds, and *convertible preferred stock*.

**residual value.** At any time, the estimated or actual, *net realizable value* (that is proceeds less removal costs) of an *asset,* usually a depreciable *plant asset*. In the context of depreciation accounting, this term is equivalent to *salvage value* and is preferable to *scrap value,* because the asset need not be scrapped. Sometimes used to mean net *book value*. In the context of a *noncancelable* lease, the estimated value of the leased asset at the end of the lease period. See *lease*.

**responsibility accounting.** Accounting for a business by considering various units as separate entities, or *profit centers,* giving management of each unit responsibility for the unit's *revenues* and *expenses*.

Sometimes called "activity accounting." See *transfer price*.

**restricted assets.** Governmental resources restricted by legal or contractual requirements for specific purposes.

**restricted retained earnings.** That part of *retained earnings* not legally available for *dividends*. See *retained earnings, appropriated. Bond indentures* and other loan contracts can curtail the legal ability of the corporation to declare dividends without formally requiring a retained earnings appropriation, but disclosure is required.

**retail inventory method.** Ascertaining *inventory* amounts for financial statements by using ratios of cost to selling price. That is, *cost of sales* = (1 − *markup percentage*) × *sales*; and *ending inventory* = (1 − *markup percentage*) × *ending inventory* at retail prices.

**retained earnings.** Net *income* over the life of a corporation less all income distributions (including capitalization through stock dividends); *owners' equity* less *contributed capital*.

**retained earnings, appropriated.** An *account* set up by crediting it and debiting *retained earnings*. Used to indicate that a portion of retained earnings is not available for dividends. The practice of appropriating retained earnings is misleading unless all capital is earmarked with its use, which is not practical. Use of formal retained earnings appropriations is declining.

**retained earnings statement.** *Generally accepted accounting principles* require that whenever *comparative balance sheets* and an *income statement* are presented, there must also be presented a *reconciliation* of the beginning and ending balances in the *retained earnings account*. This reconciliation can appear in a separate statement, in a combined statement of income and retained earnings or in the balance sheet.

**retirement method of depreciation.** No entry is recorded for *depreciation expense* until an *asset* is retired from service. Then, an entry is made *debiting* depreciation expense and *crediting* the asset account for the cost of the asset retired. If the retired asset has a *salvage value,* the amount of the debit to depreciation expense is reduced by the amount of salvage value with a corresponding debit to cash, receivables, or salvaged materials. The "replacement system of depreciation" is similar, except that the debit to depreciation expense equals the cost of the new asset less the salvage value, if any, of the old asset. These methods were used by some public utilities. For example, if ten telephone poles are acquired in year one for $60 each and are replaced in year ten for $100 each when the salvage value of the old poles is $5 each, then the accounting would be as follows:

*Retirement Method*
```
Plant Assets ...........................600
    Cash ...............................        600
To acquire assets in year one.
```

```
Depreciation Expense ...................550
Salvage Receivable ..................... 50
    Plant Assets ........................        600
To record retirement and depreciation in year ten.
```

```
Plant Assets .........................1,000
   Cash .............................     1,000
To record acquisition of new assets in year
ten.
```

*Replacement Method*
```
Plant Assets ......................... 600
   Cash .............................        600
To acquire assets in year one.
```

```
Depreciation Expense ................. 950
Salvage Receivable ...................  50
   Cash .............................   1,000
To record depreciation on old asset in amount
quantified by net cost of replacement asset in
year ten.
```

The retirement method is like *FIFO*, in that the cost of the first assets is recorded as depreciation and the cost of the second assets is put on the balance sheet. The replacement method is like *LIFO* in that the cost of the second assets determines the depreciation expense and the cost of the first assets remains on the balance sheet.

**retirement plan.** *Pension plan.*

**return.** A schedule of information required by governmental bodies, such as the tax return required by the *Internal Revenue Service*. Also the physical return of merchandise. See also *return on investment*.

**return of capital investment (capital).** A payment to owners *debited* to an *owners' equity account* other than *retained earnings*.

**return on investment (capital).** *Income* (before distributions to suppliers of capital) for a period. As a rate, this amount divided by average total assets. *Interest*, net of tax effects, should be added back to *net income* for the numerator. See *ratio*.

**revenue.** The monetary measure of a service rendered. *Sales* of products, merchandise, and services, and earnings from *interest, dividends*, rents, and the like. A revenue *transaction* results in an increase in *net assets*. Do not confuse with *receipt* of *funds*, which may occur before, when, or after revenue is recognized; contrast with *gain* and *income*. See also *holding gain*. Some writers use the term *gross income* synonymously with revenue; such usage is to be avoided.

**revenue center.** A *responsibility center* with a firm that only has control over revenues generated; contrast with *cost center*.

**revenue-cost graph.** See *breakeven chart*.

**revenue expenditure.** A phrase sometimes used to mean *expense* in contrast to a capital *expenditure* to acquire an *asset* or to discharge a *liability*. Avoid using this phrase; use *period expense* instead.

**revenue received in advance.** An inferior term for *advances from customers*.

**reversal (reversing) entry.** An *entry* in which all *debits* and *credits* are the credits and debits, respectively, of another entry, and in the same amounts. It is usually made on the first day of an *accounting period* to reverse a previous *adjusting entry*, usually an *accrual*. The purpose of such entries is to make the bookkeeper's tasks easier. Suppose that salaries are paid every other Friday, with paychecks compensating employees for the two weeks just ended. Total salaries accrue at the rate of $5,000 per five-day work

week. The bookkeeper is accustomed to making the following entry every other Friday:

```
(1) Salary Expense.......................10,000
      Cash...............................       10,000
    To record salary expense and salary
    payments.
```

If paychecks are delivered to employees on Friday, December 26, 1975, then the *adjusting entry* made on December 31 (or, perhaps, later) to record accrued salaries for December 29, 30, and 31 would be:

```
(2) Salary Expense....................... 3,000
      Salaries Payable....................      3,000
    To charge 1975 operations with all
    salaries earned in 1975.
```

The Salary Expense account would be closed as part of the December 31 *closing entries*. On the next pay day, January 9, the salary entry would have to be:

```
(3) Salary Expense....................... 7,000
    Salaries Payable....................... 3,000
      Cash...............................       10,000
    To record salary payments split between
    expense for 1976 (7 days) and liability
    carried over from 1975 (3 days).
```

To make entry (3), the bookkeeper must look back into the records to see how much of the debit is to Salaries Payable accrued from the previous year so that total debits are properly split between 1976 expense and the liability carried over from 1975. Notice that this entry forces the bookkeeper both (a) to refer to balances in old accounts and (b) to make an entry different from the one customarily made, entry (1).

The reversing entry, made just after the books have been closed for 1975, makes the salary entry for January 9, 1976, the same as that made on all other Friday pay days. The reversing entry merely *reverses* the adjusting entry (2):

```
(4) Salaries Payable....................... 3,000
      Salary Expense.....................      3,000
    To reverse the adjusting entry.
```

This entry results in a zero balance in the Salaries Payable account and a *credit* balance in the Salary Expense account. If entry (4) is made just after the books are closed for 1975, then the entry on January 9 will be the customary entry (1). Entries (4) and (1) together have exactly the same effect as entry (3).

The procedure for using reversal entries is as follows: The required adjustment to record an accrual (*payable* or *receivable*) is made at the end of an *accounting period*; the closing entry is made as usual; as of the first day of the following period, an entry is made reversing the adjusting entry; when a payment is made (or received), the entry is recorded as though no adjusting entry had been recorded. Whether or not reversal entries are used affects the record-keeping procedures, but not the financial statements.

Also used to describe the entry reversing an incorrect entry before recording the correct entry.

**reverse stock split.** A stock split in which the number of shares *outstanding* is decreased. See *stock split*.

**revolving fund.** A *fund* whose amounts are continually expended and then replenished; for example, a *petty cash fund*.

**revolving loan.** A *loan* which is expected to be renewed at *maturity*.

**right.** The privilege to subscribe to new *stock* issues or to purchase stock. Usually, rights are contained in securities called *warrants* and the warrants may be sold to others. See also *preemptive right*.

**risk.** A measure of the variability of the *return on investment*. For a given expected amount of return, most people prefer less risk to more risk. Therefore, in rational markets, investments with more risk usually promise, or are expected to yield, a higher rate of return than investments with lower risk. Most people use "risk" and "uncertainty" as synonyms. In technical language, however, these terms have different meanings. "Risk" is used when the probabilities attached to the various outcomes are known, such as the probabilities of heads or tails in the flip of a fair coin. "Uncertainty" refers to an event where the probabilities of the outcomes, such as winning or losing a lawsuit, can only be estimated.

**risk-adjusted discount rate.** In a *capital budgeting* context, a decision maker compares projects by comparing their *net present values* for a given *interest* rate, usually the *cost of capital*. If a given project's outcome is considered to be much more or much less risky than the normal undertakings of the company, then the interest rate will be increased (if the project is more risky) or decreased (if less risky) and the rate used is said to be risk-adjusted.

**risk premium.** Extra compensation paid to an employee or extra interest paid to a lender, over amounts usually considered normal, in return for their undertaking to engage in activities more risky than normal.

**ROI.** *Return on investment,* but usually used to refer to a single project and expressed as a ratio: *income* divided by average *cost* of *assets* devoted to the project.

**royalty.** Compensation for the use of property, usually copyrighted material or natural resources, expressed as a percentage of receipts from using the property or as an amount per unit produced.

**rule of 69.** An amount of money invested at r percent per period will double in 69/r + .35 periods. This approximation is accurate to one-tenth of a period for interest rates between 1/4 and 100 percent per period. For example, at 10 percent per period, the rule says a given sum will double in 69/10 + .35 = 7.25 periods. At 10 percent per period, a given sum doubles in 7.27 + periods.

**rule of 72.** An amount of money invested at r percent per period will double in 72/r periods. A reasonable approximation but not nearly as accurate as the *rule of 69*. For example, at 10 percent per period, the rule says a given sum will double in 72/10 = 7.2 periods.

**rule of 78.** The rule followed by many finance companies for allocating earnings on *loans* among the months of a year on the sum-of-the-months'-digits basis when equal monthly payments from the borrower are to be received. The sum of the digits from 1 through 12 is 78, so 12/78 of the year's earnings are allocated to the first month, 11/78 to the second month, and so on. See *sum-of-the-years'-digits depreciation*.

**ruling (and balancing) an account.** The process of summarizing a series of entries in an *account* by computing a new *balance* and drawing double lines to indicate the information above the double lines has been summarized in the new balance. The process is illustrated below. The steps are as follows. (1) Compute the sum of all *debit* entries including opening debit balance, if any—$1,464.16. (2) Compute the sum of all credit entries including opening credit balance, if any—$413.57. (3) If the amount in (1) is larger than the amount in (2), then write the excess as a credit with a check mark—$1,464.16 − $413.57 = $1,050.59. (4) Add both debit and credit columns, which should both now sum to the same amount, and show that identical total at the foot of both columns. (5) Draw double lines under those numbers and write the excess of debits over credits as the new debit balance with a check mark. (6) If the amount in (2) is larger than the amount in (1), then write the excess as a debit with a check mark. (7) Do steps (4) and (5) except that the excess becomes the new credit balance. (8) If the amount in (1) is equal to the amount in (2), then the balance is zero and only the totals with the double lines beneath them need be shown.

This process is illustrated below.

### AN OPEN ACCOUNT, RULED AND BALANCED
(Steps indicated in parentheses correspond to steps described in "ruling an account".)

| | Date 1977 | Explanation | Ref. | Debit (1) | | Date 1977 | Explanation | Ref. | Credit (2) | | |
|---|---|---|---|---|---|---|---|---|---|---|---|
| | Jan. 1 | Balance | √ | 100 | 00 | | | | | | |
| | Jan. 13 | | VR | 121 | 37 | Sept. 15 | | J | | 42 | |
| | Mar. 20 | | VR | 56 | 42 | Nov. 12 | | J | 413 | 15 | |
| | June 5 | | J | 1,138 | 09 | Dec. 31 | Balance | √ | 1,050 | 59 | (3) |
| | Aug. 18 | | J | 1 | 21 | | | | | | |
| | Nov. 20 | | VR | 38 | 43 | | | | | | |
| | Dec. 7 | | VR | 8 | 64 | | | | | | |
| (4) | | | | 1,464 | 16 | | | | 1,464 | 16 | (4) |
| (5) | 1978 Jan. 1 | Balance | √ | 1,050 | 59 | 1978 | | | | | |

# S

**SAB.** *Staff Accounting Bulletin* of the *SEC*.

**salary.** Compensation earned by managers, administrators, professionals, not based on an hourly rate. Contrast with *wage*.

**sale.** A *revenue* transaction where *goods* or *services* are delivered to a customer in return for cash or a contractual obligation to pay.

**sale and leaseback.** Phrase used to describe a *financing* transaction where improved property is sold but is taken back for use on a long-term *lease*. Such transactions often have advantageous income tax effects, but usually have no effect on *financial statement income*.

**sales allowance.** A reduction in sales *invoice* price usually given because the goods received by the buyer are not exactly what was ordered. The amounts of such adjustments are often accumulated by the seller in a temporary *revenue contra account* having this, or a similar, title. See *sales discount*.

**sales basis of revenue recognition.** *Revenue* is recognized, not as goods are produced nor as orders are received, but only when the sale (delivery) has been consummated and cash or a legal receivable obtained. Most revenue is recognized on this basis. Compare with the *percentage of completion method* and the *installment method*. Identical with the *completed contract method* but this latter term is ordinarily used only for *long-term* construction projects.

**sales discount.** Reduction in sales *invoice* price usually offered for prompt payment. See *terms of sale* and *2/10, n/30*.

**sales return.** The physical return of merchandise; the amounts of such returns are often accumulated by the seller in a temporary *revenue contra account*.

**sales, uncollectible accounts adjustment.** The preferred title for the *contra-revenue account* to recognize estimated reductions in income caused by accounts receivable that will not be collected. Called *bad debt expense* and treated as an expense, rather than an adjustment to revenue, when the write-off method is used. See *allowance for uncollectibles* and *allowance method*.

**sales value method.** *Relative sales value method*.

**salvage value.** Actual or estimated selling price, net of removal or disposal costs, of a used *plant asset* to be sold or otherwise retired. See *residual value*.

**SAS.** *Statement on Auditing Standards* of the *AICPA*.

**schedule.** Supporting set of calculations which show how figures in a statement or tax return are derived.

**scientific method.** *Effective interest method* of *amortizing bond discount* or *premium*.

**scrap value.** *Salvage value* assuming item is to be junked. A *net realizable value*.

**SEC.** Securities and Exchange Commission, an agency authorized by the U.S. Congress to regulate, among other things, the financial reporting practices of most public corporations. The SEC has indicated that it will usually allow the *FASB* to set accounting principles but it reserves the right to require more disclosure than required by the FASB. The SEC's accounting requirements are stated in its *Accounting Series Releases* (ASR) and *Regulation S-X*. See also *registration statement* and *10-K*.

**secret reserve.** *Hidden reserve*.

**Securities and Exchange Commission.** *SEC*.

**security.** Document that indicates ownership or indebtedness or potential ownership, such as an *option* or *warrant*.

**segment (of a business).** As defined by *APB Opinion* No. 30, "a component of an *entity* whose activities represent a separate major line of business or class of customer... [It may be] a *subsidiary*, a division, or a department, ... provided that its *assets,* results of *operations,* and activities can be clearly distinguished, physically and operationally for financial reporting purposes, from the other assets, results of operations, and activities of the entity." In *FASB Statement No. 14* a segment is defined as "A component of an enterprise engaged in promoting a product or service or a group of related products and services primarily to unaffiliated customers ... for a profit."

**segment reporting.** Reporting of *income* and *assets* by *segments of a business,* usually classified by nature of products sold but sometimes by geographical area where goods are produced or sold. Sometimes called "line of business reporting." *Central corporate expenses* are usually allocated to the segments although these reports may be more useful when such expenses are separately disclosed. See the excerpt from the General Electric annual report on GE's page 3, page 59 of this book, for an example.

**self-balancing.** A set of records with equal *debits* and *credits* such as the *ledger* (but not individual accounts), the *balance sheet,* and a *fund* in nonprofit accounting.

**self-insurance.** See *insurance*.

**selling and administrative expenses.** *Expenses* not specifically identifiable with, nor assigned to, production.

**semifixed costs.** *Costs* that increase with activity as a step function.

**semivariable costs.** *Costs* that increase strictly linearly with activity but that are positive at zero activity level. Royalty fees of two percent of sales are variable; royalty fees of $1,000 per year plus two percent of sales are semivariable.

**senior securities.** *Bonds* as opposed to *preferred stock; preferred stock* as opposed to *common stock*. The senior security has a claim against *earnings* or *assets* that must be met before the claim of less senior securities.

**serial bonds.** An *issue* of *bonds* that mature in part at one date, another part on another date, and so on; the various maturity dates usually are equally spaced; contrast with *term bonds*.

**service basis of depreciation.** *Production method*.

**service department.** A department, such as the personnel or computer department, that provides services to other departments, rather than direct work on a salable product; contrast with *production department*.

**service life.** Period of expected usefulness of an asset; may not coincide with *depreciable life* for income tax purposes.

**service potential.** The future benefits embodied in an item that cause the item to be classified as an *asset*. Without service potential, there are no future benefits and the item should not be classified as an asset.

**services.** Useful work done by a person, a machine, or an organization. See *goods and services*.

**setup.** The time or costs required to prepare production equipment for doing a job.

**share.** A unit of *stock* representing ownership in a corporation.

**shareholders' equity.** See *stockholders' equity.*

**short-term.** Current; ordinarily, due within one year.

**shrinkage.** An excess of *inventory* shown on the *books* over actual physical quantities on hand. Can result from theft or shoplifting as well as from evaporation or general wear and tear.

**sight draft.** A demand for payment drawn by a person to whom money is owed. The *draft* is presented to the borrower's (the debtor's) bank in expectation that the borrower will authorize its bank to disburse the funds. Such drafts are often used when a seller sells goods to a new customer in a different city. The seller is not sure whether the buyer will pay the bill. The seller sends the *bill* of lading, or other evidence of ownership of the goods, along with a sight draft to the buyer's bank. The buyer is therefore notified that if the goods are to be released to the buyer, the bank must be instructed to honor the sight draft. Once the sight draft is honored, the bill of lading or other document evidencing ownership is handed over to the buyer and the goods become the property of the buyer.

**simple interest.** *Interest* calculated on *principal* where interest earned during periods before maturity of the loan is neither added to the principal nor paid to the lender. *Interest = principal × interest rate × time.* Seldom used in economic calculations except for periods less than one year; contrast with *compound interest.*

**single-entry accounting.** Accounting that is neither *self-balancing* nor *articulated*; that is, it does not rely on equal *debits* and *credits. No journal entries* are made. *Plugging* is required to derive *owners' equity* for the *balance sheet.*

**single proprietorship.** *Sole proprietorship.*

**single step.** Said of an *income statement* where all *ordinary revenue* and *gain* items are shown first and totaled. Then all ordinary *expenses* and *losses* are totaled. Their difference, plus the effect of *income from discontinued operations* and *extraordinary items,* is shown as *net income;* contrast with *multiple-step* and see *proprietorship theory.*

**sinking fund.** *Assets* and their earnings earmarked for the retirement of *bonds* or other long-term obligations. Earnings of sinking fund investments are taxable income of the company.

**sinking fund method of depreciation.** The periodic charge is an amount so that when the charges are considered to be an *annuity,* the value of the annuity at the end of depreciable life is equal to the *acquisition cost* of the asset. In theory, the charge for a period ought also to include interest on the accumulated depreciation at the start of the period as well. A *fund* of cash is not necessarily, or even usually, accumulated. This method is rarely used.

**skeleton account.** *T-account.*

**slide.** The name of the error made by a bookkeeper in recording the digits of a number correctly with the decimal point misplaced; for example, recording $123.40 as $1,234.00 or as $12.34.

**soak-up method.** The *equity method.*

**Social Security taxes.** Taxes levied by the federal government on both employers and employees to provide *funds* to pay retired persons (or their survivors) who are entitled to receive such payments, either because they paid Social Security taxes themselves or because the Congress has declared them eligible. See *Old Age, Survivors, Disability,* and *(Hospital) Insurance.*

**sole proprietorship.** All *owner's equity* belongs to one person.

**solvent.** Able to meet debts when due.

**sound value.** A phrase used mainly in appraisals of *fixed assets* to mean *fair market value* or *replacement cost* in present condition.

**source of funds.** Any *transaction* that increases *working capital.*

**sources and uses statement.** *Statement of changes in financial position.*

**SOYD.** *Sum-of-the-years'-digits depreciation.*

**special assessment.** A compulsory levy made by a governmental unit on property to pay the costs of a specific improvement, or service, presumed not to benefit the general public but only the owners of the property so assessed. Accounted for in a special assessment fund.

**special journal.** A *journal,* such as a sales journal or cash disbursements journal, to record *transactions* of a similar nature that occur frequently.

**special revenue debt.** Debt of a governmental unit backed only by revenues from specific sources such as tolls from a bridge.

**specific identification method.** Method for valuing *ending inventory* and *cost of goods sold* by identifying actual units sold and in inventory and summing the actual costs of those individual units. Usually used for items with large unit value such as jewelry, automobiles, and fur coats.

**specific price changes.** Changes in the market prices of specific *goods and services;* contrast with *general price level changes.*

**specific price index.** A measure of the price of a specific good or service, or a small group of similar goods or services, at one time relative to the price during a base period; contrast with *general price index.* See *dollar-value LIFO method.*

**spending variance.** In *standard cost systems,* the *rate* or *price variance* for *overhead costs.*

**split.** *Stock split.* Sometimes called "splitup."

**splitoff point.** The point where all costs are no longer *joint costs* but can be identified with individual products or perhaps with a smaller number of *joint products.*

**spoilage.** See *abnormal spoilage* and *normal spoilage.*

**spread sheet.** A *work sheet* organized like a *matrix* that provides a two-way classification of accounting data. The rows and columns are both labeled with *account* titles. An entry in a row represents a *debit* while an entry in a column represents a *credit.* Thus, the number "100" in the "cash" row and the "accounts receivable" column records an entry debiting cash and crediting accounts receivable for $100. A given row total indicates all debit entries to the account represented by that row and a given column total indicates the sum of all credit entries to the account represented by that column.

**squeeze.** A term sometimes used for *plug.*

**stabilized accounting.**   General *price-level adjusted accounting.*

**stable monetary unit assumption.**   In spite of *inflation* that appears to be a way of life, the assumption that underlies *historical cost* accounting—namely that current dollars and dollars of previous years can be meaningfully added together. No specific recognition is given to changing values of the dollar in the usual *financial statements.* See *price level adjusted statements.*

**Staff Accounting Bulletin.**   An interpretation issued by the Staff of the Chief Accountant of the *SEC* "suggesting" how the various *Accounting Series Releases* should be applied in practice. A substantial fraction of the first twenty or so SAB's are concerned with the implementation of *replacement cost* accounting, as required by *ASR* No. 190.

**standard cost.**   Anticipated *cost* of producing a unit of output; a predetermined cost to be assigned to products produced.

**standard cost system.**   *Product costing* using *standard costs* rather than actual costs. May be based on either *absorption* or *direct costing* principles.

**standard price (rate).**   Unit price established for materials or labor used in *standard cost systems.*

**standard quantity allowed.**   The quantity of direct material or direct labor (inputs) that should have been used if the units of output had been produced in accordance with preset *standards.*

**standby costs.**   A type of *capacity cost,* such as property taxes, incurred even if operations are shut down completely. Contrast with *enabling costs.*

**stated capital.**   Amount of capital contributed by stockholders. Sometimes used to mean *legal capital.*

**stated value.**   A term sometimes used for the *face amount* of *capital stock,* when no *par value* is indicated. Where there is a stated value per share, it may be set by the directors (in which case, capital *contributed in excess of stated value* may come into being).

**statement of affairs.**   A *balance sheet* showing immediate *liquidation* amounts, rather than *historical costs,* usually prepared when *insolvency* or *bankruptcy* is imminent. The *going concern assumption* is not used.

**statement of changes in financial position.**   As defined by *APB Opinion* No. 19, a statement which explains the changes in *working capital* (or cash) balances during a period and shows the changes in the working capital (or cash) accounts themselves. Sometimes called the "funds statement." See *dual transactions assumption* and all *financial resources.*

**Statement of Financial Accounting Standards.**   See *FASB.*

**statement of financial position.**   *Balance sheet.*

**statement of retained earnings (income).**   A statement that reconciles the beginning-of-period and end-of-period balances in the *retained earnings* account. It shows the effects of *earnings, dividend declarations,* and *prior-period adjustments.*

**Statement on Auditing Standards.**   No. 1 of this series (1973) codifies all statements on auditing standards previously promulgated by the *AICPA.* Later numbers deal with specific auditing standards and procedures.

**static budget.**   *Fixed budget.*

**statutory tax rate.**   The tax rate specified in the *income tax* law for each type of income (for example, *ordinary income, capital gain or loss*).

**step cost.**   *Semifixed cost.*

**step-down method.**   The method for *allocating service department* costs that starts by allocating one service department's costs to *production departments* and to all other service departments. Then a second service department's costs, including costs allocated from the first, are allocated to production departments and to all other service departments except the first one. In this fashion, the costs of all service departments, including previous allocations, are allocated to production departments and to those service departments whose costs have not yet been allocated.

**stock.**   *Inventory. Capital stock.* A measure of the amount of something on hand at a specific time; in this sense, contrast with *flow.*

**stock dividend.**   A so-called *dividend* where additional *shares* of *capital stock* are distributed, without cash payments, to existing shareholders. It results in a *debit* to *retained earnings* in the amount of the market value of the shares issued and a *credit* to *capital stock* accounts. It is ordinarily used to indicate that earnings retained have been permanently reinvested in the business; contrast with a *stock split,* which requires no entry in the capital stock accounts other than a notation that the *par* or *stated value* per share has been changed.

**stockholders' equity.**   *Proprietorship* or *owners' equity* of a corporation. Because *stock* means inventory in Australian, British, and Canadian usage, the term *shareholders' equity* is usually used by Australian, British, and Canadian writers.

**stock option.**   The right to purchase a specified number of shares of *stock* for a specified price at specified times, usually granted to employees; contrast with *warrant.*

**stock right.**   See *right.*

**stock split.**   Increase in the number of common shares outstanding resulting from the issuance of additional shares to existing stockholders without additional capital contributions by them. Does not increase the total *par* (or *stated*) *value* of *common stock* outstanding because par (or stated) value per share is reduced in inverse proportion. A three-for-one stock split reduces par (or stated) value per share to one-third of its former amount. Stock splits are usually limited to distributions that increase the number of shares outstanding by 20 percent or more; compare with *stock dividend.*

**stock subscriptions.**   See *subscription* and *subscribed stock.*

**stock warrant.**   See *warrant.*

**stores.**   *Raw materials,* parts, and supplies.

**straight debt value.**   An estimate of what the *market value* of a *convertible bond* would be if the bond did not contain a conversion privilege.

**straight-line depreciation.**   If the *depreciable life* is n periods, then the periodic *depreciation* charge is 1/n of the *depreciable cost.* Results in equal periodic charges and is sometimes called "straight-time depreciation."

**Sub-chapter S Corporation.**   A firm legally organized as a *corporation* but taxed as if it were a *partnership.*

**subject to.**   Qualifications in an *auditor's report* usually caused by a *material* uncertainty in the valuation of an item, such as future promised payments from a foreign government or outcome of pending litigation.

**subordinated.** Said of *debt* whose claim on income or assets is junior to, or comes after, claims of other debt.

**subscribed stock.** A *stockholders' equity* account showing the capital that will be contributed as soon as the subscription price is collected. A subscription is a legal contract so that an entry is made debiting a receivable and crediting subscribed stock as soon as the stock is subscribed.

**subscription.** Agreement to buy a *security*, or to purchase periodicals such as magazines.

**subsequent events.** *Post-statement events.*

**subsidiary.** Said of a company more than 50 percent of whose voting stock is owned by another.

**subsidiary (ledger) accounts.** The *accounts* in a *subsidiary ledger.*

**subsidiary ledger.** The *ledger* that contains the detailed accounts whose total is shown in a *controlling account* of the *general ledger.*

**successful-efforts accounting.** In petroleum accounting, the *capitalization* of the drilling costs of only those wells which contain oil. See *discovery value accounting* for an example.

**summary of significant accounting principles.** *APB* Opinion No. 22 requires that every *annual report* summarize the significant *accounting principles* used in compiling the annual report. This summary may be a separate exhibit or the first *note* to the financial statements.

**sum-of-the-years'-digits depreciation.** An *accelerated depreciation* method for an asset with *depreciable life* of n years where the charge in period $i$ ($i = 1, \ldots, n$) is the fraction $(n + 1 - i)/[n(n + 1)/2]$ of the *depreciable cost*. If an asset has a depreciable cost of $15,000 and a five-year depreciable life, for example, the depreciation charges would be $5,000 (= 5/15 × $15,000) in the first year, $4,000 in the second, $3,000 in the third, $2,000 in the fourth, and $1,000 in the fifth.

**sunk cost.** *Costs* incurred in the past that are not affected by, and hence irrelevant for, current decisions, aside from *income tax* effects; contrast with *incremental costs* and *imputed costs*. For example, the *acquisition cost* of machinery is irrelevant to a decision of whether or not to scrap the machinery. The current *exit value* of the machine is the imputed cost of continuing to own it and the cost of, say, electricity to run the machine is an incremental cost of its operation.

**supplementary statements (schedules).** Statements (schedules) in addition to the four basic *financial statements* (including the retained earnings reconciliation as a basic statement).

**surplus.** A word once used but now considered poor terminology; prefaced by "earned" to mean *retained earnings* and prefaced by "capital" to mean *capital contributed in excess of par* (or *stated) value.*

**surplus reserves.** Of all the words in accounting, *reserve* is the most objectionable and *surplus* is the second most objectionable. This phrase, then, has nothing to recommend it. It means, simply, *appropriated retained earnings.*

**suspense account.** A *temporary account* used to record part of a transaction prior to final analysis of that transaction. For example, if a business regularly classifies all sales into a dozen or more different categories but wants to deposit the proceeds of cash sales every day, it may credit a sales suspense account pending detailed classification of all sales into sales, type 1; sales, type 2; and so on.

**sustainable income.** The part of *distributable income* (computed from *replacement cost* data) that the firm can be expected to earn in the next accounting period if operations are continued at the same levels as during the current period. *Income from discontinued operations,* for example, may be distributable but not sustainable.

**S-X.** See *Regulation S-X.*

**SYD.** *Sum-of-the-years'-digits depreciation.*

### T

**T-account.** Account form shaped like the letter T with the title above the horizontal line. *Debits* are shown to the left of the vertical line, *credits* to the right.

**take-home pay.** The amount of a paycheck; earned wages or *salary* reduced by deductions for *income taxes, Social Security taxes,* contributions to fringe benefit plans, union dues, and so on. Take-home pay might be as little as 60 percent of earned compensation.

**taking a bath.** To incur a large loss. See *big bath.*

**tangible.** Having physical form. Accounting has never satisfactorily defined the distinction between tangible and *intangible assets.* Typically, intangibles are defined by giving an exhaustive list and everything not on the list is defined as tangible.

**target cost.** *Standard cost.*

**tax.** A nonpenal, but compulsory, charge levied by a government on income, consumption, wealth, or other bases for the benefit of all those governed. The term does not include fines or specific charges for benefits accruing only to those paying the charges, such as licenses, permits, special assessments, admissions fees, and tolls.

**tax allocation: inter-period.** See *deferred income tax liability.*

**tax allocation: intra-statement.** The showing of income tax effects on *extraordinary items, income from discontinued operations,* and *prior period adjustments* along with these items, separately from income taxes on other income. See *net of tax reporting.*

**tax avoidance.** See *tax shelter.*

**tax credit.** A subtraction from taxes otherwise payable, contrast with *tax deduction.*

**tax deduction.** A subtraction from *revenues* and *gains* to arrive at taxable income. Tax deductions are technically different from tax *exemptions,* but the effect of both is to reduce gross income in computing taxable income. Both are different from *tax credits,* which are subtracted from the computed tax itself in determining taxes payable. If the tax rate is t percent of pretax income, then a *tax credit* of $1 is worth $1/t of *tax deductions.*

**tax evasion.** The fraudulent understatement of taxable income or overstatement of deductions and expenses or both; contrast with *tax shelter.*

**tax exempts.** See *municipal bonds.*

**tax shelter.** The legal avoidance of, or reduction in,

*income taxes* resulting from a careful reading of the complex income tax regulations and the subsequent rearrangement of financial affairs to take advantage of the regulations. Often the term is used pejoratively, but the courts have long held that an individual or corporation has no obligation to pay taxes any larger than the legal minimum. If the public concludes that a given tax shelter is "unfair," then the laws and regulations can be changed. Sometimes used to refer to the investment that permits tax avoidance.

**tax shield.** The amount of an *expense* that reduces taxable income but does not require *working capital*, such as *depreciation*. Sometimes this term is expanded to include expenses that reduce taxable income and use working capital. A depreciation deduction (or *R & D expense* in the expanded sense) of $10,000 provides a tax shield of $4,800 when the marginal tax rate is 48 percent.

**temporary account.** *Account* that does not appear on the *balance sheet*. *Revenue* and *expense* accounts, their *adjuncts* and *contras, production cost accounts, income distribution accounts,* and purchases-related accounts (which are closed to the various inventories). Sometimes called a "nominal account."

**temporary difference.** See *timing difference*.

**temporary investments.** Investments in *marketable securities* that the owner intends to sell within a short time, usually one year, and hence classified as *current assets*.

**10-K.** The name of the annual report required by the *SEC* of nearly all publicly-held corporations. This report contains more information than the *annual report* to stockholders. Corporations must send a copy of the 10-K to those stockholders who request it.

**term bonds.** A *bond issue* whose component bonds all mature at the same time; contrast with *serial bonds*.

**term loan.** A loan with a *maturity* date, as opposed to a demand loan which is due whenever the lender requests payment. In practice bankers and auditors use this phrase only for loans for a year or more.

**terms of sale.** The conditions governing payment for a sale. For example, the terms *2/10, n(et)/30* mean that if payment is made within ten days of the invoice date, a *discount* of two percent from *invoice* price can be taken; the invoice amount must be paid, in any event, within thirty days or it becomes overdue.

**tickler file.** A collection of vouchers or other memorandums arranged chronologically to remind the person in charge of certain duties to make payments (or to do other tasks) as scheduled.

**time-adjusted rate of return.** *Internal rate of return*.

**time cost.** *Period cost*.

**time deposit.** Cash in a bank earning interest; contrast with *demand deposit*.

**time series analysis.** See *cross section analysis* for definition and contrast.

**times-interest earned.** Ratio of pre-tax *income* plus *interest* charges to interest charges. See *ratio*.

**timing difference.** A difference between taxable income and pretax income reported to stockholders that will be reversed in a subsequent period and requires an entry in the *deferred income tax* account. For example, the use of *accelerated depreciation* for tax returns and *straight-line depreciation* for financial reporting. See *Accounting Magic* for an example.

**trade acceptance.** A *draft* drawn by a seller which is presented for signature (acceptance) to the buyer at the time goods are purchased and which then becomes the equivalent of a *note receivable* of the seller and the *note payable* of the buyer.

**trade discount.** A *discount* from *list price* offered to all customers of a given type; contrast with a *discount* offered for prompt payment and *quantity discount*.

**trade-in.** Acquiring a new *asset* in exchange for a used one and perhaps additional cash. See *boot* and *trade-in transaction*.

**trade-in transaction.** The accounting for a trade-in depends upon whether or not the asset received is "similar" to the asset traded in and whether the accounting is for *financial statements* or for *income tax* returns. Assume an old asset cost $5,000, has $3,000 of *accumulated depreciation* (after recording depreciation to the date of the trade-in), and hence has a *book value* of $2,000. The old asset appears to have a market value of $1,500, according to price quotations in used-asset markets. The old asset is traded-in on a new asset with a list price of $10,000. The old asset and $5,500 cash (*boot*) are given for the new asset. The generic entry for the trade-in transaction is:

| | | |
|---|---|---|
| New Asset .......................... | A | |
| Accumulated Depreciation (Old Asset)..... | 3,000 | |
| Adjustment on Exchange of Asset ........ | B or | B |
| Old Asset ............................ | | 5,000 |
| Cash................................. | | 5,500 |

(1) the *list-price* method of accounting for trade-ins rests on the assumption that the list price of the new asset closely approximates its market value. The new asset is recorded at its list price (A = $10,000 in the example); B is a *plug* (= $2,500 credit in the example). If B requires a *debit* plug, the Adjustment on Exchange of Asset is a *loss*; if a *credit* plug is required (as in the example), the adjustment is a *gain*.

(2) Another theoretically sound method of accounting for trade-ins rests on the assumption that the price quotation from used-asset markets gives a more reliable measure of the market value of the old asset than is the list price a reliable measure of the market value of the new asset. This method uses the *fair market value* of the old asset, $1,500 in the example, to determine B (= $2,000 book value − $1,500 assumed proceeds on disposition = $500 debit or loss). The exchange results in a loss if the book value of the old asset exceeds its market value and in a gain if the market value exceeds the book value. The new asset is recorded on the books by plugging for A (= $7,000 in the example).

(3) For income tax reporting, no gain or loss may be recognized on the trade-in. Thus the new asset is recorded on the books by assuming B is zero and plugging for A (= $7,500 in the example). In practice, firms that wish to recognize the loss currently will sell the old asset directly, rather than trading it in, and acquire the new asset entirely for cash.

(4) *Generally accepted accounting principles (APB Opinion* No. 29) require a variant of these methods. The basic method is (1) or (2), depending upon whether the list price of the new asset (1) or the quotation of the old asset's market value (2) is the more reliable indication of market value. If, when

applying the basic method, a debit entry, or loss, is required for the Adjustment on Exchange of Asset, then the trade-in is recorded as described in (1) or (2) and the full amount of the loss is recognized currently. If, however, a credit entry, or gain, is required for the Adjustment on Exchange of Asset, then the amount of gain recognized currently depends upon whether or not the old asset and the new asset are "similar." If the assets are not similar, then the entire gain is recognized currently. If the assets are similar and cash is not received by the party trading in, then no gain is recognized and the treatment is like that in (3); i.e., B = O, plug for A. If the assets are similar and cash is received by the party trading in—a rare case—then a portion of the gain is recognized currently. The portion of the gain recognized currently is the fraction *cash received/market value of old asset.* (When the list-price method, (1), is used, the market value of the old asset is assumed to be the list price of the new asset plus the amount of cash received by the party trading in.)

The results of applying GAAP to the example can be summarized as follows:

| More Reliable Information As To Fair Market Value | Old Asset Compared with New Asset | |
|---|---|---|
| | Similar | Not Similar |
| New Asset List Price..... | A =$7,500 | A =$10,000 |
| | B = 0 | B = 2,500 gain |
| Old Asset Market Price... | A =$7,000 | A =$ 7,000 |
| | B = 500 loss | B = 500 loss |

**trademark.** A distinctive word or symbol affixed to a product, its package or dispenser, which uniquely identifies the firm's products and services. See *trademark right.*

**trademark right.** The right to exclude competitors in sales or advertising from using words or symbols which may be confusingly similar to the firm's *trademarks.* Trademark rights last as long as the firm continues to use the trademarks in question. In the U.S., trademark rights arise from use and not from government registration. They therefore have a legal life independent of the life of a registration. Registrations last 20 years and are renewable as long as the trademark is being used. Thus as an asset, purchased trademark rights might, like land, not be subject to amortization if management believes the life of the trademark is indefinite. In practice, accountants usually amortize a trademark right over some estimate of its life, not to exceed 40 years. Under *FASB Statement No. 2,* internally developed trademark rights must be *expensed.*

**trade payables (receivables).** *Payable (receivables)* arising in the ordinary course of business transactions. Most accounts payable (receivable) are of this kind.

**trading on the equity.** Said of a firm engaging in *debt financing;* frequently said of a firm doing so to a degree considered abnormal for a firm of its kind. *Leverage.*

**transaction.** An exchange between the accounting *entity* and another party, or parties, that leads to an accounting entry. Sometimes used to describe any event that requires a *journal entry.*

**transfer agent.** Usually a bank or trust company *des-*

*ignated* by a corporation to make legal transfers of *stock (bonds)* and, perhaps, to pay *dividends (coupons).*

**transfer price.** A substitute for a *market,* or *arm's-length, price* used in *profit center,* or *responsibility, accounting* when one segment of the business "sells" to another segment. Incentives of profit center managers will not coincide with the best interests of the entire business unless transfer prices are properly set.

**translation gain (or loss).** *Foreign exchange gain (or loss).*

**transportation-in.** *Freight-in.*

**treasury bond.** A bond issued by a corporation and then reacquired; such bonds are treated as retired when reacquired and an *extraordinary gain* or *loss* on reacquisition is recognized. Also, a *bond* issued by the U.S. Treasury Department.

**treasury stock.** *Capital stock* issued and then reacquired by the corporation. Such reacquisitions result in a reduction of *stockholders' equity,* and are usually shown on the balance sheet as *contra* to stockholders' equity. Neither *gain* nor *loss* is recognized on transactions involving treasury stock. Any difference between the amounts paid and received for treasury stock transactions are debited (if positive) or credited (if negative) to *additional paid-in capital.* See *cost method* and *par value method.* See General Electric annual report at note 35.3.

**trial balance.** A listing of *account balances;* all accounts with *debit* balances are totaled separately from accounts with *credit* balances. The two totals should be equal. Trial balances are taken as a partial check of the arithmetic accuracy of the entries previously made. See *adjusted, pre-closing, post-closing, unadjusted trial balance.*

**turnover.** The number of times that *assets,* such as *inventory* or *accounts receivable,* are replaced on average during the period. Accounts receivable turnover, for example, is total sales on account for a period divided by average accounts receivable balance for the period. See *ratio.*

**turnover of plant and equipment.** See *ratio.*

**two-T-account method.** A method for computing either (1) *foreign exchange gains and losses* or (2) *monetary gains* and *losses* for *general price level adjusted statements.* The left-hand *T-account* shows actual net balances of *monetary items* and the right-hand T-account shows implied *(common) dollar* amounts.

**2/10, n(et)/30.** See *terms of sale.*

## U

**unadjusted trial balance.** *Trial balance* before *adjusting* and *closing entries* are made at the end of the period.

**unappropriated retained earnings.** *Retained earnings* not appropriated and therefore against which *dividends* can be charged in the absence of retained earnings restrictions. See *restricted retained earnings.*

**uncertainty.** See *risk* for definition and contrast.

**uncollectible account.** An *account receivable* that will not be paid by the *debtor.* If the preferable *allowance method* is used, the entry on judging a specific account to be uncollectible is to *debit* the allowance for uncollectibles accounts and to *credit* the specific account receivable. See *sales, uncollectible accounts adjustment*.

**unconsolidated subsidiary.** A *subsidiary* not consolidated and, hence, accounted for on the *equity method*.

**uncontrollable cost.** The opposite of *controllable cost*.

**underapplied (underabsorbed) overhead.** An excess of actual *overhead costs* for a period over costs applied, or charged, to products produced during the period. A *debit balance* remaining in an overhead account after overhead is assigned to product.

**underlying document.** The record, memorandum, *voucher*, or other signal that is the authority for making an *entry* into a *journal*.

**underwriter.** One who agrees to purchase an entire *security issue* for a specified price, usually for resale to others.

**unearned income (revenue).** *Advances from customers;* strictly speaking, a contradiction in terms.

**unemployment tax.** See *FUTA*.

**unencumbered appropriation.** In governmental accounting, portion of an *appropriation* not yet spent or *encumbered*.

**unexpired cost.** An *asset*.

**unfavorable variance.** In *standard cost* accounting, an excess of actual cost over standard cost assigned to product.

**unfunded.** Not *funded*. An obligation or *liability*, usually for *pension costs*, exists but no *funds* have been set aside to discharge the obligation or liability.

**Uniform Partnership Act.** A model law, enacted by many states, to govern the relations between partners where the *partnership* agreement fails to specify the agreed-upon treatment.

**unissued capital stock.** *Stock* authorized but not yet issued.

**units of production method.** The *production method of depreciation*.

**unlimited liability.** The liability of *general partners* or a sole proprietor for all debts of the *partnership* or *sole proprietorship*.

**unqualified opinion.** See *auditor's report*.

**unrealized appreciation.** An *unrealized holding gain;* frequently used in the context of *marketable securities*.

**unrealized gross margin (profit).** A *contra* account to *installment accounts receivable* used with the *installment method* of revenue recognition. Shows the amount of profit that will eventually be realized when the receivable is collected.

**unrealized holding gain.** See *inventory profit* for definition and an example.

**unrecovered cost.** *Book value* of an *asset*.

**usage variance.** *Quantity variance*.

**useful life.** *Service life*.

**use of funds.** Any *transaction* that reduces funds (however funds is defined).

## V

**valuation account.** A *contra account*. When *inventories* or *marketable securities* are shown at *cost* and the *lower-of-cost-or-market* valuation basis is to be used, often any declines in market value below cost will be credited to a valuation account. In this way,

the acquisition cost and the amounts of price declines below cost can both be shown.

**value.** Monetary worth; the term is usually so subjective that it ought not to be used without a modifying adjective unless most people would agree on the amount; not to be confused with *cost*. See *fair market value*.

**value added.** *Cost* of a product or *work in process*, minus the cost of the materials purchased for the product or work in process.

**value variance.** *Price variance*.

**variable annuity.** An *annuity* whose periodic payments depend upon some uncertain outcome, such as stock market prices.

**variable budget.** *Flexible budget*.

**variable costing.** *Direct costing*.

**variable costs.** *Costs* that change as activity levels change. Strictly speaking, variable costs are zero when the activity level is zero. See *semivariable costs*.

**variance.** Difference between actual and *standard costs* or between *budgeted* and actual *expenditures* or, sometimes, *expenses*. In accounting, the word has a completely different meaning from its meaning in statistics, where it is a measure of dispersion of a distribution.

**variance analysis.** The investigation of the causes of *variances* in a *standard cost system*. This term has a different meaning in statistics.

**variation analysis.** Analysis of the causes of changes in items of interest in financial statements such as net *income* or *gross margin*.

**vendor.** A seller. Sometimes spelled "vender."

**verifiable.** A qualitative *objective* of financial reporting specifying that items in *financial statements* can be checked by tracing back to supporting *invoices*, canceled *checks*, and other physical pieces of evidence.

**verification.** The auditor's act of reviewing or checking items in *financial statements* by tracing back to supporting *invoices*, canceled *checks*, and other business documents, or sending out *confirmations* to be returned. Compare with *physical verification*.

**vertical analysis.** Analysis of *percentage statements* of a single firm as of a given date, as opposed to *horizontal* or *time series analysis* where items are compared over time or across firms.

**vested.** Said of *pension plan* benefits that are not contingent on the employee continuing to work for the employer.

**volume variance.** *Capacity variance*.

**voucher.** A document that serves to recognize a *liability* and authorize the disbursement of cash. Sometimes used to refer to the written evidence documenting an *accounting entry*, as in the term *journal voucher*.

**voucher system.** A method for controlling *cash* that requires each *check* to be authorized with an approved *voucher*. No cash *disbursements* are made except from *petty cash funds*.

## W

**wage.** Compensation of employees based on time worked or output of product for manual labor. But see *take-home pay*.

**warrant.** A certificate entitling the owner to buy a

specified amount of stock at a specified time(s) for a specified price. Differs from a *stock option* only in that options are granted to employees and warrants are issued to the public. See *right*.

**warranty.** A promise by a seller to correct deficiencies in products sold. When warranties are given, good accounting practice recognizes an estimate of warranty *expense* and an *estimated liability* at the time of sale.

**wash sale.** The sale and purchase of the same or similar *asset* within a short time period. For *income tax* purposes, *losses* on a sale of stock may not be recognized if equivalent stock is purchased within thirty days before or thirty days after the date of sale.

**wasting asset.** A *natural resource* having a limited *useful life* and, hence, subject to *amortization* called *depletion*. Examples are timberland, oil and gas wells, and ore deposits.

**watered stock.** *Stock* issued for *assets* with *fair market value* less than *par* or *stated value*. The assets are put onto the books at the overstated values. In the law, for stock to be considered watered the *board of directors* must have acted in bad faith or fraudulently in issuing the stock under these circumstances. The term originated from a former practice of cattlemen who fed cattle large quantities of salt to make them thirsty. The cattle then drank a lot of water before being taken to market. This was done to make the cattle appear heavier and more valuable than they would have been otherwise.

**weighted average.** An average computed by counting each occurrence of each value, not merely a single occurrence of each value. For example, if one unit is purchased for $1 and two units are purchased for $2 each, then the simple average of the purchase prices is $1.50 but the weighted average price per unit is $5/3 = $1.67. Contrast with *moving average*.

**weighted-average inventory method.** Valuing either *withdrawals* or *ending inventory* at the *weighted average* purchase price of all units on hand at the time of withdrawal or of computing ending inventory. The *inventory equation* is used to calculate the other quantity. If the *perpetual inventory* method is in use, often called the "moving-average method."

**where-got, where-gone statement.** A term used by W. M. Cole for a statement much like the *statement of changes in financial position*.

**window dressing.** The attempt to make financial statements show *operating* results, or *financial position*, more favorable than would be otherwise shown.

**withdrawals.** *Assets* distributed to an owner. *Partner's drawings*. See *inventory equation* for another context.

**withholding.** Deductions from *salaries* or *wages*, usually for *income taxes*, to be remitted by the employer, in the employee's name, to the taxing authority.

**working capital.** *Current assets* minus *current liabilities*. The *statement of changes in financial position* usually explains the changes in working capital for a period.

**working capital provided by operations.** See *funds provided by operations*.

**working papers.** The schedules and analyses prepared by the *auditor* in carrying out investigations prior to issuing an *opinion* on *financial statements*.

**work in process.** Partially completed product; an *asset* which is classified as *inventory*.

**work sheet.** A tabular schedule for convenient summary of *adjusting* and *closing entries*. The work sheet usually begins with an *unadjusted trial balance*. Adjusting entries are shown in the next two columns, one for *debits* and one for *credits*. The horizontal sum of each line is then carried to the right into either the *income statement* or *balance sheet* columns, as appropriate. The *plug* to equate the income statement column totals is the income, if a debit plug is required, or loss, if a credit plus is required, for the period. That income will be closed to retained earnings on the balance sheet. The income statement credit columns are the revenues for the period and the debit columns are the expenses (and revenue *contras*) to be shown on the income statement.

An example work sheet is shown on page 56 for Caralex Stores, Inc. for the quarter ending September 30, 1977. The company last closed its books on June 30, 1977. The Expense Control Account is used to record various expenses not shown in separate accounts (see *control account*). The numbers in parentheses on the work sheet correspond to the adjusting entries explained below.

(1) A deposit of $1,250 was made up, journalized and posted on September 30, but actually was not deposited in the bank until October 1.

| | | |
|---|---|---|
| Undeposited Cash | 1,250 | |
| Cash in Bank | | 1,250 |
| To reverse entry prematurely recorded. | | |

(2) The net debit balances of accounts receivable from customers is $94,000. A review of individual customers' accounts reveals that several individual accounts have credit balances totaling $650. Thus, the gross amount of accounts receivable if $94,650.

| | | |
|---|---|---|
| Accounts Receivable | 650 | |
| Advances by Customers | | 650 |
| To set up advances by customers who have made payments on accounts or returned goods for credit. | | |

(3) The merchandise inventory on hand at September 30 is $130,000.

| | | |
|---|---|---|
| Cost of Goods Sold | 246,000 | |
| Merchandise Inventory | | 246,000 |
| To record reduction in inventory as cost of goods sold. $376,000 – $130,000 = $246,000. | | |

(4) The insurance policies all expire on January 1, 1979. No payments on insurance policies were made this quarter.

| | | |
|---|---|---|
| Expense Control Account | 260 | |
| Prepaid Insurance | | 260 |
| The insurance policies provide 18 months' coverage as of June 30, 1977. To record insurance expired for three months; 3/18 × $1,560 = $260. | | |

(5) The rent is $1,200 per month and has been paid through November 30, 1977. When the rent was paid, it was debited to Rent Expense, a component of the Expense Control Account.

## CARALEX STORES, INC.
### Work Sheet—Quarter Ending September 30, 1977

| | Unadjusted Trial Balance | | Adjustments | | Income Statement | | Balance Sheet | |
|---|---|---|---|---|---|---|---|---|
| | Dr. | Cr. | Dr. | Cr. | Dr. | Cr. | Dr. | Cr. |
| Undeposited Cash | 500 | | (1) 1,250 | | | | 1,750 | |
| Cash in Bank | 8,270 | | | (1) 1,250 | | | 7,020 | |
| Accounts Receivable | 94,000 | | (2) 650 | | | | 94,650 | |
| Allowance for Uncollectible Accounts | | 1,400 | | (6) 3,200 | | | | 4,600 |
| Interest Receivable | 80 | | (10) 240 | | | | 320 | |
| Merchandise Inventory | 376,000 | | | (3) 246,000 | | | 130,000 | |
| Supplies Inventory | 1,200 | | (8) 1,400 | | | | 2,600 | |
| Prepaid Rent | 1,200 | | (5) 1,200 | | | | 2,400 | |
| Prepaid Insurance | 1,560 | | | (4) 260 | | | 1,300 | |
| Notes Receivable | 9,600 | | | | | | 9,600 | |
| Furniture and Fixtures | 25,000 | | | | | | 25,000 | |
| Accumulated Depreciation | | 17,000 | | (7) 500 | | | | 17,500 |
| Accounts Payable | | 32,400 | | | | | | 32,400 |
| Advances by Customers | | | | (2) 650 | | | | 650 |
| Interest Payable | | 400 | | (11) 100 | | | | 500 |
| Bonus Payable | | | | (12) 752 | | | | 752 |
| Sales Tax Payable | | 9,600 | | | | | | 9,600 |
| Withheld Income Tax | | 1,970 | | | | | | 1,970 |
| Payroll Taxes Payable | | 360 | | (9) 1,680 | | | | 2,040 |
| Income Taxes Payable | | | | (13) 2,160 | | | | 2,160 |
| Notes Payable | | 24,000 | | | | | | 24,000 |
| Capital Stock | | 160,000 | | | | | | 160,000 |
| Retained Earnings | | 13,860 | | | | | | 13,860 |
| Sales | | 326,000 | | | | 326,000 | | |
| Sales Returns and Allowances | 6,000 | | | | 6,000 | | | |
| Sales, Uncollectible Accounts Adjustment | | | (6) 3,200 | | 3,200 | | | |
| Interest Revenue | | | | (10) 240 | | 240 | | |
| Cost of Goods Sold | | | (3) 246,000 | | 246,000 | | | |
| Expense Control Account | 62,960 | | (4) 260 | (5) 1,200 | 62,800 | | | |
| | | | (7) 500 | (8) 1,400 | | | | |
| | | | (9) 1,680 | | | | | |
| Interest Expense | 620 | | (11) 100 | | 720 | | | |
| Bonus Expense | | | (12) 752 | | 752 | | | |
| Income Tax Expense | | | (13) 2,160 | | 2,160 | | | |
| Column Totals | 586,990 | 586,990 | 259,392 | 259,392 | 321,632 | 326,240 | 274,640 | 270,032 |
| Net Income for Quarter | | | | | 4,608 | | | 4,608 |
| | | | | | 326,240 | 326,240 | 274,640 | 274,640 |

Prepaid Rent .......................... 1,200
    Expense Control Account ............. 1,200
To set up two months' prepaid rent as of September 30. Prepaid rent was $1,200. As a result of this entry, it is $2,400.

(6) The estimated uncollectibles to arise from sales of the quarter are 1 percent of sales, net of returns and allowances.

Sales, Uncollectible Accounts
    Adjustment............................ 3,200
      Allowance for Uncollectible
      Accounts......................... 3,200
.01 × ($326,000 − $6,000) = $3,200.

(7) Depreciation on furniture and fixtures is 8 percent of cost per year.

Expense Control Account ................ 500
    Accumulated Depreciation ............. 500
3/12 × .08 × $25,000 = $500.

(8) The cost of all supplies purchased is debited to Supplies Expense, a component of the Expense Control Account. The Supplies Inventory at September 30 is $2,600.

Supplies Inventory........................ 1,400
    Expense Control Account .............. 1,400
To set up supplies inventory at $2,600.

(9) The employer's share of payroll taxes has been paid through September 1. The employer's share for September is calculated to be $1,680.

Expense Control Account ................ 1,680
Payroll Taxes Payable ................. 1,680
To record Payroll Tax Expense for September as a component of the Expense Control Account.

(10) The Notes Receivable account contains a 10-percent note for $9,600 dated June 1, 1977, and due December 1, 1977.

Interest Receivable ...................... 240
Interest Revenue ...................... 240
3/12 × .10 × $9,600 = $240.

(11) The Notes Payable account contains a single 10-percent note for $24,000 dated July 15, 1977, and due January 16, 1978. Interest has been accured on the 15th of each month.

Interest Expense........................ 100
Interest Payable ...................... 100
Interest expense per month is $200 (= 1/12 × .10 × $24,000). The balance of Interest Payable on the note should be $500 (= 2½ × $200). To adjust interest expense for the quarter and interest payable as of September 30.

(12) The manager is to be paid a bonus of 10 percent of the pretax income of the enterprise exclusive of the bonus.

Bonus Expense......................... 752
Bonus Payable ...................... 752
From Income Statement columns: .10 × ($326,000 + $240 − $6,000 − $3,200 − $246,000 − $62,800 − $720) = $752.

(13) The income tax for the quarter is estimated to be $2,160.

Income Tax Expense .................... 2,160
Income Taxes Payable ................. 2,160
To record income tax expense for quarter.

Work sheet is also used to refer to *schedules* for determining other items appearing on the *financial statements* that require adjustment or compilation.

**worth.**   *Value.* See *net worth.*

**worth-debt ratio.**   Reciprocal of the *debt-equity ratio.* See *ratio.*

**write down.**   *Write off,* except that not all the asset's cost is charged to expense or *loss.* Generally used for nonrecurring items.

**write off.**   *Charge* an *asset* to *expense* or *loss;* that is, *debit* expense (or loss) and *credit* asset.

**writeoff method.**   A method for treating *uncollectible accounts* that charges *bad debt expense* and credits accounts receivable of specific customers as uncollectible amounts are identified. May not be used when uncollectible amounts are significant and can be estimated. See *sales, uncollectible accounts adjustment* and the *allowance method* for contrast.

**write up.**   To increase the recorded *cost* of an *asset* with no corresponding *disbursement* of *funds;* that is, *debit* asset and *credit revenue* or, perhaps, *owners' equity.* Seldom done since currently accepted accounting principles are based on actual transactions.

## Y

**yield.**   *Internal rate of return* on a stream of cash flows. Cash yield is cash flow divided by book value. See also *dividend yield.*

**yield to maturity.**   At a given time, the *internal rate of return* of a series of cash flows, usually said of a *bond.* Sometimes called the "effective rate."

## Z

**zero base(d) budgeting (ZBB).**   In preparing an ordinary *budget* for the next period, a manager starts with the budget for the current period and makes adjustments as seem necessary, because of changed conditions, for the next period. Since most managers like to increase the scope of the activities managed and since most prices increase most of the time, amounts in budgets prepared in the ordinary, incremental way seem to increase period after period. The authority approving the budget assumes operations will be carried out in the same way as in the past and that next period's expenditures will have to be at least as large as the current period's. Thus, this authority tends to study only the increments to the current period's budget. In ZBB, the authority questions the process for carrying out a program and the entire budget for next period: every dollar in the budget is studied, not just the dollars incremental to the previous period's amounts. The advocates of ZBB claim that in this way: (1) programs or divisions or marginal benefit to the business or governmental unit will more likely be deleted from the program, rather than being continued with costs at least as large as the present ones, and (2) alternative, more cost-effective, ways of carrying out programs are more likely to be discovered and implemented. ZBB implies questioning the existence of programs, and the fundamental nature of the way they are carried out, not merely the amounts used to fund them. Experts appear to be evenly divided as to whether the middle word should be "base" or "based."

**zero salvage value.**   If the *salvage value* of a *depreciable asset* is estimated to be less than 10 percent of its *cost,* then the tax regulations permit an assumption of zero salvage value in computing *depreciation* for federal *income tax* purposes. This convention is often used in financial reporting as well.

# GENERAL ⊛ ELECTRIC

# 1976 Annual Report

## Authors' Introduction

This is an excerpt from GE's Annual Report. GE's annual reports are consistently among the best we see. GE provides copious explanations and discloses helpful items beyond those that are currently required. The first 31 pages of the Annual Report consist of general information about the company, illustrations, and highlights of the year's operations. We have commented on various aspects of the financial statements, which follow the general information, in numbered footnotes keyed to the GE annual report. None of our criticisms is major. The page numbers of the original 32 through 44, are left intact and references, both in the report and our notes, use these numbers. The "1976 Financial Highlights" shown on the next page is taken from page 3 of GE's annual report. It is reproduced here to provide additional information for assessing GE's operating performance during 1976.

Our footnotes are numbered in the form "32.3"; the digits before the period refer to the page number in the GE report. The digits after the period refer to note number on that page. Thus "32.3" refers to our note 3 for GE's page 32. Our notes appear on a page facing (or near) the page of the annual report being commented on. Our notes begin at the bottom of this page. The bold face numbers shown in the margins of the annual report do not, of course, appear in the original. All accounting terms used in our supplementary footnotes are explained in the Glossary.

We think there is no better way to learn financial accounting than to try to understand all that appears in GE's statements. (The GE corporate signature, as it appears above is a trademark of General Electric Company. It is, perhaps, the single most valuable asset of the Company. In accord with generally accepted accounting principles, this asset does not appear anywhere in the financial statements.)

## Authors' Notes to General Electric Annual Report

**3.1** This is the style of our commentary footnotes. The report shown here appears on page 3 of the GE annual report. At the top of the page is a summary of the year's results. The schedule at the bottom of the page is a "line of business" or "segment" report.

**3.2** "Total capital invested" is defined by GE as short-term borrowings + long-term borrowings + minority interest + shareowners' equity. You cannot check this relation from the information given here, but see the Ten-year summary on pages 46 and 47 of the annual report (pages 82–83 of this book). Minority interest is discussed in note 33.5.

**3.3** The numerator of this ratio (percent earned on average total capital invested) for 1976 is net income ($930.6 million; see GE's page 32) plus minority interest in earnings of consolidated affiliates ($28.3 million; see page 32) plus interest on long-term borrowings ($94.5 million; see GE's note 6 on page 38). The denominator is the average of the "total capital invested figures" given above, $7,305 million at the end of 1976 and $6,628 million at the end of 1975.

**3.4** This is the "line of business" report. FASB *Statement No. 14* requires such reports in annual reports for years starting after December 15, 1976.

**3.5** Sales between categories and profits on these sales are shown on this line. Setting of prices on such intercategory transactions gives rise to the *transfer price* problem (see Glossary).

**3.6** The major difficulty in constructing meaningful and useful segment reports is the allocation of these "corporate items" to the major categories. They are truly common or joint costs of running the entire corporation but must be allocated to the various segments in order to present subtotals for segment earnings that add up to the total earnings, $931 million.

# 3.1 1976 Financial highlights

Data for both years include Utah International Inc. as a result of a pooling of interests consummated in 1976.
(Dollar amounts in millions; per-share amounts in dollars)

| For the year | 1976 | 1975 | Percent increase |
|---|---|---|---|
| Sales of products and services to customers | $15,697 | $14,105 | 11% |
| Net earnings applicable to common stock | 931 | 688 | 35 |
| Funds generated from operations | 1,412 | 1,172 | 20 |
| Operating funds after dividends | 1,051 | 846 | 24 |

| At year end | 1976 | 1975 | Percent increase |
|---|---|---|---|
| Short- and long-term borrowings | $ 1,933 | $ 1,907 | 1% |
| Share owners' equity | 5,253 | 4,617 | 14 |
| **3.2** Total capital invested | 7,305 | 6,628 | 10 |

| Measurements | 1976 | 1975 | |
|---|---|---|---|
| Net earnings per common share | $ 4.12 | $ 3.07 | 34% |
| Dividends declared per General Electric common share | 1.70 | 1.60 | 6 |
| Operating margin as a percentage of sales | 9.7% | 8.4% | |
| Percent earned on average share owners' equity | 18.9 | 15.7 | |
| **3.3** Percent earned on average total capital invested | 15.1 | 12.5 | |
| Borrowings as a percentage of total capital invested | 26.5 | 28.8 | |

| | Sales | | | Net earnings | | |
|---|---|---|---|---|---|---|
| **3.4** Operating results by major categories | 1976 | 1975 | Percent increase | 1976 | 1975 | Percent increase |
| Aerospace | $ 2,099 | $ 1,972 | 6% | $ 95 | $ 76 | 25% |
| Consumer | 3,307 | 2,880 | 15 | 198 | 108 | 83 |
| Industrial components and systems | 4,787 | 4,320 | 11 | 266 | 226 | 18 |
| Industrial power equipment | 3,074 | 2,922 | 5 | 72 | 65 | 11 |
| International: manufacturing exports and diversified foreign affiliates | 4,024 | 3,745 | 7 | 196 | 158 | 24 |
| Natural resources: Utah International Inc. | 1,001 | 706 | 42 | 181 | 108 | 68 |
| General Electric Credit Corporation | — | — | | 59 | 52 | 13 |
| **3.5** Corporate eliminations | (2,595) | (2,440) | | (136) | (105) | |
| Total Company | $15,697 | $14,105 | 11 | $931 | $688 | 35 |

**3.6** Sales and net earnings by major category throughout this Report include intercategory transactions. To the extent that sales and earnings are recognized in more than one category, appropriate eliminations are reflected in the "Corporate eliminations" line. Net earnings for each major category are after allocation of corporate items such as expenses of headquarters personnel, corporate research and development, other income, and interest and other financial charges. Income taxes are allocated to major categories based on the total corporate effective tax rate, except for the Credit Corporation and Utah whose income taxes are calculated separately. Unless otherwise indicated by the context, the terms "GE", "General Electric" and "Company" are used on the basis of consolidation described on page 36. Unless otherwise indicated by the context, the terms "Utah" and "Utah International" mean Utah International Inc., as well as all of its "affiliates" and "associated companies" as those terms are used on page 36.

## 32.1 Statement of Earnings

General Electric Company and consolidated affiliates

**32.2** Data for both years reflect pooling of interests with Utah International Inc. (no▮

| For the years ended December 31 (In millions) | 1976 | 1975 | Addi▮ inform |
|---|---|---|---|
| **Sales of products and services to customers** | $15,697.3 | $14,105.1 | (no▮ |
| **32.3** **Operating costs** | | | (no▮ |
| Employee compensation, including benefits | 5,849.9 | 5,136.8 | (no▮ |
| **32.4** Materials, supplies, services and other costs | 7,726.0 | 7,038.9 | |
| Depreciation, depletion and amortization | 486.2 | 470.5 | |
| Taxes, except those on income | 258.8 | 162.1 | |
| Decrease (increase) in inventories during the year | (151.5) | 110.2 | |
| | 14,169.4 | 12,918.5 | |
| **Operating margin** | 1,527.9 | 1,186.6 | |
| Other income | 274.3 | 174.2 | (no▮ |
| Interest and other financial charges | (174.7) | (186.8) | (no▮ |
| **Earnings before income taxes and minority interest** | 1,627.5 | 1,174.0 | |
| **32.5** Provision for income taxes | (668.6) | (459.8) | (no▮ |
| **32.6** Minority interest in earnings of consolidated affiliates | (28.3) | (25.7) | |
| **Net earnings applicable to common stock** | $   930.6 | $   688.5 | |
| **32.7** Earnings per common share (in dollars) | $4.12 | $3.07 | (no▮ |
| Dividends declared per General Electric common share (in dollars) | $1.70 | $1.60 | |
| Operating margin as a percentage of sales | 9.7% | 8.4% | |
| Net earnings as a percentage of sales | 5.9% | 4.9% | |

The Summary of Significant Accounting Policies on page 36 and the Notes to Financial
Statements on pages 37-43 are an integral part of this Statement.

32.1, 32.2, 33.1, 33.2, etc.: These numbers refer to Authors' Notes. The numbers before the decimal indicate the page number from the GE Annual Report; the numbers after the decimal refer to the order on that page.

**32.1**   This is the income statement.
**32.2**   General Electric merged with Utah International during 1976 in a pooling of interests. Refer to the Glossary at *pooling of interests method* and contrast with *purchase method,* particularly the valuation of the merged assets.

General Electric gave up about 41 million shares of common stock for Utah; see General Electric's note 1 on page 37. At the time of the merger, General Electric's common stock traded in the market for about $50 per share. Thus, the total consideration given up by General Electric was worth a little over $2 billion (= 41 million shares × $50 per share). The economic substance of the merger transaction would be reflected in a journal entry such as the following (which was *not* made by GE):

```
Assets (net of Liabilities) from Utah ....................   2 billion
      Common Stock plus Amounts Received for Stock
           in Excess of Par Value .........................             2 billion
Entry to record net assets of Utah acquired for $2 billion of
stock issued.
```

Instead, GE made an entry recording the acquisition of Utah's net assets at their historical cost as shown on the books of Utah, about $550 million at the time of the merger. The journal entry made by GE can be reconstructed from the information given on page 35 of the annual report. It was:

|  | Dollar Amounts in Millions |
|---|---|
| Assets (net of Liabilities) from Utah ....................... | 548 |
| Common Stock ....................................... | 103 |
| Amounts Received for Stock in Excess of Par Value ...... | 52 |
| Retained Earnings .................................. | 393 |

Entry to record acquisition of assets at historical costs to Utah in pooling of interests. See note 35.2 for derivation of amounts.

Thus, GE in an arm's length transaction with the owners of Utah acquired net assets for which it gave up $2 billion of its own stock. Yet the net assets are now recorded on GE's books for about $550 million. GE will charge to expense over the future only the $550 million. Over the life of the acquired assets, GE's consolidated income will be, aside from tax effects, $1,450 million (= $2 billion − $550 million) larger than it would have been had the economic substance of this transaction been recorded on its books.

We hasten to add that GE's accounting is required under these circumstances by APB *Opinion No. 16*. The FASB is currently considering changing the accounting rules so that assets acquired in mergers such as this would be recorded at the fair market value on the date of the acquisition.

Under pooling of interests accounting, the assumption is made that Utah had always been part of GE, so that GE's financial statements for all years are restated to include Utah data. GE's note 1 on page 37 of the annual report shows GE's results independent of Utah as well as in combination with Utah for 1975 and 1976. Note, too, that the "Ten-year summary" shown on pages 46–47 also assumes that Utah has always been part of GE. The merger actually took place in December of 1976, less than one month before the end of the year being reported on in this annual report.

**32.3** *Operating costs* is a poor term. The title would better be *Operating expenses*. Contrast *cost* and *expenses* in the Glossary. See also note 37.2.

**32.4** All manufacturing costs (as well as selling and administrative costs) incurred during the year are shown as operating costs. If inventories have increased (ending inventory > beginning inventory), some of those costs have not expired and are not expenses. Hence, the increase in inventories is deducted from total operating costs, and *vice versa* for decreases in inventories. This can, perhaps, be seen better as follows. If "additions" are defined to mean purchases of manufacturing materials, labor, and overhead, then,
*Cost of Goods Sold = Beginning Inventory + Additions − Ending Inventory.*
Rearranging terms,
*Cost of Goods Sold = Additions − (Ending Inventory − Beginning Inventory)* or
*Cost of Goods Sold = Additions − Increase in Inventory.*
All additions for manufacturing and other costs are shown as "operating costs"; thus, the increase in inventories must be subtracted from additions for proper computation of cost of goods sold.

**32.5** Provision usually means "estimated expense" in this country; see the Glossary at *provision* for the contrast in this word's meanings on the two sides of the Atlantic Ocean.

**32.6** GE does not own all the shares in all of its consolidated subsidiaries. Some of the shares belong to outsiders, called the *minority interest*. The minority interest's share of the earnings of the subsidiary companies does not belong to GE's shareholders. Hence, in deriving income to GE's shareholders the minority interest's share in earnings is subtracted from the earnings of the consolidated group of companies. Note, however, that this reduction in income uses no cash or other funds, so that there is an adjustment on the Statement of Changes in Financial Position for this charge against income. See note 34.6.

**32.7** This is primary earnings per share, as called for by APB *Opinion No. 15*. See GE's note 8 for a discussion of fully diluted earnings per share. Fully diluted earnings per share is not separately shown here since the amount is within one percent of the primary earnings per share amount. (In general, fully diluted earnings per share need not be separately shown if it is within 3 percent of primary earnings per share.)

**33.1** This is the balance sheet. GE explains most of these items in its own notes.

**33.2** GE uses the completed contract method of recognizing revenue from long-term construction contracts; see GE's Summary of Significant Accounting Policies on page 36 at "Sales". As GE incurs costs on these contracts it makes journal entries such as:

Work in Process Inventory for Long-term Contracts .........   X
   Various Assets and Liabilities .........................        X
To record cost of construction activity.

Some of GE's long-term construction contracts provide that the customer shall make progress payments to GE as the work is done. GE does not recognize revenue until the work is completed, so the journal entry made at the time cash is received is one such as:

Cash ...............................................   Y
   Advances from Customers on Long-term Contracts .......       Y
To record cash received and to set up the corresponding liability.

When the balance sheet is prepared, the amounts, X (debit balance), in the inventory accounts are netted against the amounts, Y (credit balance), in the liability accounts. If there is a net credit balance, as here, with Y greater than X, then the difference, $Y - X$, is recorded as a liability. GE shows this liability under the title "Progress Collections". On contracts where the amounts in the inventory account exceed the cash collections, then the difference, $X - Y$, is shown as an asset under a title such as "Costs Incurred on Long-term Contracts in Excess of Billings". This netting of costs incurred against cash collections and the separate showing of the excesses is called for by ARB *No. 45*.

GE told us that on many of its contracts the only cash collections received before construction is completed are for engineering costs incurred in preparation to undertake construction. GE said that it expenses these engineering costs, rather than accumulating them in work in process inventory accounts. Thus, there is no asset account to net against the liability. The "Progress collections" title is appropriate because it tends to represent gross "advances from customers," rather than a netting of work in process inventory against advances from customers.

**33.3** You can test your understanding of the accounting process by answering the question, "How much cash did GE pay out in dividends during 1976?" The answer is given in the next paragraph.

From page 35, Statement of Changes in Share Owners' Equity, we can see that total dividends declared during 1976 were $360.8 (= $332.5 + $28.3) million. The amount of dividends paid in cash must be the amount declared minus the increase in the amount payable, shown on the balance sheet. Dividends payable increased by $28.2 (= $101.7 − $73.5) million. Thus, cash payments for dividends were $332.6 (= $360.8 − $28.2) million.

**33.4** *Costs* is a poor word to use as a liability title; see Glossary at *cost* and note 41.3.

**33.5** (Refer to our note 32.6 for a description of "minority interest" on the income statement.) This account represents the equity of the minority interest in the consolidated affiliates. From the point of view of GE's shareholders, this equity belonging to the minority is a liability. From the point of view of the consolidated entity, the minority equity is part of total shareowners' equity. Thus whether one believes that minority interest is a liability or an item of owners' equity depends upon whether one views the financial statements as being prepared for the stockholders of GE (the proprietorship theory) or for all potential readers (the entity theory). Note that GE discreetly avoids the issue by not classifying "minority interest" either with liabilities or with owners' equity. The authors' views are evenly divided; two of us prefer the liability treatment (see *indeterminate-term liability* in Glossary) and two prefer the owners' equity treatment.

**33.6** GE uses the cost method of accounting for treasury stock and shows the cost of its own shares acquired on the market as contra to all of owners' equity. Refer to our note 35.3.

## .1 Statement of Financial Position

General Electric Company and consolidated affiliates

Data for both years reflect pooling of interests with Utah International Inc.                    (note 1)

| At December 31 (In millions) | 1976 | 1975 | Additional information |
|---|---|---|---|
| **Assets** | | | |
| Cash | $ 1,059.0 | $ 760.0 | (note 9) |
| Marketable securities | 554.3 | 100.3 | (note 9) |
| Current receivables | 2,717.3 | 2,687.2 | (note 10) |
| Inventories | 2,354.4 | 2,202.9 | (note 11) |
| **Current assets** | 6,685.0 | 5,750.4 | |
| | | | |
| Investments | 1,286.3 | 1,156.6 | (note 12) |
| Property, plant and equipment | 3,356.4 | 3,180.9 | (note 13) |
| Other assets | 722.0 | 653.4 | (note 14) |
| **Total assets** | $12,049.7 | $10,741.3 | |
| | | | |
| **Liabilities and equity** | | | |
| Short-term borrowings | $ 611.1 | $ 667.2 | (note 15) |
| Accounts payable | 879.7 | 776.7 | |
| .2 Progress collections and price adjustments accrued | 1,169.7 | 1,070.4 | |
| .3 Dividends payable | 101.7 | 73.5 | |
| Taxes accrued | 554.9 | 423.7 | |
| .4 Other costs and expenses accrued | 1,287.8 | 1,151.5 | (note 16) |
| **Current liabilities** | 4,604.9 | 4,163.0 | |
| | | | |
| Long-term borrowings | 1,322.3 | 1,239.5 | (note 17) |
| Other liabilities | 750.6 | 617.2 | |
| **Total liabilities** | 6,677.8 | 6,019.7 | |
| | | | |
| .5 **Minority interest in equity of consolidated affiliates** | 119.0 | 104.6 | |
| Preferred stock ($1 par value; 2,000,000 shares authorized; none issued) | — | — | |
| Common stock ($2.50 par value; 251,500,000 shares authorized; 230,368,572 shares issued 1976; 228,724,807 shares issued 1975) | 575.9 | 571.8 | |
| Amounts received for stock in excess of par value | 618.3 | 534.8 | |
| Retained earnings | 4,251.2 | 3,681.4 | |
| | 5,445.4 | 4,788.0 | |
| .6 Deduct common stock held in treasury | (192.5) | (171.0) | |
| **Total share owners' equity** | 5,252.9 | 4,617.0 | (notes 18 and 19) |
| **Total liabilities and equity** | $12,049.7 | $10,741.3 | |
| | | | |
| Commitments and contingent liabilities | | | (note 20) |

The Summary of Significant Accounting Policies on page 36 and the Notes to Financial Statements on pages 37-43 are an integral part of this Statement.

# Statement of Changes in Financial Position

General Electric Company and consolidated affiliates

Data for both years reflect pooling of interests with Utah International Inc.  (note 1)

| For the years ended December 31 (In millions) | 1976 | |
|---|---|---|
| **34.1  Source of funds** | | |
| From operations | | |
| **34.2**  Net earnings | $  930.6 | $  6 |
| **34.3**  Less earnings retained by nonconsolidated finance affiliates | (10.9) | 0 |
| **34.4**  Depreciation, depletion and amortization | 486.2 | 4 |
| **34.5**  Income tax timing differences | (22.5) | |
| **34.6**  Minority interest in earnings of consolidated affiliates | 28.3 | |
| | 1,411.7 | 1,1 |
| **34.7**  Increases in long-term borrowings | 156.7 | |
| Newly issued common stock | 87.4 | |
| **34.8**  Decrease in inventories | — | 1 |
| **34.9**  Increase in current payables other than short-term borrowings | 498.0 | 1 |
| Other — net | 141.7 | 1 |
| **Total source of funds** | 2,295.5 | 1,6 |
| **Application of funds** | | |
| Additions to property, plant and equipment | 740.4 | 5 |
| Dividends declared on General Electric common stock | 332.5 | 2 |
| Dividends declared on Utah International common stock* | 28.3 | |
| Investments | 129.7 | |
| **34.7**  Reduction in long-term borrowings | 73.9 | 2 |
| **34.10**  Increase in current receivables | 30.1 | |
| **34.8**  Increase in inventories | 151.5 | |
| **Total application of funds** | 1,486.4 | 1,1 |
| **34.11  Net increase in cash, marketable securities, and short-term borrowings** | $  809.1 | $  4 |
| **Analysis of net increase in cash, marketable securities, and short-term borrowings** | | |
| Increase in cash and marketable securities | $  753.0 | $  4 |
| Decrease (increase) in short-term borrowings | 56.1 | ( |
| **34.11** | $  809.1 | $  4 |

*Reflects transactions prior to merger date.

The Summary of Significant Accounting Policies on page 36 and the Notes to Financial
Statements on pages 37-43 are an integral part of this Statement.

**34.1**  Most companies define funds as working capital = current assets − current liabilities. GE uses a
more restrictive definition of funds; for GE, funds = cash + marketable securities − short-term
borrowings. We approve of GE's excluding inventories from its definition of funds, but we are
not sure why GE chooses also to exclude current receivables less current payables from the
definition. In any case, sufficient information is given so that the readers can convert to almost
any definition of funds that they choose. Test yourself: What is the net increase in *working capital*
for 1976? The answer is given below in note 34.11.

**34.2**  This statement, as is customary, starts with net income as shown in the income statement on page
32. The next few lines show subtractions for revenues and other credits to income that did not
produce funds and additions for expenses and other charges against income that did not use

funds. After these adjustments to income is shown the total of $1,411.7 million of funds produced by operations. An acceptable alternative format, but one that is seldom used, shows only those revenues that produce funds and subtracts only those expenses that use funds in deriving funds produced by operations.

**34.3**  All earnings of the GE Credit Corporation ($59 million in 1976) are included in income under the equity method. See "Other income" on page 38, GE's note 5. Only $47.5 million of dividends were declared by the Credit Corporation; see the "current and retained earnings statement" of the Credit Company near the bottom right-hand column on page 39. The difference, $11.5 (= $59.0 − $47.5) million, provided no funds to GE and must be subtracted from net income to derive GE's funds from operations. That is, the entire $59.0 million is included in the $930.6 million shown as net earnings by GE, but dividend declarations of the Credit Corporation provided funds of only $47.5 million. The subtraction here is not only for the $11.5 million (caused by the Credit Corporation alone), but also includes the effects of all unconsolidated finance companies. These companies as a group paid GE a net amount of $0.6 (= $11.5 − $10.9) million more than GE picked up as income from them using the equity method. See note 42.4.

**34.4**  Depreciation is *not* a source of funds. Rather, it is an expense that reduces net income without using any funds. The funds were used some time in the past when the depreciable assets were acquired. The arithmetic here is correct, but the caption is misleading.

**34.5**  Income taxes payable for the year exceeded the amount of income tax expense for the year. See the discussion at GE's note 7 on page 38 and our note 38.4. Since more funds were used for income taxes than were reported as income tax expense, there has to be a subtraction for the extra funds used in deriving funds from operations.

**34.6**  See our note 32.6. The charge on the income statement for the minority's interest in earnings (of $28.3 million) reduces the income reported to GE's shareholders, but does not reduce the amount of funds provided by operations of the consolidated entity. Thus, there is an addback to net income for $28.3 million in deriving funds produced by operations. This minority interest of $28.3 million has no direct relation with the $28.3 million shown several lines later as dividends on Utah's shares. The equality of these two numbers is a coincidence.

**34.7**  As is preferable, GE shows separately funds provided by new borrowings and funds used to reduce old borrowings. Some companies show only the net effect either as a source or as an application of funds; they provide no information about the amount of actual borrowings and repayments during the period.

**34.8**  GE's definition of funds does not include inventories. Thus an increase in inventories (as occurred in 1976) is shown as a use of funds and a decrease in inventories (as occurred in 1975) is shown as a source of funds.

**34.9**  GE's definition of funds does not include current payables. Thus, an increase in current payables provides funds in the same way any long-term new borrowing provides funds.

**34.10**  GE's definition of funds does not include current receivables. An increase in receivables uses funds just as does any increase in investments.

**34.11**  Notice the self-balance nature of this statement. The actual change in funds (= cash + marketable securities − short-term borrowings) of $809.1 million is exactly explained in the top part of the statement with the various sources and applications of funds. Some companies do not place the "Analysis" section at the bottom of the statement, thus losing the elegance of the statement; these companies show the "Analysis" in a footnote. Earlier, in our note 34.1, we asked you to test yourself by determining the change in working capital for the year from this statement. The answer might be derived from the information on page 34 as follows:

| | Dollar Amounts in Millions | |
| --- | --- | --- |
| | 1976 | 1975 |
| Increase in Cash, Marketable Securities, and Short-term Borrowings | $809.1 | $465.7 |
| Increase in Current Receivables | 30.1 | 49.2 |
| Increase (Decrease) in Inventories | 151.5 | (110.2) |
| Less Increase in Current Payables Other than Short-term Borrowings | (498.0) | (119.3) |
| Net Increase in Working Capital | $492.7 | $285.4 |

## 35.1 Statement of Changes in Share Owners' Equity

General Electric Company and consolidated affiliates

Data for both years reflect pooling of interests with Utah International Inc.   (note 1)

| For the years ended December 31 (Dollar amounts in millions) | 1976 | 1975 | 1976 | |
|---|---|---|---|---|
| **Common stock issued** | | | (Thousands of shar| |
| Balance January 1, as previously reported | $ 469.3 | $ 465.2 | 187,720 | 186 |
| 35.2   Shares issued to effect merger with Utah International | 102.5 | 102.5 | 41,002 | 41 |
| | 571.8 | 567.7 | 228,722 | 227 |
| New shares issued: | | | | |
| Stock options and appreciation rights | 0.3 | 0.1 | 137 | |
| Employee savings plans | 3.8 | 4.0 | 1,510 | 1 |
| Balance December 31 | 575.9 | 571.8 | 230,369 | 228 |
| **Amounts received for stock in excess of par value** | | | | |
| Balance January 1, as previously reported | 482.7 | 414.5 | | |
| 35.2   Effect of merger with Utah International | 52.0 | 52.1* | | |
| | 534.7 | 466.6 | | |
| Excess over par value of amounts received for newly issued shares.. | 83.3 | 71.3 | | |
| 35.3   Gain on disposition of treasury stock | 0.3 | 0.5 | | |
| Conversion of Canadian General Electric preferred stock | — | (3.6) | | |
| Balance December 31 | 618.3 | 534.8 | | |
| **Retained earnings** | | | | |
| Balance January 1, as previously reported | 3,288.2 | 3,000.5 | | |
| 35.2   Retained earnings of Utah International | 393.2 | 318.6 | | |
| | 3,681.4 | 3,319.1 | | |
| Net earnings | 930.6 | 688.5 | | |
| Dividends declared on General Electric common stock | (332.5) | (293.1) | | |
| Dividends declared on Utah International common stock* | (28.3) | (33.1) | | |
| Balance December 31 | 4,251.2 | 3,681.4 | | |
| **Common stock held in treasury** | | | | |
| Balance January 1 | (171.0) | (175.9) | (3,362) | (3 |
| Purchases | (27.1) | (12.8) | (508) | |
| Dispositions: | | | | |
| Employee savings plans | — | 0.1 | — | |
| Incentive compensation plans | 5.5 | 8.5 | 121 | |
| Conversion of Overseas Capital Corporation 1985 bonds .... | 0.1 | 9.1 | 1 | |
| Balance December 31 | (192.5) | (171.0) | (3,748) | (3, |
| **Total share owners' equity December 31** | $5,252.9 | $4,617.0 | 226,621 | 225, |

*Reflects transactions prior to merger date.

The Summary of Significant Accounting Policies on page 36 and the Notes to Financial
Statements on pages 37-43 are an integral part of this Statement.

35.1   Generally accepted accounting principles call for a reconciliation of changes in all of the owners' equity accounts during the year. Ordinarily, the only major changes in GE's owners' equity accounts are caused by the earning of income and the declaration of dividends. In each year for the past decade or so, GE had merely shown those events at the bottom of the income statement in a combined "Statement of Current and Retained Earnings". Because of the merger with Utah in 1976, the changes in the owners' equity accounts are more complex and GE uses a separate statement to show all the changes.

35.2   In merging with Utah, GE brings Utah's assets and liabilities onto GE's books at Utah's current book values. The shareholders' equity of Utah is brought intact, but in different account amounts, onto GE's books. The journal entries to effect the transaction are as shown below. Note that the amount for "Amounts received for stock in excess of par value" has to be a plug, derived by GE to give equal debits and credits in the entire transaction.

**GE Annual Report and Authors' Notes**

Assets (Net of Liabilities) from Utah .......................... 547.7
Common Stock Issued (41,002,000 Shares Issued × $2.50
Per Share Par Value) .................................. 102.5
Retained Earnings (from Utah's Books) .................. 393.2
Amounts Received for Stock in Excess of Par Value (plug). 52.0

**35.3** Neither gain nor loss can be recognized on transactions by a company in its own shares (called *treasury shares*). GE's accounting is correct, but the use of the term *gain* may be misleading. When GE reissues previously-acquired treasury shares, the adjustment to achieve equal debits and credits is not to a gain or loss account (to appear on the income statement), but to the account "Amounts received for stock in excess of par value." If treasury shares are acquired for an outlay of $1,000 and then are reissued for $1,200, then the entries would be:

Common Stock Held in Treasury ........................ 1,000
Cash ............................................... 1,000
To record acquisition of treasury shares.

Cash ............................................... 1,200
Common Stock Held in Treasury ...................... 1,000
Amounts Received for Stock in Excess of Par Value (not Gain
on Disposition of Treasury Shares) .................. 200
To record reissue of treasury shares for an amount greater than
outlay to acquire them.

**36.1** APB *Opinion No. 22* requires that all annual reports include a summary of significant accounting principles used so that the reader can know which accounting alternatives have been chosen by the company.

**36.2** A parent, such as GE, usually consolidates a subsidiary when all three of the following criteria are met:
1. The parent owns more than 50 percent of the voting shares of the subsidiary.
2. There are no important restrictions on the ability of the parent to exercise control of the subsidiary.
3. The asset and equity structure of the subsidiary is not significantly different from that of the parent.

**36.3** GE tells us here that it consolidates all "majority-owned" (greater than 50 percent) and "controlled" companies except the finance companies which are not similar to the others in the consolidated group. Instead, the finance affiliates are accounted for under the equity method. As can be seen from GE Credit Corporation's balance sheet on page 39, most (92 percent) of the Credit Corporation's assets are receivables and most (89 percent) of its equities is debt, rather than owners' equity. In this sense, the operations of the finance affiliates "are not similar to those of the consolidated group." As our note 39.8 points out, the nonconsolidation of the finance companies makes GE's balance sheet look quite different than it would if the finance affiliates were consolidated. There is no effect on final net income, but the components of income are affected.

**36.4** Consolidated financial statements present information about a group of affiliated companies essentially as if the group were one company. Consequently, gains or losses on sales of assets between companies in the consolidated group must be eliminated. The recognition of such gains or losses is postponed until the assets are sold by one company of the consolidated group to a buyer outside of the consolidated group.

**36.5** GE tells us that it uses the equity method for nonconsolidated finance affiliates in which it holds more than 20 percent of the voting stock. Under the equity method, GE's net earnings include its share of the earnings, not just the dividends, of these companies. See note 34.3.

**36.6** GE uses the completed contract method of recognizing revenue on long-term construction projects. See note 33.2.

**36.7** GE tells us that it charges vacation pay to expense (or product cost) accounts, as employees earn vacations, rather than charging income when employees take their vacations. We would not have thought that the implied alternative, charging income only when vacations are taken, would ever be permitted (for material amounts), so that we are somewhat surprised to see this disclosure.

**36.8** That is, in computing future values of pension fund investments and interest on unfunded obligations for prior service costs, a six-percent rate is used. GE's note 4 (p. 37) indicates that the rates earned in 1976 and 1975 were 6.4 and 6.6 percent respectively.

**36.9** See note 37.7.

## Summary of Significant
## 36.1 Accounting Policies

The most significant of the accounting policies followed by General Electric are described below to help users of these Financial Statements understand and evaluate them.

### 36.2 Basis of consolidation
The Financial Statements consolidate the accounts of the parent General Electric Company and those of all majority-owned and controlled companies ("affiliated companies"),

**36.3** except finance companies whose operations are not similar to those of the consolidated group. All significant items relating to transactions among the parent and affiliated companies

**36.4** are eliminated from the consolidated statements. The statements are restated to reflect the merger with Utah International Inc. as a pooling of interests (see note 1).

The nonconsolidated finance companies are included in the Statement of Financial Position under Investments and are

**36.5** valued at equity plus advances. In addition, companies in which GE and/or its consolidated affiliates own 20% to 50% of the voting stock ("associated companies") are included under Investments, valued at the appropriate share of equity plus advances. After-tax earnings of nonconsolidated finance companies and associated companies are included in the Statement of Earnings under Other income.

A nonconsolidated uranium mining company (see note 12) is also included under investments and is valued at cost.

### 36.6 Sales
The Company and its consolidated affiliates record a transaction as a sale only when title to products passes to the customer or when services are performed in accordance with contract terms.

### 36.7 Vacation expense
Most employees earn credits during the current year for vacations to be taken in the following year. The expense for this liability is accrued during the year vacations are earned rather than in the year vacations are taken.

### Pensions
Investments of the General Electric Pension Trust, which funds the obligations of the General Electric Pension Plan, are carried at amortized cost plus programmed appreciation in the common stock portfolio. Recognition of programmed appreciation is carried out on a systematic basis which does not give undue weight to short-term market fluctuations. This recognition of programmed appreciation is limited by a maximum ratio, calculated on a moving basis, of book to market values over a multiyear period.

**36.8** The funding program for the Pension Trust uses 6% as the estimated rate of future income. This rate includes systematic recognition of appreciation in the common stock portfolio.

Unfunded liabilities of the Trust are being amortized over a 20-year period.

Costs of a separate, supplementary pension plan, primarily

affecting long-service professional and managerial employees, are not funded. Current service costs and amortization of past service costs over a period of 20 years are being charged to Company operating costs currently.    **36**

### Investment tax credit    **36**
The investment tax credit is recorded by the "deferral method." Under this method the credit is amortized as a reduction of the provision for taxes over the lives of the facilities to which the credit applies, rather than being "flowed through" to income in the year the asset is acquired.

### Inventories    **36**
Substantially all manufacturing inventories located in the United States are valued on a last-in first-out, or "LIFO" basis. Manufacturing inventories outside the U.S. are generally valued on a first-in first-out, or "FIFO" basis. Valuations are based    **36** on the cost of material, direct labor and manufacturing overhead, and do not exceed net realizable values. Certain indirect manufacturing expenses are charged directly to operating    **36** costs during the period incurred rather than being inventoried.

Mining inventories, which include principally mined ore and coal, metal concentrates, and mining supplies, are stated at the lower of average cost and market. The cost of mining inventories includes both direct and indirect costs consisting of labor, purchased supplies and services, and depreciation, depletion and amortization of property, plant and equipment.

### Property, plant and equipment
Manufacturing plant and equipment includes the original cost of land, buildings and equipment less depreciation, which is the estimated cost consumed by wear and obsolescence. An accelerated depreciation method, based principally on a sum-of-the-years digits formula, is used to record depreciation of the original cost of manufacturing plant and equipment purchased and installed in the United States subsequent to 1960. Acquisitions prior to 1961, and most manufacturing plant and equipment located outside the United States, are    **36** depreciated on a straight-line basis. If manufacturing plant and equipment is subject to abnormal economic conditions or obsolescence, additional depreciation is provided. Expenditures for maintenance and repairs of manufacturing plant and equipment are charged to operations as incurred.

The cost of mining properties includes expenditures which substantially increase the useful lives of existing assets. The cost of mining properties is depreciated, depleted or amortized over the useful lives of the related assets by use of unit-of-production, straight-line or declining-balance methods. Maintenance and repairs on major mining equipment and facilities are provided for principally over useful lives of the assets. Minor maintenance and repairs and minor replacements of mining equipment and facilities are charged to operating costs as incurred. Maintenance and repairs associated with development of new mining projects are capitalized.

Mining exploration costs are expensed until it is determined that the development of a mineral deposit is likely to be economically feasible. After this determination is made, all costs related to further development, including financing costs of    **36** identifiable new borrowings associated with the development of new mining projects, are capitalized and amortized over the lesser of 10 years or the productive life of the property.

Oil and gas properties are accounted for by use of the full    **36** cost method.

*(See page 67 for Authors' Notes 36.1–36.9.)*

**36.10** See note 38.15 for a discussion of the investment credit and the effect of GE's using the conservative deferral method.

**36.11** See GE's note 11 and our note 39.4 for more about inventories and cost of goods sold.

**36.12** Most foreign governments do not allow the use of LIFO for tax purposes.

**36.13** Since GE will not show an item of inventory on the balance sheet at an amount greater than net realizable value, it must be using a lower-of-cost-or-market valuation basis.

# Notes to Financial Statements

Supplemental details are as follow:

| (In millions) | 1976 | 1975 | |
|---|---|---|---|
| Company-funded research and development | $411.5 | $357.1 | **37.5** |
| Maintenance and repairs | 535.3 | 421.4 | |
| Social security taxes | 302.2 | 268.4 | |
| Advertising | 175.5 | 143.8 | |
| Rent | 134.6 | 119.7 | |
| Mineral royalties and export duties | 125.9 | 51.2 | |

**1** **1. Pooling of Interests**
A merger with Utah International Inc. ("Utah" or "Utah International") was effected as of December 20, 1976, whereby Utah became a wholly-owned affiliate of General Electric through the exchange of 41,002,034 shares of General Electric $2.50 par value common stock for all of the outstanding shares of Utah. The principal business of Utah is the extraction and sale of natural resources. The merger was accounted for as a pooling of interests, and accordingly the accompanying financial statements include the accounts of Utah from January 1, 1975.
   The sales of products and services to customers and the net earnings applicable to common stock of General Electric and Utah for the years ended December 31, 1976 and December 31, 1975 are shown below.

| (In millions) | 1976 | 1975 |
|---|---|---|
| Sales of products and services to customers: | | |
| General Electric | $14,696.7 | $13,399.1 |
| Utah International | 1,000.6 | 706.0 |
| | $15,697.3 | $14,105.1 |
| Net earnings applicable to common stock: | | |
| General Electric | $ 749.3 | $ 580.8 |
| Utah International | 181.3 | 107.7 |
| | $ 930.6 | $ 688.5 |

Prior to the merger, the fiscal year of Utah ended on October 31. Utah's financial results have been conformed to the calendar-year period used by General Electric.

**2. Sales**
Approximately one-seventh of sales in 1976 and 1975 were to agencies of the U.S. government, which is the Company's largest single customer.

**2** **3** **3. Operating costs**
Operating costs as classified for reporting to the Securities and Exchange Commission are shown below.

| (In millions) | 1976 | 1975 |
|---|---|---|
| **4** Cost of goods sold | $11,481.2 | $10,624.2 |
| Selling, general and administrative expenses | 2,688.2 | 2,294.3 |
| | $14,169.4 | $12,918.5 |

**4. Employee benefits**
General Electric and its affiliates have a number of pension plans, the total Company cost of which was $240.1 million in 1976 and $193.1 million in 1975. The most significant of these plans is the General Electric Pension Plan, in which substantially all employees in the U.S. are participating. Obligations of the Pension Plan are funded through the GE Pension Trust.
   The limit described under Pensions on page 36 for recognizing programmed appreciation in the common stock portfolio was not reached at year-end 1976 or 1975.
   Earnings of the Trust, including the programmed recognition of appreciation, as a percentage of book value of the portfolio were 6.4% for 1976 and 6.6% for 1975.
   Unfunded liabilities of the Trust were estimated to be $707 **37.6** million at December 31, 1976, compared with $581 million at the end of 1975, the increase resulting primarily from amendments to the Plan which became effective July 1, 1976. Unfunded vested liabilities included in these amounts were $568 million and $447 million at December 31, 1976 and 1975, respectively. Estimated market value of Trust assets at the end of 1976 was $3,636 million and $2,993 million at the end of 1975.
   Financial statements of the Pension Trust are on page 38.
   Costs of a separate supplementary pension plan, primarily affecting long-service professional and managerial employees, were $9.5 million in 1976 and $4.3 million in 1975. **37.7** Unamortized liabilities for this supplementary plan were $74 million and $31 million at December 31, 1976 and 1975, respectively. The increase in costs and unamortized liabilities resulted principally from amendments to the plan effective January 1, 1976.
   Utah has separate pension plans which are substantially fully funded and the costs of which are included in the total Company costs reported above.
   Incentive compensation plans apply to over 3,000 key employees. Amounts included in costs and expenses for incentive compensation, including Utah's Bonus Program, were $40.1 million in 1976 and $35.2 million in 1975.

---

**37.1**   See our discussion in note 32.2. In later years, we are not likely to be shown the separate sales and earnings applicable to GE and to Utah, except as part of segment reports. (See our note 3.4.)
**37.2**   *Operating expenses* would be a better term. See the Glossary at *cost* and at *expense*.

*(Authors' Notes are continued on page 72.)*

---

**36.14**   Many foreign governments do not allow accelerated depreciation for tax purposes. This probably explains GE's use of straight-line depreciation abroad.
**36.15**   GE uses a form of "successful efforts accounting" for its mining operations. See the Glossary at *discovery value accounting* for a discussion of the options. See also the next note.
**36.16**   GE uses "full cost" accounting for its oil and gas operations. See the Glossary at *discovery value accounting* for a discussion of the options. The U.S. Congress has passed a law that requires the SEC (and FASB) to set uniform accounting in the petroleum industry by the end of 1977. If additional time for securing uniformity is not allowed by Congress, GE will no longer have a choice of methods by the time the 1978 annual report is issued.

## General Electric Pension Trust

| (In millions) | 1976 | 1975 |
|---|---|---|
| **Operating statement** | | |
| Total assets at January 1 | $3,047.5 | $2,762.0 |
| Company contributions | 204.5 | 170.2 |
| Employee contributions | 59.4 | 47.2 |
| | 263.9 | 217.4 |
| Dividends, interest and sundry income | 144.9 | 128.0 |
| Common stock appreciation: | | |
| Realized | 11.7 | 16.7 |
| Accrued | 76.6 | 70.7 |
| Total programmed | 88.3 | 87.4 |
| Pensions paid | (158.5) | (147.3) |
| Total assets at December 31 | $3,386.1 | $3,047.5 |
| **Financial position — December 31** | | |
| U.S. government obligations and guarantees | $ 103.6 | $ 97.2 |
| Corporate bonds, notes and mineral interests | 318.0 | 335.5 |
| Real estate and mortgages | 672.3 | 589.2 |
| Common stocks and convertibles | 2,177.4 | 1,831.1 |
| | 3,271.3 | 2,853.0 |
| Cash and short-term investments | 57.4 | 123.1 |
| Other assets — net | 57.4 | 71.4 |
| Total assets | $3,386.1 | $3,047.5 |
| Funded liabilities: | | |
| Liability to pensioners | $1,265.9 | $1,153.8 |
| Liability for pensions to participants not yet retired | 2,120.2 | 1,893.7 |
| Total funded liabilities | $3,386.1 | $3,047.5 |

### 5. Other income

| (In millions) | 1976 | 1975 |
|---|---|---|
| Net earnings of the Credit Corporation | $ 59.0 | $ 52.2 |
| Income from: | | |
| Marketable securities and bank deposits | 60.3 | 28.7 |
| Customer financing | 44.6 | 40.9 |
| Royalty and technical agreements | 34.7 | 43.6 |
| Associated companies | (2.3) | (34.3) |
| Other investments: | | |
| Interest | 20.4 | 22.0 |
| Dividends | 7.7 | 8.0 |
| Other sundry income | 49.9 | 13.1 |
| | $274.3 | $174.2 |

**38.1**

Income from associated companies for 1976 includes a $6.2 million gain as Utah's share of a partial recovery to date for the expropriation by the government of Peru of assets owned by a company in which Utah has a 46% interest. The 1975 amount includes a $28.9 million loss recorded as a result of the expropriation.

Other sundry income for 1976 includes a gain of $20.7 million realized on the sale of equity and convertible investments in AEG-Telefunken (Germany).

### 6. Interest and other financial charges

Amounts applicable to principal items of long-term borrowings were $94.5 million in 1976 and $101.6 million in 1975.

### 7. Provision for income taxes

| (In millions) | 1976 | 1975 |
|---|---|---|
| U.S. federal income taxes: | | |
| Estimated amount payable | $407.2 | $229.3 |
| Effect of timing differences | (21.7) | 15.4 |
| Investment credit deferred — net | 13.4 | 13.6 |
| | 398.9 | 258.3 |
| Foreign income taxes: | | |
| Estimated amount payable | 253.5 | 208.4 |
| Effect of timing differences | (0.8) | (17.3) |
| | 252.7 | 191.1 |
| Other (principally state and local income taxes) | 17.0 | 10.4 |
| | $668.6 | $459.8 |

**Effect of timing differences on U.S. federal income taxes**

| (In millions) Increase (decrease) in provision for income taxes | 1976 | 1975 |
|---|---|---|
| Undistributed earnings of affiliates and associated companies | $ 4.3 | $11.2 |
| Tax over book depreciation | 7.8 | 12.7 |
| Margin on installment sales | 2.1 | 28.3 |
| Provision for warranties | (21.6) | (21.6) |
| Other — net | (14.3) | (15.2) |
| | $ (21.7) | $15.4 |

The cumulative net effect of timing differences has resulted in a deferred-tax asset which is shown under Other assets.

**Reconciliation of statutory and effective income tax rates**

| | 1976 | 1975 |
|---|---|---|
| U.S. federal statutory rate | 48.0% | 48.0% |
| Reduction in taxes resulting from: | | |
| Consolidated affiliate earnings (including DISC) subject to aggregate effective tax rates generally less than 48% | (3.9) | (5.7) |
| Inclusion of earnings of the Credit Corporation in before-tax income on an "after-tax" basis | (1.7) | (2.1) |
| Investment credit | (1.2) | (1.3) |
| Income taxed at capital gains rate | (0.9) | (0.4) |
| Other — net | 0.8 | 0.7 |
| Effective tax rate | 41.1% | 39.2% |

Provision has been made for federal income taxes to be paid on that portion of the undistributed earnings of affiliates and associated companies expected to be remitted to the parent company. Undistributed earnings intended to be reinvested indefinitely in affiliates and associated companies totaled $579 million at the end of 1976 and $512 million at the end of 1975.

All U.S. federal income tax returns have been settled through 1971 except for the year 1970.

Investment credit amounted to $31.4 million in 1976, compared with $28.7 million in the prior year. In 1976, $18.0 million was added to net earnings, compared with $15.1 million in 1975. At the end of 1976, the amount still deferred and to be included in net earnings in future years was $112.2 million.

**1** **8. Earnings per common share**

Earnings per share are based on General Electric average shares outstanding plus outstanding average shares previously reported by Utah multiplied by 1.3. Any dilution which would result from the potential exercise or conversion of such items as stock options or convertible debt outstanding is insignificant (less than 1% in 1976 and 1975).

**9. Cash and marketable securities**

Time deposits and certificates of deposit aggregated $875.2 million at December 31, 1976 and $595.4 million at December 31, 1975. Deposits restricted as to usage and withdrawal or
**2** used as partial compensation for short-term borrowing arrangements were not material.

Marketable securities (none of which are equity securities) are carried at the lower of amortized cost or market value. Carrying value was substantially the same as market value at year-end 1976 and 1975.

**10. Current receivables**

| (In millions)          December 31 | 1976 | 1975 |
|---|---|---|
| Customers' accounts and notes | $2,330.1 | $2,312.2 |
| Associated companies | 87.5 | 100.9 |
| Nonconsolidated affiliates | 2.1 | 1.1 |
| Other | 353.4 | 326.8 |
| | 2,773.1 | 2,741.0 |
| **3** Less allowance for losses | (55.8) | (53.8) |
| | $2,717.3 | $2,687.2 |

**11. Inventories**

| (In millions)          December 31 | 1976 | 1975 |
|---|---|---|
| Raw materials and work in process | $1,529.6 | $1,470.1 |
| Finished goods | 700.7 | 607.1 |
| Unbilled shipments | 124.1 | 125.7 |
| | $2,354.4 | $2,202.9 |

About 81% of total inventories were in the United States at year-end 1976 and 1975.

If the FIFO method of inventory accounting had been used
**4** by the Company, manufacturing inventories would have been $1,160.8 million higher than reported at December 31, 1976 ($963.7 million higher than reported at December 31, 1975).

**12. Investments**

| (In millions)          December 31 | 1976 | 1975 | |
|---|---|---|---|
| Nonconsolidated finance affiliates | $ 552.9 | $ 508.6 | **39.5** |
| Nonconsolidated uranium mining affiliate | 86.7 | — | |
| Miscellaneous investments (at cost): | | | |
| Government and government-guaranteed securities | 248.0 | 268.0 | |
| Other | 72.4 | 79.1 | |
| | 320.4 | 347.1 | **39.6** |
| Marketable equity securities: | | | |
| Honeywell Inc. and Honeywell Information Systems Inc. | 77.1 | 100.3 | |
| Other | 39.9 | 72.1 | |
| | 117.0 | 172.4 | **39.7** |
| Associated companies | 223.9 | 143.6 | |
| Less allowance for losses | (14.6) | (15.1) | |
| | $1,286.3 | $1,156.6 | |

Condensed consolidated financial statements for the General Electric Credit Corporation, the principal nonconsolidated finance affiliate, are shown below.

**General Electric Credit Corporation**
**Financial position**

| (In millions)          December 31 | 1976 | 1975 | |
|---|---|---|---|
| Cash and marketable securities | $ 233.9 | $ 185.3 | |
| Receivables | 5,311.0 | 5,017.0 | |
| Deferred income | (496.9) | (522.1) | |
| Allowance for losses | (142.9) | (126.1) | |
| Net receivables | 4,671.2 | 4,368.8 | |
| Other assets | 151.5 | 120.0 | |
| Total assets | $5,056.6 | $4,674.1 | **39.8** |
| Notes payable: | | | |
| Due within one year | $2,164.1 | $2,131.3 | |
| Long-term — senior | 1,186.9 | 1,074.1 | |
| — subordinated | 276.6 | 249.5 | |
| Other liabilities | 312.3 | 290.6 | |
| Total liabilities | 3,939.9 | 3,745.5 | **39.8** |
| Deferred credits | 569.6 | 428.0 | **39.8** |
| Capital stock | 344.2 | 309.2 | |
| Additional paid-in capital | 11.5 | 11.5 | |
| Retained earnings | 191.4 | 179.9 | |
| Equity | 547.1 | 500.6 | |
| Total liabilities, deferred credits and equity | $5,056.6 | $4,674.1 | |

**Current and retained earnings**

| (In millions)          For the year | 1976 | 1975 | |
|---|---|---|---|
| Earned income | $ 613.3 | $ 585.1 | |
| Expenses: | | | |
| Interest and discount | 220.0 | 223.6 | |
| Operating and administrative | 222.2 | 184.6 | |
| Provision for losses — receivables | 72.0 | 85.9 | |
| — other assets | 15.3 | 10.7 | |
| Provision for income taxes | 24.8 | 28.1 | |
| | 554.3 | 532.9 | |
| Net earnings | 59.0 | 52.2 | **39.9** |
| Less dividends | (47.5) | (41.7) | |
| Retained earnings at January 1 | 179.9 | 169.4 | |
| Retained earnings at December 31 | $ 191.4 | $ 179.9 | |

Copies of General Electric Credit Corporation's 1976 Annual Report may be obtained by writing to General Electric Credit Corporation, P.O. Box 8300, Stamford, Conn. 06904.

**37.3** In the income statement shown on page 32, GE uses a *natural classification,* rather than a *functional classification;* see the Glossary for an explanation of the difference. The SEC requires that companies like GE, who use a natural classification, report results using a functional classification in the notes, as GE does here.

**37.4** Cost of goods sold includes depreciation of production facilities. Most of GE's depreciation charges ($365 million out of $419 million) are product costs, included in the cost of inventory. Exactly how much can be ascertained from GE's disclosure on replacement costs. See Exhibit 4 on page 99 of this book. See the Glossary at *flow of costs.*

**37.5** FASB Statement No. 2 requires the expensing of research and development costs, and the disclosure, as GE does here, of the costs incurred during the year for R & D. FASB Statement No. 2 allows the capitalizing of R & D costs that are incurred under contract and that are reimbursable. GE is making clear that these costs ($411.5 million in 1976) do not qualify for capitalization.

**37.6** The present value of GE's promises to its work force under pension plans exceeds the amount of investments in the Pension Trust by $707 million. (Of this amount only $568 million is vested.) GE's balance sheet, in accord with current GAAP (APB *Opinion No. 8*), does not show these promises as a liability. Since this amount does not appear on the balance sheet, it would be better to call them "unfunded obligations" rather than "unfunded liabilities."

If the unfunded obligations for pensions, which are like liabilities, were shown as liabilities in the balance sheet, some companies would have their debt-equity ratios drastically increased.

Often a pension plan is sweetened and the sweetenings are granted retroactively. That is, the company gives the employee credit for years worked before the sweetening. In these circumstances, a *prior service cost* (see Glossary) arises. GE's "amendments" to the plan at July 1, 1976, resulted in new prior service costs.

**37.7** Refer to the GE annual report near our reference to note 36.8. GE states that the costs of this pension plan are not funded. For its primary pension plan referred to in the context of the GE Pension Trust, GE funds pension liabilities as they are recognized. Thus the ordinary pension-related entries are, first, to debit pension expense and to credit pension liability:

Pension Expense ........................................ X
    Pension Liability ........................................ X

and then to fund the liability with a debit to Pension Liability and a credit to Cash:

Pension Liability ........................................ X
    Cash ................................................ X
The actual funding need not be, but usually is, exactly equal to the amount of pension expense recognized in the entry just preceding.

For this supplementary pension plan, the first entry is being made (with prior service costs being amortized over 20 years; see page 36), but the liability is not being funded. Therefore an explicit pension liability, amounting to $74 million by the end of 1976, is included in GE's balance sheet on page 33. The amount is so small in relation to other liabilities, however, that it is merely included on the line called "Other liabilities".

---

**38.1** GE uses the equity method of accounting for its 100-percent ownership of the GE Credit Corporation. Hence it shows 100 percent of the earnings of the Credit Corporation as "Other income". See notes 34.3 and 39.8.

**38.2** GE's income statement on page 32 shows $174.7 million of interest charges. This note enables us to separate the amounts of interest for short-term and long-term borrowings and to make the calculation in our note 3.3.

**38.3** Nothing in current GAAP is more confusing for beginners and accounting experts alike than the accounting for corporate income taxes. There is a wealth of information in GE's note 7, but one must keep one's wits in order to follow it all. This first schedule shows the details of income tax expense, unfortunately called a "provision". The bottom line of the first schedule is the total expense reported on the statement of earnings on page 32 shown near our reference 32.5. It is the sum of U.S. federal, foreign, and other income tax expenses. The U.S. federal and foreign income tax expense amounts are derived in essentially two steps: first is shown the amount of taxes payable; then there is an adjustment for timing differences; GE also shows the effect of the investment credit, which is discussed below in our note 38.15.

**38.4** In 1975 and 1976 income taxes payable exceeded income tax expense because of timing differences; taxable income was larger than financial statement pretax income. The details of the U.S. federal timing differences are shown in the next schedule. Total timing differences (federal and foreign) are treated together in the statement of changes in financial position on page 34 at our reference to note 34.5. Although U.S. federal timing differences were positive (tax expenses exceeded taxes payable) by $15.4 million in 1975, there was a $17.3 million excess of taxes payable over taxes expense abroad resulting in the net $1.9 million excess of taxes payable over tax expense shown on page 34 of the Annual Report.

38.5 GE uses the deferral method of accounting for the investment credit; see the discussion at note 38.15.

38.6 This schedule shows the components of the timing differences on U.S. federal income taxes.

38.7 Revenues from subsidiaries ("affiliates") shown on the financial statements under the equity method exceeded taxable revenue from these subsidiaries. Taxable revenue from this source is based primarily on the amount of dividends received. (Note that 85 percent of dividends received by one corporation from another corporation are not taxed. This is, however, a permanent difference that would not appear here.)

38.8 Depreciation on the tax return exceeded the amount included in cost of goods sold and other expenses on the financial statements. For most companies, tax depreciation exceeds book depreciation because an accelerated method is used for taxes and the straight-line method is used for financial reporting. GE, however, uses an accelerated method (based on sum-of-the-years' digits) in its financial statements; see page 36 in the Summary of Significant Accounting Policies near our reference to note 36.14. The excess of tax deductions for depreciation over book depreciation expense for GE arises from GE's using shorter depreciable lives for tax than for book calculations. See the Glossary at *asset depreciation range*. We can compute the excess of tax depreciation deductions over the book depreciation expense reported in the financial statements by using the $7.8 million timing difference shown here for 1976. If income tax expense exceeds income taxes payable by $7.8 million because of depreciation timing differences and if the marginal income tax rate is 48 percent of pretax income, then depreciation on the tax return must have exceeded depreciation on the financial statements by $x$ where

$$.48x = \$ \ 7.8 \text{ million, or}$$
$$x = \$ \ 7.8 \text{ million}/.48, \text{ or}$$
$$x = \$16.25 \text{ million.}$$

38.9 GE makes sales on credit, with cash payments from the customer to GE spread over time. Such sales are called "installment sales". GAAP (APB *Opinion No. 10*) requires that revenue from most such sales be recognized in the financial statements for the period of sale. For tax purposes, GE recognizes revenue when the cash payments are collected. Thus a timing difference is created. The amount shown here for GE is relatively small because GE tends not to have large percentages of its sales on the installment method. Refer, however, to the financial statements of Sears and our Note A.4. There you will see Sears has saved over $800 million in income taxes by reporting revenues on the tax return only when cash is collected.

38.10 Estimated warranty expense recognized by the "allowance method" does not qualify as a tax deduction. GE uses the "allowance method" of recognizing warranty expense for financial reporting. As products carrying guarantees or warranties are sold, GE makes the following entry recognizing the estimated liability for future repairs and replacements:

| Estimated Warranty Expense (Provision) ................. | X | |
| --- | --- | --- |
|    Estimated Warranty Liability ........................... | | X |
| Entry made in the period of sale for expected warranty costs. | | |

Later, when repairs are made, and warranty costs are incurred, the entry is:

| Estimated Warranty Liability ............................ | Y | |
| --- | --- | --- |
|    Assets Used and Liabilities Incurred ................... | | Y |
| To recognize cost of actual repairs and replacements. | | |

The repair and, therefore, the second entry often occur in a year subsequent to the year of sale. The cost of providing the warranty services does not become a tax deduction until the repair is actually made. Thus timing differences are created: an expense is subtracted on the financial statements in one year but is deducted on the tax return in a later year. We can make the following statements about both 1976 and 1975: The provision for warranties (the estimated expense) results in income taxes payable being larger than income tax expense. Therefore, it must be true that the estimated expense of rendering warranty service in future years for sales in the current year is greater than the actual costs of warranty repairs made in the current year, most of which related to sales of earlier years.

**38.11** Primarily because of the accounting (explained just above) for warranties, GE's cumulative income tax payments have exceeded cumulative income tax expense reported in the financial statements. This has resulted in a "deferred tax debit" (whereas most companies have the reverse situation and a "deferred tax credit") which GE reports among its "Other assets;" see GE's note 14 on page 41.

**38.12** Most readers of financial statements are aware that the U.S. federal tax rate on most corporate income is 48 percent of pretax income. The SEC requires that companies report in its footnotes why reported income tax expense differs from 48 percent of pretax book income. Income from a DISC is taxed at a rate less than 48 percent. The $59 million of income from GE Credit reported in GE's Note 5 on page 38 is after taxes. Yet it appears in GE's income statement before the income tax calculation. GE need pay no further taxes on the income from GE Credit; this accounts for part of the difference between GE's effective tax rate on "pretax income", 41.1 percent in 1976, and the statutory rate, 48 percent. (See also note 38.13.) The investment credit (See Glossary and note 38.15 below) reduces taxes otherwise payable and this accounts for another part of the difference.

**38.13** APB Opinion No. 11 says that income of affiliates that is expected to be indefinitely reinvested in the affiliate need not be subject to income tax provisions by the parent. If the parent expects to receive dividends from the affiliate in the foreseeable future, then the parent must make an income tax provision.

**38.14** Are you surprised to learn that the Internal Revenue Service and GE are still negotiating about GE's tax return for 1970? Some companies, see for example U.S. Steel, still have unsettled tax returns from more than ten years ago.

**38.15** GE uses the deferral method of accounting for the investment credit, rather than the less conservative flow-through method. (The great majority of U.S. corporations use the flow-through method.) GE earned $31.4 million of tax credits during 1976. A portion (which cannot be determined from the published data) of this $31.4 million reduced reported tax expense in 1976; the remainder is shown as a deferred investment credit on the balance sheet (under "Other liabilities"). A portion of previous years' investment credits, which had been deferred, also served to reduce 1976 reported tax expense. The total of these two reductions of reported tax expense in 1976 was $18.0 million. If GE had used the flow-through method, income tax expense would have been reduced by an additional $13.4 (= $31.4 − $18.0) million and 1976 net income would have been $13.4 million larger. Under the flow-through method, retained earnings at the end of 1976, would have been $112.2 million larger. Total deferred investment credits of $112.2 million are part of "Other liabilities" on the balance sheet. See also the income tax calculation for Conservative Company in the *Accounting Magic* section of this book, (p. 118).

---

**39.1** GE reports only primary earnings per share. Since it has so few dilutive securities outstanding, fully diluted earnings per share would be less than one percent below the primary earnings per share. A dual presentation of earnings per share is required only when fully diluted earnings per share is 97 percent or less of primary earnings per share.

**39.2** See *compensating balance* in the Glossary. Compensating balances increase the stated cost of borrowing; accordingly, the SEC requires disclosure of such amounts, if they are significant. GE is stating that its compensating balances are not significant.

**39.3** *Allowance for losses* might better be called *Allowance for uncollectible accounts*. See *allowance for uncollectibles* in the Glossary for an explanation of the accounting method GE uses for estimated uncollectible receivables.

**39.4** GE provides information that allows us to calculate what the operating income would have been if a FIFO cost flow assumption had been used. (See Glossary at *LIFO* and the *Accounting Magic* section for an explanation of why LIFO leads to lower reported net income in periods of rising prices.) The IRS does not allow companies using LIFO for tax purposes to disclose directly what income would have been under FIFO, but the SEC requires (and the IRS allows) the disclosure of beginning and ending inventories as they would have been under FIFO, if these amounts are significantly different from the LIFO amounts. The SEC's required disclosure of inventory differences allows the reader to compute the income difference that the IRS will not allow direct disclosure of. See note 32.4 for an explanation of why an increase in ending inventory implies a reduction in cost of goods sold and hence an increase in income. As of December 31, 1976, cumulative pretax income is $1,160.8 million less than it would have been under FIFO. As of January 1, 1976, cumulative pretax income is $963.7 million less than it would have been under

FIFO. This difference increased by $197.1 (= $1,160.8 − $963.7) million during the year 1976. Hence 1976 pre-tax income would have been $197.1 million, or about 12 percent, larger if FIFO had been used.

This calculation may be seen more clearly in the following exhibit:

### General Electric Company Inventory Data from Financial Statements and Footnotes for 1976

(Amounts shown in **boldface** type are given in GE's financial statements.
Other amounts are computed as indicated.)

**Dollar Amounts in Millions**

|  | LIFO Cost-Flow Assumption (Actually Used) | + | Excess of FIFO over LIFO Amount | = | FIFO Cost-Flow Assumption (Hypothetical) |
|---|---|---|---|---|---|
| Beginning Inventory ..................... | **$ 2,202.9** |  | **$ 963.7** |  | $ 3,166.6 |
| Purchases ............................ | 11,632.7 [a] |  | 0 |  | 11,632.7 |
| Cost of Goods Available for Sale ......... | $13,835.6 |  | $ 963.7 |  | $14,799.3 |
| Less Ending Inventory .................. | **2,354.4** |  | **1,160.8** |  | 3,515.2 |
| Cost of Goods Sold ..................... | **$11,481.2** |  | ($ 197.1) |  | $11,284.1 |
| Sales ................................. | **$15,697.3** |  | $ 0 |  | $15,697.3 |
| Less Cost of Goods Sold ............... | **11,481.2** |  | ( 197.1) |  | 11,284.1 |
| Gross Margin on Sales ................. | $ 4,216.1 |  | $ 197.1 |  | $ 4,413.2 |

a. Purchases = Cost of Goods Sold + Ending Inventory − Beginning Inventory
   $11,632.7 =  **$11,481.2**  +  **$2,354.4**  −  **$2,202.9**

**39.5**  After reading note 39.8, test your understanding by convincing yourself that GE's investment in "nonconsolidated finance affiliates" *other* than GE Credit Corporation decreased by $2.2 million during 1976. We show the derivation of this amount in note 39.9.

**39.6**  See note 40.2 for discussion of the unrealized holding gains and losses on these miscellaneous investments.

**39.7**  See notes 40.3 and 40.4 for discussion of the unrealized holding gains on these marketable equity securities.

**39.8**  If the Credit Corporation were consolidated, rather than accounted for on the equity method, all these assets, liabilities, and deferred credits would be shown on GE's balance sheet, page 33. GE's consolidated retained earnings would be no different, however, since the equity method records income of unconsolidated subsidiaries as earned. The $547.1 (= $5,056.6 − $3,939.9 − $569.6) million of net assets added to GE's balance sheet would be offset with the elimination of $547.1 million from "Nonconsolidated finance affiliates," one component of "Investments," shown on the balance sheet and detailed in GE's note 12 in the right-hand column of page 39.

If GE were to consolidate GE Credit Corporation, the results would be as shown in the exhibit on page 76. It shows the income statement and balance sheet as reported (on pages 32 and 33) and as they would appear if GE Credit Corporation were consolidated. We also show two key financial ratios, as they would be calculated from year-end account balances. The consolidation policy with respect to GE Credit Corporation makes an enormous difference in the financial statements. For an even larger difference, look at the financial statements of General Motors Corporation and go through the exercise of consolidating GMAC (General Motors Acceptance Corporation), which GM accounts for by the equity method.

**39.9**  Observe the effect of the equity method on page 38 in the "Other income" schedule shown in GE's note 5. GE reports $59.0 million for 1976 from GE Credit, not just the $47.5 million in dividends. See also note 34.3.

In note 39.5 we asked you to understand that GE's investment in "nonconsolidated finance affiliates" *other* than GE Credit decreased by $2.2 million during the year. The total increase in the investment amount (see data by reference 39.5 in GE's report) is $44.3 = ($552.9 − $508.6) million. The increase in GE's investment in GE Credit (see "Equity" line of GE Credit's balance sheet) is $46.5 (= $547.1 − $500.6) million. Thus, all other investments must have decreased by $2.2 (= $44.3 − $46.5) million.

## Exhibit For Note 39.8
## General Electric and GE Credit Corporation, 1976

| Income Statement | Equity Method (as Reported) | Adjustments Debit | Adjustments Credit | Consolidated |
|---|---|---|---|---|
| Revenues (other than from Credit Corporation) .. | $15,912.6 | $ | $ 613.3 (1) | $16,525.9 |
| Equity Method Revenues from Credit Corporation | 59.0 | 59.0 (1) | | |
| Total Revenues[a] | $15,971.6 | | | |
| Total Expenses[b] | 15,041.0 | 554.3 (1) | | 15,595.3 |
| Net Income | $  930.6 | | | $  930.6 |

| Balance Sheet | | | | |
|---|---|---|---|---|
| All Assets Except Investment in Credit Corporation | $11,502.6 | 5,056.6 (2) | 0.7[c](3) | $16,558.5 |
| Investment in Credit Corporation | 547.1 | | 547.1 (2) | |
| Total Assets | $12,049.7 | | | $16,558.5 |
| Liabilities (including Minority Interest) | $ 6,796.8 | 0.7[c](3) | 4,509.5[d](2) | $11,305.6 |
| Owners' Equity | 5,252.9 | | | 5,252.9 |
| Total Equities | $12,049.7 | $5,670.6 | $5,670.6 | $16,558.5 |

All capital earnings rate:
(See Glossary for definition)

$$\frac{\$930.6 + \$28.3^e + (.52 \times 174.7^f)}{\$12,049.7} \qquad \frac{\$930.6 + 28.3^e + .52 \times (\$174.7^f + \$220.0^g)}{\$16,558.5}$$

$$= \frac{\$ 1,049.7}{\$12,049.7} = 8.7\% \qquad \frac{\$ 1,164.1}{\$16,558.5} = 7.0\%$$

Debit-equity ratio:
(See Glossary for definition)

$$\frac{\$ 6,796.8}{\$12,049.7} = 56\% \qquad \frac{\$11,305.6}{\$16,558.5} = 68\%$$

a. $15,697.3 shown as sales on page 32 of the annual report plus $274.3 of other income.

b. $14,169.4 (operating costs) + $174.7 (interest) + $668.6 (income taxes) + $28.3 (minority interest).

c. Advances to nonconsolidated finance affilitates of $0.7 (see top of page 40) are all treated as advances from GE to GE Credit.

d. GE Credit's "liabilities" ($3,939.9) plus "deferred credits" ($569.6).

e. Minority interest in net income from the income statement.

f. GE's interest expense. Multiply by .52 to state on aftertax basis.

g. GE Credit's interest expense. Multiply by .52 to state on aftertax basis.

---

**40.1** In order for GE and Utah to be allowed to merge, the U.S. Justice Department had to give a "clearance" (approval). At the time of the negotiations, there was governmental concern about a shortage of uranium for electric utilities which owned or planned nuclear generating plants. (Westinghouse Electric Corporation had recently announced it was short some 65 million pounds of uranium that it had contracted to deliver to electric utilities over the next several decades.) The Justice Department became concerned that if GE possessed its own uranium (via Utah), then other manufacturers of nuclear generating plants would be at a competitive disadvantage when compared to GE. Thus, the Justice Department allowed the merger provided that GE agreed not to acquire any uranium from Utah. The elaborate financial details spelled out in this paragraph and the next go into the details of the agreement GE and Utah reached with the Justice Department as a condition of the merger.

**40.2** The disclosure of both historical cost and current market values follows from the requirement of FASB *Statement No. 12*. The net realizable value of these securities at year-end 1976 is $310 million; the cost (see page 39 at note 39.6) was $320 million. Thus GE has an unrealized holding loss on these securities of $10 (= $320 cost − $310 value) million at year-end 1976. At year-end 1975, the unrealized holding loss was $12 (= $347 cost − $335 value) million. Thus the unrealized holding loss decreased during the year by $2 million from $12 to $10 million. GE therefore had unrealized holding gains during 1976 of $2 million on these securities.

Advances to nonconsolidated finance affiliates aggregated $0.7 million at the end of 1976 and 1975.

**1**   Investment in the nonconsolidated uranium mining affiliate consists of investment in a wholly-owned affiliate (established in the course of obtaining a U.S. Department of Justice Business Advisory Clearance Procedure Letter in connection with the Utah merger) to which all uranium business of Utah has been transferred. All common stock of this affiliate has been placed in a voting trust controlled by independent voting trustees. Prior to the year 2000, General Electric and its affiliates may not withdraw the common stock from the voting trust except for sale to unaffiliated third parties. Directors and officers of the affiliate may not be directors, officers, or employees of General Electric, Utah or of any of their affiliates. Uranium may not be sold by this affiliate, in any state or form, to, or at the direction of, General Electric or its affiliates.

All outstanding shares of preferred stock of the uranium affiliate are retained by Utah as an affiliate of General Electric. Payment of cumulative quarterly dividends out of legally available funds on this preferred stock is mandatory commencing in May 1977 in amounts equal to 85% of the affiliate's net after-tax income for the previous quarter (without taking account of any deduction for exploration expense as defined). Utah, as holder of the preferred stock, must make loans with up to 10-year maturities when requested by the affiliate, provided that the aggregate amount of such loans does not at any time exceed preferred dividend payments for the immediately preceding two calendar years.

**2**   The estimated realizable value of miscellaneous investments at December 31, 1976 was $310 million ($335 million at December 31, 1975).

**3**   Marketable equity securities are valued at the lower of cost or market. Aggregate market value of marketable equity securities was $209 million and $224 million at year-end 1976 and 1975, respectively.

**4**   At December 31, 1976, gross unrealized gains on marketable equity securities were $92 million. In April 1976, the Company sold all of its investment in equity securities of AEG-Telefunken for a realized gain of $18.6 million (see note 5).

Market value calculations for equity securities include the Company's investment in Honeywell Information Systems Inc. (HIS) as being equivalent to 1,400,000 shares of Honeywell Inc. common stock at December 31, 1976 (2,200,000 shares at December 31, 1975). Cost of the investment in Honeywell Inc. and HIS is the appraised fair value recorded on October 1, 1970, when the General Electric information systems equipment business was transferred to HIS. The recorded value is substantially less than tax cost.

General Electric held an 18½ % ownership in HIS at December 31, 1975. In 1976, in accordance with an Agreement between General Electric and Honeywell, General Electric exercised certain partial option rights and received 800,000 Honeywell shares in return for reducing its interest in HIS to an 11.7% ownership. The Agreement further provides that GE can require Honeywell to purchase its interest in HIS at any

time during 1977 for 1,000,000 shares of Honeywell stock, and at any time during 1978 for 1,400,000 shares of Honeywell stock. In addition, during 1977 Honeywell may at any time require GE to sell all of its HIS interest to Honeywell for 1,400,000 shares of Honeywell stock, or may make one or more partial exercises of this right in return for shares of Honeywell stock proportionate to the portion of GE's interest in HIS then being acquired. During 1978, Honeywell has the right to purchase GE's HIS interest at any time but only in its entirety, for 1,400,000 shares of Honeywell stock.

At December 31, 1976, GE held 584,000 shares of Honeywell common stock, compared with 380,800 shares at December 31, 1975. GE sold 596,800 shares of Honeywell common stock in 1976 and 1,056,916 shares in 1975. Using average cost, realized gains entering into the determination of net income were nominal in both 1976 and 1975.

**40.5**   General Electric is committed to the U.S. Department of Justice to dispose of its year-end 1976 holding of Honeywell common stock and all other shares of Honeywell common stock GE receives for its interest in HIS by December 31, 1980.

A voting trust has been established in which General Electric must deposit all shares of Honeywell common stock received as part of these transactions.

### 13. Property, plant and equipment

| (In millions) | 1976 | 1975 |
|---|---|---|
| Major classes at December 31: | | |
| Manufacturing plant and equipment | | |
| Land and improvements | $ 111.7 | $ 111.8 |
| Buildings, structures and related equipment | 1,770.5 | 1,686.4 |
| Machinery and equipment | 3,930.1 | 3,659.6 |
| Leasehold costs and manufacturing plant under construction | 180.3 | 198.4 |
| Mineral property, plant and equipment | 962.2 | 845.2 |
| | $6,954.8 | $6,501.4 |
| Cost at January 1 | $6,501.4 | $6,161.7 |
| Additions | 740.4 | 588.2 |
| Dispositions | (287.0) | (248.5) |
| Cost at December 31 | $6,954.8 | $6,501.4 |

**40.6**

| Accumulated depreciation, depletion and amortization | | |
|---|---|---|
| Balance at January 1 | $3,320.5 | $3,011.5 |
| Current year provision | 486.2 | 470.5 |
| Dispositions | (202.1) | (159.6) |
| Other changes | (6.2) | (1.9) |
| Balance at December 31 | $3,598.4 | $3,320.5 |
| **Property, plant and equipment less depreciation, depletion and amortization at December 31** | $3,356.4 | $3,180.9 |

**40.3**   The aggregate market value of these securities at year-end 1976 is $209 million; the cost (see page 39 at note 39.7) is $117 million. Thus the unrealized holding gain at year end is $92 (= $209 value − $117 cost) million. At year-end 1975, the unrealized holding gain was $52 (= $224 value − $172 cost) million. Thus, the unrealized holding gain increased by $40 million during the year. GE had an increase in wealth of $40 million which is not reported in the conventional financial statements.

**40.4**   GE does part of the calculation as in the preceding note here.

**40.5**   Many years ago, GE attempted to enter the computer business (in competition with companies like IBM, Burroughs, and Control Data). GE was not successful and decided to discontinue the business by selling off its computer business to Honeywell. The Justice Department became involved and placed certain restrictions on GE and Honeywell's behavior after the sale. These paragraphs describe some of the financial implications of the current restrictions.

**40.6**   These mineral assets were the major assets that GE acquired in the merger with Utah.

### 14. Other assets

| (In millions)   December 31 | 1976 | 1975 |
|---|---|---|
| Long-term receivables | $322.0 | $326.7 |
| Customer financing | 89.5 | 87.7 |
| Real estate development projects | 71.0 | 7.7 |
| Deferred charges | 60.6 | 66.8 |
| Deferred income taxes | 59.4 | 44.8 |
| Recoverable engineering costs on government contracts | 55.4 | 57.0 |
| Licenses and other intangibles — net | 29.5 | 28.7 |
| Other | 34.6 | 34.0 |
| | $722.0 | $653.4 |

**41.1**

**41.2**

**41.2**

The principal reason for the increase in Real estate development projects was the inclusion in 1976 consolidated financial statements of certain projects in which General Electric Real Estate Credit Corporation increased its equity position.

Licenses and other intangibles acquired after October 1970 are being amortized over appropriate periods of time.

### 15. Short-term borrowings

The average balance of short-term borrowings, excluding the current portion of long-term borrowings, was $573.3 million during 1976 (calculated by averaging all month-end balances for the year) compared with an average balance of $577.6 million in 1975. The maximum balance included in these calculations was $606.0 million and $644.0 million at the end of July 1976 and February 1975, respectively. The average effective interest rate for the year 1976 was 11.6% and for 1975 was 11.3%. These average rates represent total short-term interest expense divided by the average balance outstanding. A summary of short-term borrowings and the applicable interest rates is shown below.

**Short-term borrowings**

| (In millions)   December 31 | 1976 Amount | 1976 Average rate at Dec. 31 | 1975 Amount | 1975 Average rate at Dec. 31 |
|---|---|---|---|---|
| Parent notes with Trust Departments | $310.9 | 4.73% | $274.7 | 5.92% |
| Consolidated affiliates: | | | | |
| Banks | 201.2 | 22.82 | 213.8 | 15.69 |
| Commercial paper | 6.3 | 9.50 | — | — |
| Other, including current portion of long-term borrowings | 92.7 | | 178.7 | |
| | $611.1 | | $667.2 | |

Parent borrowings are from U.S. sources. Borrowings of consolidated affiliated companies are from both U.S. and foreign sources. Current portion of long-term borrowings for 1975 includes General Electric 3½% debentures ($84.3 million) retired in May 1976.

Although the total unused credit available to the Company through banks and commercial credit markets is not readily quantifiable, informal credit lines in excess of $1 billion had been extended by approximately 130 U.S. banks at year-end 1976.

### 16. Other costs and expenses accrued

**41**

The balance at the end of 1976 included compensation and benefit costs accrued of $453.9 million and interest expense accrued of $30.5 million. At the end of 1975, compensation and benefit costs accrued were $424.0 million and interest expense accrued was $31.0 million.

### 17. Long-term borrowings

| (In millions) Outstanding December 31 | 1976 | 1975 | Due Date | Sinking fund/ pre-payment period |
|---|---|---|---|---|
| **General Electric Company:** | | | | |
| 6¼ % Debentures | $ 125.0 | $ 125.0 | 1979 | None |
| 5¾% Notes | 87.5 | 93.7 | 1991 | 1972-90 |
| 5.30% Debentures | 123.3 | 133.3 | 1992 | 1973-91 |
| 7½% Debentures | 179.2 | 185.3 | 1996 | 1977-95 |
| 8½% Debentures | 300.0 | 300.0 | 2004 | 1985-03 |
| **Utah International Inc:** | | | | |
| 7½% Guaranteed Notes | 20.0 | 20.0 | 1979 | None |
| Notes with banks | 115.1 | 108.9 | 1985 | 1977-85 |
| 7.2% Note | 27.1 | — | 1986 | 1981-86 |
| 8% Guaranteed Sinking Fund Debentures | 19.6 | 20.0 | 1987 | 1977-87 |
| 7.6% Notes | 43.0 | 46.0 | 1988 | 1974-88 |
| Other | 9.5 | 6.4 | | |
| **General Electric Overseas Capital Corporation:** | | | | |
| 4¼% Bonds | 31.9 | 31.9 | 1985 | 1976-84 |
| 4¼% Debentures | 50.0 | 50.0 | 1987 | None |
| 5½% Sterling/Dollar Guaranteed Loan Stock | 6.1 | 7.3 | 1993 | None |
| Other | 49.1 | 45.7 | | |
| All other | 135.9 | 66.0 | | |
| | $1,322.3 | $1,239.5 | | |

The amounts shown above are after deduction of the face value of securities held in the treasury as shown below.

**Face value of long-term borrowings in treasury**

| (In millions)   December 31 | 1976 | 1975 |
|---|---|---|
| **General Electric Company:** | | |
| 5.30% Debentures | $36.7 | $36.7 |
| 7½% Debentures | 20.8 | 14.7 |
| **General Electric Overseas Capital Corporation:** | | |
| 4¼% Bonds | 4.9 | 6.9 |

**41.1** See notes 38.10 and 38.11.

**41.2** Licenses and other intangibles acquired before October 1970 need not be amortized. APB Opinion No. 17 requires that licenses and intangibles acquired after October 1970 be amortized over a period of not more than 40 years.

**41.3** "Other costs and expenses accrued" is one of our least favorite account titles used by GE. First, *costs* (see Glossary) should be used for assets, not for liabilities as here. Second, the word *accrued* (see Glossary) adds little meaning to an account title and probably should not be used.

During 1976, General Electric 5.30% Debentures having a face value of $10.0 million ($10.0 million in 1975) and a reacquired cost of $8.2 million ($8.4 million in 1975) were retired in accordance with sinking fund provisions, and General Electric 5¾% Notes having a value of $6.2 million ($6.3 million in 1975) were retired in accordance with prepayment provisions.

Utah International Inc. notes with banks are payable in varying installments to 1985 and were subject to average interest rates at year-end 1976 and 1975 of 6.7% and 7.7%, respectively. The 7.2% Note is payable to an associated company.

Borrowings of General Electric Overseas Capital Corporation are unconditionally guaranteed by General Electric as to payment of principal, premium if any, and interest. This Corporation primarily assists in financing capital requirements of foreign companies in which General Electric has an equity interest, as well as financing certain customer purchases. The Corporation's 4¼% Guaranteed Bonds due in 1985 were convertible through November 1975 into General Electric common stock at $65.50 a share. Bonds having a face value of $11.2 million were converted in 1975. Borrowings also include 4¼% Guaranteed Debentures due in 1987, which are convertible until June 15, 1987 into General Electric common stock at $80.75 a share; and 5½% Sterling/Dollar Guaranteed Loan Stock due in 1993 in the amount of £3.6 million ($6.1 million), convertible from October 1976 into General Electric common stock at $73.50 a share. During 1976, General Electric Overseas Capital Corporation 4¼% Guaranteed Bonds having a face value of $2.0 million and a reacquired cost of $1.4 million were retired in accordance with sinking fund provisions.

All other long-term borrowings were largely by foreign and real estate development affiliates with various interest rates and maturities.

**.2**  Long-term borrowing maturities during the next five years, including the portion classified as current, are $66.0 million in 1977, $90.1 million in 1978, $212.5 million in 1979, $64.0 million in 1980 and $45.8 million in 1981. These amounts are after deducting reacquired debentures held in the treasury for sinking fund requirements.

### 18. Share owners' equity

Common stock held in treasury at December 31, 1976 included 1,443,110 shares for the deferred compensation provisions of incentive compensation plans (1,386,845 shares at December 31, 1975). These shares are carried at market value at the time of allotment, which amounted to $70.0 million and $66.2 million at December 31, 1976 and 1975, respectively. The liability is recorded under Other liabilities. Other common stock in treasury, which is carried at cost, aggregated 2,304,794 and 1,974,887 shares at December 31, 1976 and 1975, respectively. These shares are held for future corporate requirements, including distributions under employee savings plans, incentive compensation awards and possible conversion of General Electric Overseas Capital Corporation convertible indebtedness. The maximum number of shares required for conversions was 737,725 at December 31, 1976 and 1975. Corporate requirements of shares for benefit plans and conversions may be met either from unissued shares or from shares in treasury.

Retained earnings at year-end 1976 included approximately $204.3 million representing the excess of earnings of nonconsolidated affiliates over dividends received since their **42.3** formation. In addition, retained earnings have been increased by $47.3 million, which represents the change in equity in associated companies since acquisition. At the end of 1975, **42.4** these amounts were $192.2 million and $52.1 million, respectively.

### 19. The stock option and stock appreciation rights plan

The plan approved by the share owners in 1973, and previous plans under which options remain outstanding, provide continuing incentives for more than 500 employees. Option price under these plans is the full market value of GE common stock **42.5** on date of grant. Employees can only exercise options to the extent that annual installments have matured, normally over a period of nine years. The 1973 plan also provides for granting stock appreciation rights to holders of options under present and past plans, which permit them to surrender exercisable options or a portion of an option in exchange for an amount equal to the excess of the market price of the common stock on the date the right is exercised over the option price. The Management Development and Compensation Committee of the Board of Directors has determined that this amount will be distributed in GE common shares.

At the end of 1976, there were 2,485,979 shares reserved for the 1973 plan and 1,399,232 shares covered by outstanding options granted under prior plans, for a total of 3,885,211 shares. Of this total amount, 1,292,530 shares were subject to exercisable options, 1,689,572 shares were under options not yet exercisable, and 903,109 shares were available for granting options in the future. Appreciation rights relating to unexpired options for 972,294 and 1,020,791 shares were outstanding at December 31, 1976 and 1975, respectively. The number of shares available for granting options at the end of 1975 was 1,123,897. A summary of stock option transactions during the last two years is shown below.

**Stock Options**                                                              **42.5**

|  | Shares subject to option | Average per share Option price | Average per share Market price |
|---|---|---|---|
| Balance at Jan. 1, 1975 | 3,170,482 | $50.94 | $33.38 |
| Options granted | 167,062 | 47.81 | 47.81 |
| Options exercised | (35,378) | 41.81 | 46.94 |
| Options surrendered on exercise of appreciation rights | (795) | 35.25 | 48.63 |
| Options terminated | (243,154) | 53.33 | — |
| Balance at Dec. 31, 1975 | 3,058,217 | 50.69 | 46.13 |
| Options granted | 316,053 | 52.62 | 52.62 |
| Options exercised | (133,542) | 45.25 | 53.42 |
| Options surrendered on exercise of appreciation rights | (21,987) | 46.08 | 53.56 |
| Options terminated | (236,639) | 52.92 | — |
| Balance at December 31, 1976 | 2,982,102 | 51.00 | 55.63 |

Utah International Inc. does not have a stock option and stock appreciation rights plan. Although no options or appreciation rights had been granted as of December 31, 1976 under the Company's plan to any employees of Utah, options and rights may be granted to certain Utah employees in the future.

**42.1**  See note 39.1. Fully diluted earnings per share is less than primary earnings per share probably because some of these convertible bonds are not common stock equivalents (for primary earnings per share) but are dilutive for fully diluted earnings per share. The total dilution is immaterial, so that GE's fully diluted earnings per share need not be separately disclosed.

**42.2**  GE's note 15 gives the details of its short-term borrowings. GE's note 17 gives the details of its long-term borrowings. This paragraph helps the analyst to understand GE's intermediate-term

*(Authors' Notes are continued on the following page.)*

borrowings. From these data, the analyst can estimate cash requirements for debt retirement over the next several years.

**42.3**  Test yourself: How much of the $204.3 million represents equity in earnings of GE Credit Corporation? To answer the question, refer to the Credit Corporation's balance sheet on page 39. Note that GE's equity includes $191.4 million of earnings retained by the Credit Corporation. Thus, the answer is $191.4 million.

**42.4**  Associated companies are 20-percent to 50-percent owned by GE. APB 18 requires GE to use the equity method for its investment in those companies. GE's share of total undistributed earnings from associated companies decreased by $4.8 million (= $47.3 million at 12/31/76 − $52.1 million at 12/31/75) during 1976. GE's note 5 indicates that its share of associated companies losses was $2.3 million. If losses were $2.3 million but the total investment declined by $4.8 million, then dividends must have been $2.5 (= $4.8 − $2.3) million. Thus associated companies despite their losses in 1976 paid dividends to GE in 1976 of $2.5 million. See also the last part of note 34.3.

**42.5**  The unwary reader might mistakenly infer that these options do not dilute the equity of other stockholders. Options will not be exercised unless the market price at time of exercise exceeds the exercise price. If the option exercise price exceeds the market price, then the holder of the option can obtain a share at lower cost by merely purchasing it on the stock market. At the time options are exercised, shares are issued at a price less than would be realized if the shares were issued to the general investing public. Notice, for example, that if the 2.98 million options outstanding were exercised at the end of 1976, the average share should be issued for about $4.63 (= $55.63 − $51.00) less than the market price and the dilution of owners' equity would be about $14 million of stockholders' equity as of that time. This phenomenon is not as easy to demonstrate as of the end of 1975 when, because of stock market declines in GE share prices, the *average* option exercise price exceeded market price.

---

**43.1**  Both the SEC and the FASB (*Statement No. 13*) require disclosure of material commitments under long-term uncancelable leases. GE has no such material commitments. In general, the disclosures must include the effects on both the income statement and the balance sheet of capitalizing such leases. See, however, our note 9 to the Sears report.

**43.2**  As a result of FASB *Statement No. 8,* GE tells us that it is reporting over $40 ($16.5 gain versus $24.0 loss) million more income for 1976 than it would have reported before GAAP were changed.

**43.3**  1976 corporate annual reports include, for the first time, a section of "unaudited notes." During 1976 the SEC defined a new class of footnote with which the auditor is "associated" (to use the SEC's term), but which is not audited.

**43.4**  During the year, GE (and other companies) are required to send quarterly (interim) financial statements to shareholders. The SEC requires companies to show in the annual statements the amounts of the interim earnings *after* all information for the year is available. If there is a difference, the company must explain why its interim reported numbers differ from the corresponding numbers shown in the annual report. GE explains that the acquisition of Utah did not formally take place until the fourth quarter. Since the Utah acquisition was treated as a pooling of interests, the financial reports for all previous periods, including the first three quarters of 1976, required restatement.

**43.5**  In its Accounting Series Release No. 190, the SEC requires disclosure of certain replacement cost data in the Form 10-K. Many companies, including GE, are merely referring to those data in the annual report and mentioning the availability of the Form 10-K. We reproduce the GE replacement cost disclosure from its Form 10-K on pages 99–100 of this book in Exhibit Four. On page 84 of this book we show the material from GE's pages 30 and 31 where GE discusses the effects of inflation.

### 20. Commitments and contingent liabilities

Lease commitments and contingent liabilities, consisting of guarantees, pending litigation, taxes and other claims, in the opinion of management, are not considered to be material in relation to the Company's financial position.

### 21. Foreign operations

Foreign currency translation gains, calculated in accordance with Financial Accounting Standards Board Statement No. 8, and after recognizing related income tax effects and minority interest share, were $16.6 million in 1976 and $24.7 million in 1975. Prior to implementation of FASB Statement No. 8, effective January 1976, the Company included in these amounts translation gains and losses on certain accounts such as inventories which are now required to be translated at exchange rates in effect when the assets were acquired. This change had no significant effect on operating results, but changed the definition of gains and losses attributed to foreign currency translation. Appropriate amounts, consistent with the definition the Company formerly used, were losses of $24 million and $17 million for 1976 and 1975, respectively.

A summary of certain information, before elimination of intercompany transactions, for all foreign operations of General Electric except for exports from the United States is shown below.

**Foreign operations**

| (In millions) December 31 | 1976 | 1975 |
|---|---|---|
| **Operating results** | | |
| Sales | $3,982.9 | $3,398.2 |
| Net earnings | 339.6 | 239.5 |
| General Electric share of net earnings | 311.5 | 213.9 |
| **Financial position** | | |
| Total assets | $3,250.2 | $2,898.4 |
| Total liabilities | $1,831.2 | $1,721.8 |
| Minority interest in equity | 118.9 | 104.4 |
| General Electric interest in equity | 1,300.1 | 1,072.2 |
| Total liabilities and equity | $3,250.2 | $2,898.4 |

## Unaudited Notes to Financial Statements

43.3

In accordance with requirements of the United States Securities and Exchange Commission, the information in the following two notes (A and B) is presented to supplement the Company's audited financial statements and notes. In the opinion of management the information presented conforms with the requirements of the SEC.

### A. Operations by quarter for 1976 (unaudited)

43.4

A summary of certain information pertaining to operating results for each quarter of calendar year 1976 is shown below.

| (Dollar amounts in millions; per-share amounts in dollars) | First Quarter | Second Quarter | Third Quarter | Fourth Quarter |
|---|---|---|---|---|
| Sales of products and services to customers | $3,483.5 | $3,917.0 | $3,774.3 | $4,522.5 |
| Operating margin | 295.9 | 375.4 | 376.5 | 480.1 |
| Net earnings | 172.5 | 238.6 | 227.3 | 292.2 |
| Net earnings per common share | 0.77 | 1.05 | 1.01 | 1.29 |

The amounts shown for the first three quarters differ from those reported to share owners during 1976 because the amounts originally reported have been restated to include the operating results of Utah International Inc. which was merged with General Electric on December 20, 1976 in a transaction accounted for as a pooling of interests.

### B. Estimated current replacement cost of certain assets and certain costs and expenses (unaudited)

43.5

In inflationary periods the cost of replacing certain assets, such as plant and equipment and inventories, with equivalent productive capacity or goods is generally higher than the cost incurred when such assets were originally acquired. The Securities and Exchange Commission (SEC) has required for 1976 that estimates be made of replacement costs for certain assets and the effect of the assumed replacement on certain costs and expenses. In accordance with the SEC's requirement, the Company has made such estimates and will include them in its "10-K Report" to be filed with that Agency at the end of March 1977. For further information about the effect of inflation, see page 30 of this Report.

**Note that GE's "Ten-year summary" appears on the following pages.**

## Ten-year summary (a)

| (Dollar amounts in millions; per-share amounts in dollars) | 1976 | 1975 | 1974 | 1973 | 1972 |
|---|---|---|---|---|---|
| Summary of operations | | | | | |
| Sales of products and services | $15,697.3 | $14,105.1 | $13,918.2 | $11,944.6 | $10,473.7 |
| Materials, engineering and production costs | 11,481.2 | 10,624.2 | 10,458.1 | 8,762.8 | 7,676.3 |
| Selling, general and administrative expenses | 2,688.2 | 2,294.3 | 2,289.4 | 2,112.1 | 1,920.8 |
| Operating costs | 14,169.4 | 12,918.5 | 12,747.5 | 10,874.9 | 9,597.1 |
| Operating margin | 1,527.9 | 1,186.6 | 1,170.7 | 1,069.7 | 876.6 |
| Other income | 274.3 | 174.2 | 206.7 | 202.9 | 207.3 |
| Interest and other financial charges | (174.7) | (186.8) | (196.5) | (142.8) | (120.8) |
| Earnings before income taxes and minority interest | 1,627.5 | 1,174.0 | 1,180.9 | 1,129.8 | 963.1 |
| Provision for income taxes | (668.6) | (459.8) | (457.4) | (456.5) | (385.5) |
| Minority interest | (28.3) | (25.7) | (18.2) | (11.9) | (5.0) |
| Net earnings | $ 930.6 | $ 688.5 | $ 705.3 | $ 661.4 | $ 572.6 |
| Earnings per common share (b) | $ 4.12 | $ 3.07 | $ 3.16 | $ 2.97 | $ 2.57 |
| Dividends declared per common share (c) | $ 1.70 | $ 1.60 | $ 1.60 | $ 1.50 | $ 1.40 |
| Earnings as a percentage of sales | 5.9% | 4.9% | 5.1% | 5.5% | 5.5% |
| Earned on average share owners' equity | 18.9% | 15.7% | 17.8% | 18.4% | 17.5% |
| Dividends–General Electric | $ 332.5 | $ 293.1 | $ 291.2 | $ 272.9 | $ 254.8 |
| Dividends–Utah International Inc. (d) | $ 28.3 | $ 33.1 | $ 23.9 | $ 14.0 | $ 12.8 |
| Shares outstanding–average (in thousands) (e) | 225,791 | 224,262 | 222,921 | 222,631 | 222,503 |
| Share owner accounts–average | 566,000 | 582,000 | 566,000 | 543,000 | 542,000 |
| Market price range per share (c) (f) | 59¼-46 | 52⅞-32⅜ | 65-30 | 75⅞-55 | 73-58¼ |
| Price/earnings ratio range (c) | 14-11 | 17-10 | 19-9 | 24-17 | 25-20 |
| Current assets | $ 6,685.0 | $ 5,750.4 | $ 5,334.4 | $ 4,597.4 | $ 4,056.8 |
| Current liabilities | 4,604.9 | 4,163.0 | 4,032.4 | 3,588.2 | 2,920.8 |
| Working capital | $ 2,080.1 | $ 1,587.4 | $ 1,302.0 | $ 1,009.2 | $ 1,136.0 |
| Short-term borrowings | $ 611.1 | $ 667.2 | $ 655.9 | $ 675.6 | $ 453.3 |
| Long-term borrowings | 1,322.3 | 1,239.5 | 1,402.9 | 1,166.2 | 1,191.2 |
| Minority interest in equity of consolidated affiliates | 119.0 | 104.6 | 86.4 | 62.4 | 53.4 |
| Share owners' equity | 5,252.9 | 4,617.0 | 4,172.2 | 3,774.3 | 3,420.2 |
| Total capital invested | $ 7,305.3 | $ 6,628.3 | $ 6,317.4 | $ 5,678.5 | $ 5,118.1 |
| Earned on average total capital invested | 15.1% | 12.5% | 13.4% | 13.7% | 12.7% |
| Property, plant and equipment additions | $ 740.4 | $ 588.2 | $ 812.9 | $ 734.6 | $ 500.8 |
| Depreciation, depletion and amortization | 486.2 | 470.5 | 415.0 | 371.9 | 343.7 |
| Employees–average worldwide | 380,000 | 380,000 | 409,000 | 392,000 | 373,000 |

(a) Unless specifically noted, all years are adjusted to include Utah International Inc., which became a wholly-owned affiliate of General Electric on December 20, 1976 through the exchange of 41,002,034 shares of General Electric common stock for all of the outstanding shares of Utah.
(b) Computed using outstanding shares as described in note (e).
(c) For General Electric common stock as reported in the years shown.
(d) Reflects transactions prior to merger date.

(e) Includes General Electric average shares outstanding plus outstanding average shares previously reported by Utah multiplied by 1.3. Adjustments have been made for a two-for-one GE stock split in 1971 and the two-for-one and three-for-one Utah stock splits effected in the form of stock dividends in 1973 and 1969, respectively.
(f) Represents high and low market prices as reported on New York Stock Exchange through January 23, 1976 and as reported on the Consolidated Tape thereafter.

| 1971 | 1970 | 1969 | 1968 | 1967 |
|---|---|---|---|---|
| $9,556.7 | $8,833.8 | $8,526.4 | $8,448.8 | $7,787.7 |
| 7,053.4 | 6,491.3 | 6,399.2 | 6,298.0 | 5,809.5 |
| 1,731.3 | 1,758.7 | 1,619.5 | 1,485.6 | 1,324.0 |
| 8,784.7 | 8,250.0 | 8,018.7 | 7,783.6 | 7,133.5 |
| 772.0 | 583.8 | 507.7 | 665.2 | 654.2 |
| 176.6 | 127.7 | 120.0 | 101.2 | 103.2 |
| (102.1) | (105.5) | (83.8) | (75.0) | (65.9) |
| 846.5 | 606.0 | 543.9 | 691.4 | 691.5 |
| (332.8) | (237.2) | (240.8) | (319.1) | (325.5) |
| (4.2) | (5.8) | 2.3 | 5.8 | 12.5 |
| $ 509.5 | $ 363.0 | $ 305.4 | $ 378.1 | $ 378.5 |
| $ 2.30 | $ 1.66 | $ 1.41 | $ 1.75 | $ 1.75 |
| $ 1.38 | $ 1.30 | $ 1.30 | $ 1.30 | $ 1.30 |
| 5.3% | 4.1% | 3.6% | 4.5% | 4.9% |
| 17.2% | 13.4% | 11.8% | 15.3% | 16.2% |
| | | | | |
| $ 249.7 | $ 235.4 | $ 235.2 | $ 234.8 | $ 234.2 |
| $ 11.4 | $ 8.9 | $ 7.6 | $ 6.5 | $ 5.8 |
| 221,591 | 218,938 | 217,048 | 216,332 | 215,700 |
| 529,000 | 535,000 | 525,000 | 534,000 | 533,000 |
| 66½-46½ | 47¼-30⅛ | 49⅛-37 | 50¼-40⅛ | 58-41¼ |
| 26-18 | 26-17 | 32-24 | 25-20 | 29-21 |
| | | | | |
| $3,700.0 | $3,383.1 | $3,362.6 | $3,395.5 | $3,273.5 |
| 2,893.8 | 2,689.4 | 2,398.2 | 2,130.0 | 2,005.5 |
| $ 806.2 | $ 693.7 | $ 964.4 | $1,265.5 | $1,268.0 |
| $ 581.7 | $ 670.2 | $ 351.5 | $ 288.0 | $ 276.6 |
| 1,016.2 | 691.3 | 813.6 | 884.4 | 817.8 |
| 50.4 | 45.0 | 42.3 | 40.3 | 38.2 |
| 3,105.4 | 2,819.1 | 2,610.8 | 2,556.4 | 2,379.3 |
| $4,753.7 | $4,225.6 | $3,818.2 | $3,769.1 | $3,511.9 |
| 12.3% | 10.2% | 8.8% | 11.2% | 11.7% |
| | | | | |
| $ 710.8 | $ 685.3 | $ 567.3 | $ 542.9 | $ 578.5 |
| 289.5 | 348.1 | 365.0 | 312.2 | 292.3 |
| | | | | |
| 366,000 | 398,000 | 412,000 | 402,000 | 391,000 |

**Dividends declared** for the last two quarters of 1976 were at a rate of 45 cents per share; dividends declared during the first two quarters of 1976 and all of 1975 were at a rate of 40 cents per share.

**Supplemental information:** The information in the financial statements in this Report, in the opinion of management, substantially conforms with or exceeds the information required in the annual statements constituting part of the "10-K Report" submitted to the Securities and Exchange Commission, except for current replacement cost data. Certain supplemental information, considered nonsubstantive, is included in that report, however, and copies will be available without charge from: Investor Relations, General Electric Company, Fairfield, Connecticut 06431.

### New York Stock Exchange market prices (c) (f)

| (High and low by quarter) | 1976 | | 1975 | |
|---|---|---|---|---|
| First Quarter | $56¾ | $46 | $49½ | $32⅜ |
| Second Quarter | 58¼ | 49⅞ | 52⅞ | 44¼ |
| Third Quarter | 59¼ | 52⅛ | 52¾ | 41⅜ |
| Fourth Quarter | 55¾ | 50⅛ | 50 | 42¼ |

### Transfer Agents

General Electric Company
Securities Transfer Operation
570 Lexington Avenue
New York, New York 10022

The First National Bank of Boston
Stock Transfer Division
P.O. Box 644
Boston, Massachusetts 02102

The 1976 Annual Report is one of four quarterly issues of *The General Electric Investor*, published to inform share owners and investors about activities of the General Electric Company. Others may receive the *Investor* on request.

**Editor:** Frederick N. Robinson
**Associate Editors:** Devere E. Logan; Edna Vercini
**Financial Editor:** Sidney D. Spencer
**Editorial Board:** David W. Burke, *Manager, Corporate Communications;* J. Hervie Haufler, *Manager, Corporate Editorial Programs;* John L. Ingersoll, *Manager, Corporate Institutional Relations*
**Cover concept:** Ron V. Taylor
**Photographers:** Chris Anderson, Stan Blanchard, Bill Bridges, Joseph B. Brignolo, John Conboy, Ralph Crane, Arthur d'Arazien, Walter B. Halstead, Ty Hyon, Tony Kelly, Dan Montross, Lance Nelson, Horst Oesterwinter, John Olson
**Art Direction:** Jack Hough and Associates, Inc.

## 44.1 Report of Independent Certified Public Accountants

To the Share Owners and Board of Directors of
General Electric Company

We have examined the statement of financial position of
General Electric Company and consolidated affiliates as of
December 31, 1976 and 1975, and the related statements of
earnings, changes in financial position and changes in share
owners' equity for the years then ended. Our examination was
made in accordance with generally accepted auditing standards, and accordingly included such tests of the accounting
records and such other auditing procedures as we considered
necessary in the circumstances.

The financial statements as of and for the year ended
December 31, 1975 have been restated to reflect the pooling
of interests with Utah International Inc. described in note 1
of the Notes to Financial Statements. We did not examine the
financial statements of Utah International Inc. and consolidated affiliates, which statements reflect total assets constituting 10% and 9% and sales constituting 6% and 5% in
1976 and 1975, respectively, of the related consolidated
totals. These statements were examined by other auditors
whose report thereon has been furnished to us, and our
opinion expressed herein, insofar as it relates to the amounts
included for Utah International Inc. and consolidated affiliates
is based solely upon the report of the other auditors.

In our opinion, based upon our examination and the report
of other auditors, the aforementioned financial statements
present fairly the financial position of General Electric
Company and consolidated affiliates at December 31, 1976
and 1975, and the results of their operations and the changes
in their financial position for the years then ended, in conformity with generally accepted accounting principles applied
on a consistent basis.

*Peat, Marwick, Mitchell & Co.*

Peat, Marwick, Mitchell & Co.
345 Park Avenue, New York, N.Y. 10022
February 18, 1977

## 44.2 1976 Financial comments

**Accounting for inflation:** The search for adequate ways of accounting for inflation, which has justly been called "the unseen tax
collector," continued in 1976. The significance of this issue is
clearly apparent when comparing the effective tax rate on *real*
profits with either reported or statutory rates. According to Department of Commerce data, the impact in 1976 of "understated"
depreciation expense and inventory costs due to inflation is estimated to result in an effective tax rate nearly *20 percentage points*
over the reported rate. While no adequate resolution has been
found, various authorities throughout the world continue to focus on
this important accounting and economic issue.

Related to the inflation accounting issue is the Securities and
Exchange Commission's 1976 requirement that larger companies
make estimates of "replacement costs" of inventories and property,
plant and equipment, as well as the impact of these restated
amounts on certain costs and expenses. Such estimates must be
filed with the Commission in GE's form 10-K for 1976.

The impact of restating inventories to replacement cost is mini-
mized for General Electric by the fact that approximately 81% of
these assets are already accounted for by the LIFO method. The
impact of restating property, plant and equipment to estimated
replacement costs will represent an inflation-caused gap which
generally will continue to accumulate as long as inflation persists.
The SEC has noted that the information required must be estimated
on the basis of numerous assumptions and untested techniques
which may not have been fully developed. Recognizing the experimental character of its requirement, the Commission has cautioned
against simplistic use of the data presented. The lack of definitive
guidelines will almost certainly lead to the use of substantially different methodologies in determining the data to be reported and
will undoubtedly frustrate meaningful comparisons among companies. In addition, a requirement which concentrates on only the
*cost* side of the asset replacement equation risks unintentional
confusion by ignoring related factors such as productivity gains
often associated with new technologies and equipment. Using the
SEC-sponsored approach, GE's depreciation expense for 1976
applicable to manufacturing property, plant and equipment would
have been approximately $230 million greater than the amount
reported on an original or historical cost basis. This amount, of
course, does not represent a net reduction in before-tax income
inasmuch as the significant productivity gains which would result
from new equipment and related technologies have not been
considered.

Notwithstanding the conceptual and implemental difficulties with
the SEC replacement cost concept as presently understood, it does
represent an effort to focus on key problems facing businesses from
inflation. Depreciation is normally intended only to allocate the
original purchase cost over the useful life of the related asset and
not to provide for its replacement during periods of inflation.
However, so long as inflation persists, an inflation-caused gap
accumulates between the time a depreciable asset is acquired and
is replaced. Unless tax laws and regulations are changed to give
much more recognition to this readily understood inflation phenomenon, the funds to fill the gap must come entirely from retained
earnings or new capital.

The gap resulting from under-depreciation takes on a larger significance when viewed against the serious question of whether U.S.
business will be able to fund the investments required to meet the
nation's needs and aspirations. Unless the U.S. adopts changes in
national policy with respect to capital formation, GE's economists
foresee the nation's capital investment requirements outrunning
the fund-raising ability of business. Foremost among the changes
needed is a broader understanding of the long-term effect of inflation and the early initiation of steps to help offset and reduce its
damage to the productive growth of our country's businesses.

Note that GE's "Ten-year summary" appears on pages 82 and 83 of this book.

**44.1**   This is the auditors' report. This particular report is nonqualified ("clean"), but nonstandard
since it contains a middle paragraph referring to the work of other auditors. Reliance on the work
of another auditor technically results in a "scope limitation" that does not result in a "qualified
opinion," but in a "shared unqualified opinion." In general, the first paragraph of the auditors'
report is the scope paragraph—telling the work done—and the last paragraph is the opinion.
Ordinarily, auditors' reports have only two paragraphs.

**44.2**   This material is taken from pages 30 and 31 of GE's report. It is management's discussion of
inflation.

# An Annual Report for a Company Approaching Bankruptcy

On June 21, 1970, the Penn Central Company filed a bankruptcy petition for its major subsidiary, the Penn Central Transportation Company. On March 12, 1970, only three months before, the 1969 financial statements of the Penn Central Transportation Company had been issued. The income statement and balance sheet from those statements are shown here. They indicate one important point: analysis of the stockholders' equity section of a balance sheet need not give any indication of impending insolvency or bankruptcy.

Notice that at the end of 1969, Penn Central Transportation Company had retained earnings of almost half a billion dollars which was a part of stockholders' equity of over $1.8 billion. Much of this equity, however, was invested in track and roadbed, assets for which there is no ready market. Penn Central could not dispose of these assets to raise working capital. You can compute that at the end of 1968 and 1969, the Transportation Company had negative working capital; that is, current liabilities (as shown, plus debt due within one year) exceeded current assets. Working capital increased by about $18 million during 1969, but net quick assets—cash and receivables less current liabilities—decreased. The Company was in a less liquid position at the end of the year than at the start.

At the end of 1969, the Transportation Company had over $100 million of debt to repay in the following year. Although the Transportation Company had sufficient "net worth" to show almost half a billion dollars of retained earnings and almost two billion dollars of stockholders' equity, it did not have the funds to meet "only" a few hundred million dollars in current obligations. The company was approaching insolvency by the end of 1969, as can be discerned from these statements. (The declaration of $43 million in dividends during the first three quarters of 1969 under these circumstances seems a questionable step.)

Like Penn Central Transportation Company, many bankrupt firms have positive net assets, or stockholders' equity, on the books at the time of bankruptcy.

**Penn Central Transportation Company**
## Statement of Earnings and Retained Earnings

| Current Earnings | | *Year ended December 31* | 1969 | 1968 |
|---|---|---|---|---|
| *Income* | Railway operating revenues................ | | $1,651,978,000 | $1,514,071,000 |
| | Income from rental of properties, net........ | | 33,772,000 | 27,131,000 |
| | Dividends and interest—consolidated subsidiaries........................... | | 66,324,000 | 40,155,000 |
| | Dividends and interest—other.............. | | 2,661,000 | 15,451,000 |
| | Net gain on sales of properties and investments........................ | | 12,587,000 | 35,437,000 |
| | Income under tax allocation agreements (note 5)............................ | | 21,543,000 | 19,038,000 |
| | | *Total Income* | 1,788,865,000 | 1,651,283,000 |
| *Costs and Expenses* | Railway operating expenses, excluding items listed below........................ | | 1,296,397,000 | 1,173,761,000 |
| | Depreciation, including depreciation on leased lines (note 3)................... | | 91,279,000 | 94,135,000 |
| | Taxes, except Federal income............. | | 144,059,000 | 125,602,000 |
| | Equipment and other rents, net (note 13).... | | 183,802,000 | 169,292,000 |
| | Interest on debt........................ | | 96,764,000 | 68,787,000 |
| | Guaranteed dividends and interest— leased lines................ | | 26,173,000 | 26,315,000 |
| | Miscellaneous, net.... ................ | | 6,719,000 | (1,454,000) |
| | | *Total Costs and Expenses* | 1,845,193,000 | 1,656,438,000 |
| *Earnings (Loss)* | From ordinary operations (note 13)........ | | (56,328,000) | (5,155,000) |
| | Extraordinary item (loss on investment in long-haul passenger service facilities) (note 12).. | | (126,000,000) | — |
| *Net Earnings (Loss)* | For the year (notes 12 and 13)............. | | (182,328,000) | (5,155,000) |
| *Retained Earnings* | From prior years: | | | |
| | As previously reported................. | | 730,047,000 | 788,220,000 |
| | Adjustment (note 13)................ | | (8,818,000) | (6,436,000) |
| | As adjusted......................... | | 721,229,000 | 781,784,000 |
| | | | 538,901,000 | 776,629,000 |
| | Cash dividends........................ | | 43,396,000 | 55,400,000 |
| | Balance at end of year.................. | | $ 495,505,000 | $ 721,229,000 |

# Balance Sheet

| Assets | December 31 | 1969 | 1968 |
|---|---|---|---|
| **Current Assets** | Cash and temporary cash investments....... | $ 80,331,000 | $ 46,915,000 |
| | Accounts receivable and unbilled revenue.... | 293,181,000 | 240,211,000 |
| | Material and supplies, etc., at cost.......... | 104,303,000 | 88,692,000 |
| | *Total Current Assets* | 477,815,000 | 375,818,000 |
| **Noncurrent Assets** | Investments and advances, at cost or less (notes 2 and 7)...................... | 1,139,038,000 | 1,217,796.000 |
| | New Haven—net assets acquired, at cost (note 1)............................. | — | 127,544,000 |
| | Properties (notes 3, 6, 7 and 12) | | |
| | Road, structures, etc................... | 2,066,769,000 | 1,904,536,000 |
| | Revenue equipment (rolling stock)....... | 1,662,759,000 | 1,745,448,000 |
| | Other............................ | 96,051,000 | 90,541,000 |
| | | 3,825,579,000 | 3,740,525,000 |
| | Less accumulated depreciation and losses upon merger................. | 902,731,000 | 992,036,000 |
| | *Total Properties—Net* | 2,922,848,000 | 2,748,489,000 |
| | Deferred charges and sundry assets........ | 56,939,000 | 43,703,000 |
| | *Total Assets* | $4,596,640,000 | $4,513,350,000 |

**Liabilities and Shareholder's Equity**

| | | 1969 | 1968 |
|---|---|---|---|
| **Current Liabilities*** | Notes payable (none to subsidiaries in 1969; $19,420,000 in 1968)................... | $ 102,048,000 | $ 87,420,000 |
| | Accounts payable and accrued expenses..... | 396,407,000 | 356,519,000 |
| | *Total Current Liabilities* (excluding debt due within one year)* | 498,455,000 | 443,939,000 |
| **Long-Term Debt** | Due within one year..................... | 106,058,000 | 76,716,000 |
| | Due after one year..................... | 1,585,585,000 | 1,407,610,000 |
| | *Total Long-Term Debt (note 7)* | 1,691,643,000 | 1,484,326,000 |
| **Other** | Estimated liabilities incurred upon merger (note 6)............................ | 101,935,000 | 119,346,000 |
| | Casualty and other claims................ | 90,667,000 | 81,803,000 |
| | Amounts payable to subsidiary companies... | 167,711,000 | 122,582,000 |
| | Other............................ | 240,857,000 | 231,015,000 |
| | *Total Other* | 601,170,000 | 554,746,000 |
| **Shareholder's Equity** | Capital stock—$10 par value. Authorized 27,000,000 shares; issued 24,113,703 shares (1968—24,085,329) (note 8)....... | 241,137,000 | 240,853,000 |
| | Additional paid-in capital (note 8).......... | 1,068,730,000 | 1,068,257,000 |
| | Retained earnings (note 13).............. | 495,505,000 | 721,229,000 |
| | *Total Shareholder's Equity* | 1,805,372,000 | 2,030,339,000 |
| | *Total Liabilities and Shareholder's Equity* | $4,596,640,000 | $4,513,350,000 |

# Annual Report 1976
### Fiscal Year Ending January 31, 1977

## A.1 Statement of Income

| $ in thousands | Year Ended January 31 | |
| --- | --- | --- |
| | 1977 | 1976* |
| Net sales (including finance charge revenues–note 3) | $14,950,208 | $13,639,887 |
| Cost of sales, buying and occupancy expenses | 9,408,238 | 8,543,844 |
| Selling and administrative expenses | 4,293,933 | 3,941,369 |
| | 13,702,171 | 12,485,213 |
| Operating income from sales and services | 1,248,037 | 1,154,674 |
| Other income | 3,731 | 96 |

**A.2** Equity in income of Allstate Group (note 1)
Insurance companies

**A.3** In accordance with prescribed standards, unrealized increases in the market value of equity investments of $129,564 and $271,803 are not included in the determination of net income.

| | 1977 | 1976* |
| --- | --- | --- |
| Underwriting and investment income | 187,311 | 52,606 |
| Realized capital gains | 8,003 | 11,847 |
| Allstate Enterprises, Inc. | 15,015 | 11,464 |
| | 210,329 | 75,917 |
| Other unconsolidated subsidiaries and affiliates (note 1) | 41,946 | 51,367 |
| Other companies (dividends) | 622 | 1,799 |
| | 252,897 | 129,083 |
| Income before general expenses | 1,504,665 | 1,283,853 |
| General expenses | | |
| Interest (less capitalization of $4,265 and $7,411) | 260,088 | 271,169 |
| Contribution to Employes' Profit Sharing Fund | 114,455 | 86,442 |
| Belgian subsidiary loss (note 2) | 54,058 | 11,151 |
| Income taxes (notes 2 and 4) | | |
| Current operations | 435,200 | 392,500 |
| Belgian subsidiary disposal | (53,652) | — |
| | 810,149 | 761,262 |
| Net income | $ 694,516 | $ 522,591 |
| Per share (average shares 158,899 and 158,034) | $4.37 | $3.31 |

*Reclassified (see note 2, page 22).
See accompanying statement of accounting policies and notes to financial statements.

## Authors' Notes on Sears Annual Report

**A.1**  There are certain items in this report of Sears, Roebuck and Co. that are not illustrated in the General Electric report. Many items in the Sears report are, however, illustrated in GE; in the interest of saving space, we do not repeat all comments here.

**A.2**  Sears owns 100 percent of Allstate Insurance Company ("the good hands"). Because the nature of Sears' business is so different from that of Allstate, Sears does not consolidate Allstate, but instead uses the equity method. General Electric's treatment of GE Credit Corporation parallels this treatment.

**A.3**  In accord with generally accepted accounting principles in the insurance industry, Allstate (and thus Sears) does not recognize in income the unrealized holding gains in Allstate's investment portfolio. Note, from the information given here, that if changes in the market value of Allstate's investments were included in income, Sears' net income for the year ending January 31, 1977, would have been about $130 million larger ignoring income tax effects.

**A.4**  Note the large amount, $856 million, of "current liability" for deferred income taxes. This current liability for deferred taxes and the $172 million of noncurrent liability for deferred income taxes will, in all likelihood, never become payable. (In earlier reports, Sears used to say about its income taxes that "Because of expected future income tax deferrals, it is not expected that tax

*(Authors' Notes are continued on page 91.)*

## A.1 Statement of Financial Position

| $ in thousands | January 31 | |
| --- | --- | --- |
|  | 1977 | 1976 |
| **Assets** | | |
| Current Assets | | |
| Cash | $ 223,112 | $ 277,437 |
| Receivables | 5,672,270 | 5,200,660 |
| Inventories (note 6) | 2,215,141 | 1,877,609 |
| Prepaid advertising and other charges | 90,445 | 97,904 |
| Total Current Assets | 8,200,968 | 7,453,610 |
| Investments (note 1) | | |
| **A.2** Allstate Insurance Company (cost $62,072 and $61,874) | 1,433,945 | 1,148,915 |
| Other investments and advances | 695,368 | 645,025 |
|  | 2,129,313 | 1,793,940 |
| Property, Plant and Equipment | 2,372,267 | 2,322,556 |
| Deferred Charges | 8,928 | 6,467 |
| Total Assets | $12,711,476 | $11,576,573 |
| **Liabilities** | | |
| Current Liabilities | | |
| Short-term borrowings (note 10) | | |
| Commercial paper | $ 1,940,578 | $ 1,706,286 |
| Banks | 305,869 | 217,567 |
| Agreements with bank trust departments | 655,046 | 634,384 |
| Current maturity of long-term debt | 48,900 | 125,000 |
| Accounts payable and accrued expenses | 990,762 | 1,119,604 |
| Unearned maintenance agreement income | 242,143 | 221,562 |
| **A.4** Deferred income taxes | 855,893 | 782,673 |
| Total Current Liabilities | 5,039,191 | 4,807,076 |
| **A.4** Deferred Income Taxes | 171,849 | 140,804 |
| Long-Term Debt | 1,563,512 | 1,326,252 |
| Total Liabilities | $ 6,774,552 | $ 6,274,132 |
| **A.5** Shareholders' Equity | $ 5,936,924 | $ 5,302,441 |

See accompanying detail, statement of accounting policies and notes to financial statements.

## Notes to Financial Statements (Excerpts)

**A.4** ### 4. Income taxes
Federal and state income taxes on current operations include:

| (millions) | Year Ended January 31 | |
|---|---|---|
| | 1977 | 1976 |
| Current portion (before investment tax credit) ............... | $341 | $363 |
| Investment tax credit (flow-through method) | (13) | (13) |
| Deferred tax expense— | | |
| Current | | |
| Installment sales .................. | 93 | 24 |
| Receivable reserves .............. | (8) | 7 |
| Maintenance agreement income ...... | (11) | (10) |
| Supplemental pension costs ......... | 9 | (9) |
| Other............................ | (4) | (5) |
| Long-term | | |
| Depreciation ..................... | 28 | 30 |
| Other.......................... | — | 6 |
| Total Deferred..................... | 107 | 43 |
| Financial statement income tax provision... | $435 | $393 |

**A.6**

The financial statement tax expense for 1976 and 1975 includes state income tax expense of $43 million ($11 million deferred) and $41 million ($5 million deferred), respectively. A reconciliation of effective rates, based upon income before taxes, equity in income of unconsolidated subsidiaries, and the Belgian subsidiary loss (note 2), with the statutory federal tax rate is:

| | Year Ended January 31 | |
|---|---|---|
| | 1977 | 1976 |
| Statutory federal income tax rate ........ | 48.0% | 48.0% |
| State income taxes, net of federal income taxes ........... | 2.6 | 2.7 |
| Investment tax credit (flow-through method) | (1.4) | (1.7) |
| Miscellaneous items................... | .4 | .2 |
| Effective income tax rate .............. | 49.6% | 49.2% |

**A.7** ### 5. Supplemental pension plan
This noncontributory plan provides pension benefits to salaried employes based upon length of service and remuneration over $15,000 per year. For fiscal years 1976 and 1975, the company provided $33,309,000 and $26,783,000, respectively, for this plan.

At January 31, 1977, the actuarially computed value of vested benefits was $55,533,000 in excess of the market value of the plan's assets. The actuarially computed unfunded past service costs (amortizable over 40 years), which includes provision for both vested and non-vested benefits, were $227,689,000 at January 31, 1977.

**A.8** ### 6. Inventories
Effective February 1, 1975, the company adopted the last-in, first-out (LIFO) method of inventory valuation for substantially all domestic inventories. If the company had used the first-in, first-out (FIFO) method of inventory accounting, inventories would have been $88,188,000 and $6,892,000 higher at January 31, 1977 and January 31, 1976.

### 7. Long-term debt
The indentures provide that the company cannot take certain actions, including the declaration of cash dividends, which would cause its unencumbered assets to drop below 150 per cent of liabilities. The excess unencumbered assets at January 31, 1977, were $1.159 billion.

Aggregate long-term debt maturities, including minimum sinking fund payments (excludes $500 million of 5.43% notes which have no specified maturity and amounts classified as current liabilities) through January 31, 1982, are:

Year Ending January 31 (millions)

| | | | |
|---|---|---|---|
| 1979..$24 | 1980..$25 | 1981..$25 | 1982..$25 |

### 8. Commitments
*Leases:*
Rental payments are based upon contractual minimum rates and, for certain retail stores, amounts in excess of these minimum rates are payable based upon specified percentages of sales. Certain of the leases include renewal or purchase provisions at the company's option. Minimum fixed rentals exclusive of taxes, insurance and other expenses payable directly by the company under leases (over one year) in effect as of January 31, 1977, are:

| (millions) | | |
|---|---|---|
| 1977—$74* | 1980—$52* | 1987–1991—$143 |
| 1978—$68* | 1981—$48 | 1992–1996—$ 91 |
| 1979—$58* | 1982–1986—$198 | after 1996—$ 89 |

*Includes computer rentals of $12, $9, $3 and $1 million, respectively.

The present value (interest rates range from 3.4% to 8.5% with a 6.5% weighted average interest rate) of all future contractual minimum rental payments on the above leases (all presented on a net lease basis) as of January 31, 1977, is $423 million.

If financing leases, as defined by the Securities and Exchange Commission, had been recorded as long-term debt and the related property rights depreciated under the straight-line method, net income for the years ended January 31, 1977 and 1976, would have been decreased by $1.7 million and $1.8 million. The present value of these financing leases (6% weighted average interest rate) at January 31, 1977, is $359 million.

*Capital expenditures:*
At January 31, 1977, the company's commitment for capital expenditures for new and enlarged facilities is $208 million for the period 1977–79.

*Pending acquisition:*
Allstate Enterprises, Inc., has agreed to purchase for a total consideration of $63,500,000, subject to certain conditions, substantially all of the assets and liabilities of California Financial Corporation which principal asset is Security Savings and Loan Association.

## Notes to Financial Statements, continued

### 12. Estimated replacement cost data (unaudited)

The Securities and Exchange Commission (SEC) has published rules which require disclosure of management's estimate of the replacement cost of inventories and productive capacity of the company. In its rules the SEC cautions, and the company concurs, that the information cannot be used simplistically to adjust reported net income because of the substantial unresolved theoretical problems, the subjective judgments involved, and the fact that this data does not purport to quantify all costs and savings involved or all effects of inflation. These estimates are not representative of management's intention for the orderly replacement of existing facilities, nor are they necessarily representative of costs that might be incurred in the future or of current market values.

The estimated replacement cost data presented below was prepared in accordance with general guidelines developed by the retail industry. Various acceptable, alternative methods, which were considered appropriate in each instance, were used to estimate replacement cost; but, no significant degree of comparability may exist between the data presented and similar information reported by other companies.

The estimated replacement cost data is based upon the following guidelines and assumptions: (1) productive facilities, including those owned and those under noncapitalized financing leases, but excluding land and construction-in-progress, sufficient to generate current sales volume were designed using the technology now incorporated in new facilities and were valued by applying current construction costs; (2) accumulated depreciation and depreciation expense have been computed by applying historical relationships, adjusted to the straight-line method, to estimated replacement costs classified by type and location,

and (3) cost of merchandise sold was computed using inventories valued at the lower of cost (last-in, first-out) or market determined by the retail method. This method, which is also used in the historical financial statements, does not differ materially from replacement cost amounts for 1976.

The following condensed information is from the company's annual report on SEC Form 10-K:

| (millions) | At January 31, 1977 | |
| --- | --- | --- |
| | Plant and equipment | Accumulated depreciation |
| Per financial statements . . . . . . . | $3,795 | $1,423 |
| Adjusted for: | | |
| Land, capitalized carrying costs and construction in progress . | (425) | (16) |
| Non-capitalized financing leases . . . . . . . . . . . . . . . . | 395 | 139 |
| Historical costs, as adjusted . . . | $3,765 | $1,546 |
| Estimated replacement cost . . . . | $5,252 | $2,107 |

The additional depreciation expense resulting from the replacement cost calculation would be approximately $75 million. Additionally, operating cost savings of approximately $65 million for the year 1976 would be realized based on the replacement assumptions used. These savings relate primarily to new technology in distribution facilities. In accordance with SEC instructions, general expenses (interest, profit sharing and income taxes) have not been adjusted. Interest and income taxes are two of many variables considered in replacement cost decisions. Also, the company has followed and will continue to follow a policy of adjusting selling prices, competitive conditions permitting, for cost increases. Therefore, we repeat the SEC caution to investors against simplistic use of the aforementioned data.

**A.12**

**A.13**

**A.14**

**A.15**

### A.4 continued

payments will exceed the tax expense shown in the financial statements in the foreseeable future.'' We have been told by Sears that they still hold this belief but have taken the statement out of this report in the interest of saving space. We wish they had left it in.)

Almost all of the ''current liability'' for deferred income taxes arises from Sears use of the accrual (completed sales) method of revenue recognition on its financial statements and the installment (cash collection) method of revenue recognition on its tax return. Virtually all retailers, like Sears, make most of their sales on credit, through ''charge accounts.'' Sears recognizes revenue for the financial statements on the date of sale; it reports the taxable income sometime later when the customer pays and the cash is collected. When the cash is collected in a year different from the year of sale, then a timing difference arises, deferred income tax expenses must be reported on the income statement, and the liability for deferred taxes must be shown on the balance sheet. We think this required accounting flies in the face of economic reality. Sears is going to make credit sales each year that will be collected in the next year. Thus the deferred taxes will not be paid until a year when Sears' collections on the sales of prior years are less than their uncollected sales of the current year. This, in effect, means a decline in credit sales from one year to the next. When Sears has a reduction in credit sales in a given year, it is unlikely that it will be a profitable company. If there are no profits, however, then there are no income taxes to pay, no matter how large the deferred income tax liability.

For example, at the start of 1974, W. T. Grant Co. (a former retailer, much like Sears in its lines of business) showed $118 million of liability for deferred income taxes (analogous to Sears' $1,028 million). By the end of 1974, Grant's liability had been reduced to $2 million. Not a single penny of the $116 million reduction in (debit to) the liability account was matched with a cash payment. Grant's went bankrupt. Bankrupt companies generally are not expected to pay taxes. The credits were to tax loss carryforwards and carrybacks of various kinds.

Sears is unlikely ever to have to pay the items shown as deferred taxes. If GAAP did not require income tax allocation, then Sears' reported income for 1976 would be about $107 million, or about 15 percent, larger (see Sears' Note 4).

**A.5** If we were analyzing Sears' financial statements, we would (see previous note) reclassify the deferred tax items, $1,028 (= $856 + $172) million, on the balance sheet as shareholder's equity, increasing it by about 17 percent.

**A.6** See Note A.4. $93 million of the current deferred income tax expense in 1976 arises because Sears uses the sales basis of revenue recognition on financial statements, but the installment method on tax returns.

**A.7** See the Glossary for definitions of *noncontributory, vested, unfunded,* and *past service costs.* GAAP requires, incorrectly many think, that Sears' liabilities not include the $228 million of obligations for unfunded past service costs.

**A.8** Test yourself. How much larger would Sears' pretax income for the year ended January 31, 1977, have been if Sears had used FIFO instead of LIFO? See our Note 39.4 to the General Electric Report for a description of how to answer this question. The answer is $81 million.

**A.9** The disclosure in Sears' note 8 conforms to the requirements of SEC ASR No. 147. Sears gives us the increase in liabilities ($359 million) and reduction in income ($1.7 million) that would occur if certain long-term noncancelable leases were treated as the acquisition of assets that they are in economic substance. (See also our discussion in the *Pronouncements* section under "Leases".)

**A.10** Sears provides some detail about its replacement cost data. The disclosure here is not as complete as the version shown in the Form 10-K, but it, along with the information in Sears' note 6 on Inventories, tells us virtually everything we want to know. See the following five notes.

**A.11** Observe that Sears uses functional pricing (see Glossary) and defines its productive capacity in terms of sales volume. Other retailers have (less imaginatively) defined productive capacity in terms of square feet of selling space and cubic feet of storage space. Sears recognizes that with modern store and warehousing designs, one can generate sales revenue using smaller physical quantities of store space.

**A.12** Sears tells us that replacement cost of goods sold and LIFO historical cost of goods sold are immaterially different in amount. This is the expected result for companies with a relatively smooth pattern of acquisitions for inventory over a year and with a relatively high inventory turnover (above 3 times per year). We cannot calculate Sears' inventory turnover precisely because Sears includes "occupancy expenses" with cost of goods sold (see its income statement). The turnover calculated from the numbers shown on the income statement is 4.6 times per year. This number is the result of the following calculation (see Glossary at *ratio*):
$$4.6 = \$9,408/[.5 \times (\$2,215 + \$1,878)].$$

**A.13** Sears does not disclose the replacement cost of ending inventory here. That figure is required for Form 10-K disclosure. The information in the Sears' note 6 enables us to estimate that Sears' inventory at year-end (January 31, 1977) has a replacement cost that is approximately $88.2 million larger than historical cost. (See the Glossary at *FISH* and *LISH*. Under FIFO, balance sheet historical costs are LISH—last-in, still here—which is approximately replacement cost at year-end.) Sears' Form 10-K discloses that the replacement cost of ending inventory is $88.2 million larger than historical cost; Sears uses the same relationships mentioned above.

**A.14** Sears, unlike many companies, attempts to quantify the amount of operating cost savings that would occur if existing assets were replaced with modern functional equivalents. If an old asset is replaced with a new one, the new one might have a greater acquisition cost, but lower operating costs (such as for labor and fuel). Sears projects operating cost savings of $65 million that almost offset the extra replacement cost depreciation charges of $75 million. Thus, the impact of inflation on Sears' replacement cost of plant is not severe. This fact, plus the fact that Sears uses LIFO for its cost flow assumption, means that Sears' distributable income (see Glossary and the discussion in the section on *Accounting for Changing Prices*) is not significantly different from its conventionally-reported historical-cost income. See the discussion on pages 101–102 of this book.

**A.15** Nearly all companies repeat the SEC's warning against using the replacement cost data in a "simplistic" way. The SEC's warning appears in Accounting Series Release No. 190.

# Accounting for the Effects of Changing Prices: Inflation Accounting and Replacement Cost Accounting

The conventional financial accounting model rests on the assumption that a *common* or *uniform measuring unit* is used in recording the results of transactions and events in the accounting records. That is, the measuring unit (the dollar) applied in recording the acquisition of a machine costing $10,000 five years ago is treated as if it has the same dimension as the measuring unit applied in recording the purchase of merchandise inventory one week ago for $10,000. The conventional accounting model also rests on the *realization convention:* increases in the market prices of individual assets are generally not recognized as gains in determining net income until the assets are sold (or otherwise retired) and higher values are realized in arm's length transactions. Only at the time of sale is the determination of the amount of the gain considered to be sufficiently objective to warrant recognition in the accounts. That is, assets are generally carried in the accounting records at *historical* or *acquisition* cost, less amortization if appropriate.

During earlier periods of relative price stability, the common measuring unit assumption presented no special problems. Since 1945, however, the general level of prices in the United States has increased at an average rate of approximately 4 percent per year. In recent years, the rate of inflation has been substantially greater. Even during periods when prices in general have remained relatively stable, the prices of some goods and services have increased or decreased significantly. Changing prices, either in general or in specific goods and services, raise serious questions about the appropriateness of the common monetary measuring unit assumption and the realization convention. The accounting problems associated with changing prices should be separated into those related to *changes in the general price level* and those associated with *changes in prices of specific goods and services.*

## General Price Level Adjusted Financial Statements

The objective of general price level adjusted financial statements is to state all amounts in dollars of uniform general purchasing power, thereby obtaining a common, or uniform, measuring unit. The purchasing power of the dollar on the date of the most recent balance sheet is usually recommended as the unit of measurement for all financial statements. General price level indices, such as the Gross National Product Implicit Price Deflator or Consumer Price Index, are used to measure the general purchasing power of the dollar on various dates. The general approach is to convert the number of dollars received or expended at various price levels to an equivalent number of dollars in terms of the price level on the date of the current financial statements.

For example, assume that two parcels of land are held on December 31, 19X9, at which time an index of the general price level is 155. Tract A was acquired during 19X1 for $100,000, when the general price index was 100. Tract B was acquired during 19X3 for $100,000, when the general price index was 106. The acquisition cost of these parcels of land would be restated from 19X1 and 19X3 dollars to an equivalent number of 19X9 dollars as shown in Exhibit 1.

**EXHIBIT 1**
**Illustration of General Price Level Restatement Procedure for Land**

| Item | Conventionally Reported Acquisition Cost | Conversion Factor as of 12/31/X9 | General Price Level Restated Acquisition Cost as of 12/31/X9 |
|---|---|---|---|
| Tract A ..... | $100,000 | 155/100 | $155,000 |
| Tract B ..... | $100,000 | 155/106 | $146,226 |

The sacrifice in general purchasing power made during 19X1 when Tract A was acquired for $100,000 is equivalent to sacrificing $155,000 (= 155/100 × $100,000) in general purchasing power on December 31, 19X9. Likewise, the sacrifice in general purchasing power made during 19X3 when Tract B was acquired for $100,000 is equivalent to sacrificing $146,226 (= 155/106 × $100,000) in general purchasing power on December 31, 19X9. The restated amounts in Exhibit 1 use a measuring unit of uniform general purchasing power.

Two important aspects of the general price level restatement procedure should be noted. First, the procedure does *not* represent a departure from the use of acquisition cost as the principal valuation basis in preparing financial statements. Second, the amounts shown for general price level restated acquisition cost do *not* attempt to reflect the current market prices of these two parcels of land. The market prices of the land could have changed in an entirely different direction and pattern from that of the general price level changes. The focus of the general price level restatement procedure is on stating the acquisition cost data in comparable units and not on reflecting current market prices of individual assets and equities.

General price level adjusted income statements differ in essentially five important respects from conventional income statements. These differences, illustrated in Exhibit 2 with data estimated from the General Electric Company's annual report, are explained next.[1]

1. *Revenues and expenses occurring fairly evenly throughout the year.*  Sales and expenses, other than cost of goods sold and depreciation, usually occur fairly evenly through the year. To restate them in terms of dollars of end-of-year general purchasing power, they are adjusted for half a year of general price change. Since the price increase in 1976 (as measured by the GNP deflator) was about 4.7 percent, the price change for half a year was about 2.3 percent. Sales and other income (except revenue recognized on the equity method—see next item) as well as expenses (except cost of goods sold and depreciation) are increased by about 2.3 percent in the adjustment process.

2. *Revenue recognized under the equity method.*  In the conventional income statement, the investor company uses the equity method and recognizes its share of the income of the investee company (in GE's case, "unconsolidated finance subsidiaries"). In general price level adjusted income statements, the investor recognizes its share of the adjusted income of the investee. The 100-percent owned GE Credit Corporation reported income of $59.0 million on a conventional basis; restated on a general price level adjusted basis, this would have been only $19 million. (For simplicity, the estimated restatement of the Credit Company is not presented here.) The large reduction from conventional income to adjusted income for GE Credit is caused almost entirely by its loss on holding net monetary assets during the period of general price increases—see adjustment 5 below.

3. *Cost of goods sold.*  With rising prices, cost of goods sold on a price level adjusted basis will be higher than that reported in conventional financial statements. How much higher depends in large part on the cost flow assumption—FIFO, LIFO, etc.—used. During periods of rising prices and increasing inventory quantities, the adjustment will be greatest for firms using a FIFO assumption. GE uses a LIFO flow assumption for 81 percent of its inventory and a FIFO flow assumption for 19 percent. Our analysis indicates that this results in an average increase of about 2.5 percent in cost of goods sold in the adjusted income statement. (We subtract depreciation from cost of goods sold and adjust depreciation expense separately; see next item.)

4. *Depreciation.*  General price level adjusted depreciation is almost always much larger than depreciation as conventionally reported. For most firms, many of the depreciable assets are acquired many years before the period being reported on; price levels have increased substantially since acquisition. The depreciation adjustment reflects a portion (equal to the depreciation rate) of the cumulative change in prices since the depreciable assets were acquired. (For example, if the depreciation rate for an asset is 10 percent and the general price level has increased by 60 percent since that asset was acquired, then depreciation will be increased by 6 percent (= .10 × .60) of the asset's acquisition cost. Our analysis indicates that GE's depreciable assets were acquired, on average, just under 6 years before December 31, 1976. The cumulative price increase over that time has been about 48 percent; the depreciation expense is correspondingly increased.

5. *Gain or loss on monetary items.*  Price level adjusted income statements explicitly show the gain for the period in purchasing power captured by a debtor (or the loss suffered by a creditor) during a period of rising general price levels. Since most industrial companies are typically net debtors, they will usually show purchasing power gains from this debt. (The liabilities will be paid off, or discharged, with dollars of smaller general purchasing power than was originally borrowed. The difference between the purchasing power borrowed and that repaid is the gain on a monetary liability during the term of the

---

[1]The techniques for making these estimates are described in detail in Sidney Davidson, Clyde P. Stickney, and Roman L. Weil, *Inflation Accounting,* New York: McGraw-Hill Book Co., 1976.

## EXHIBIT 2
### General Electric Company Income Statement for 1976

|  |  | Historical Dollars (Shown in Annual Report) | In 12/31/76 Dollars (As Estimated) | Percentage Change |
|---|---|---|---|---|
| | **Revenues** | | | |
| (1)[a] | Sales and Other Income .............. | $15,913 | $16,283 | + 2.3% |
| (2) | Equity Method Revenue ................ | 59 | 19 | −67.8 |
| | Total ............................. | $15,972 | $16,302 | + 2.1 |
| | **Expenses and Deductions** | | | |
| (3) | Cost of Goods Sold[b] ................... | $11,048 | $11,325 | + 2.5 |
| (4) | Depreciation (SYD)[c] ................... | 486 | 718 | +47.7 |
| (1) | Other Expenses and Deductions ........ | 3,507 | 3,588 | + 2.3 |
| | Total ............................. | $15,041 | $15,631 | + 3.9 |
| | Income before Gain on Monetary Items .. | $    931 | $    671 | −27.9 |
| (5) | Gain on Monetary Items[d] .............. | — | 26 | — |
| | Net Income ......................... | $    931 | $    697 | −25.1 |

[a]Adjustment number, keyed to description in text.
[b]Inventories are 81 percent LIFO; 19 percent FIFO. Amounts shown exclude depreciation.
[c]Average life of depreciable assets is estimated to be 6.1 years; the general price index increased by 47.7 percent during the 6.1 years preceding December 31, 1976.
[d]The net monetary liabilities for GE are computed as follows:

| | (Historical Dollars in Millions) | |
|---|---|---|
| | 12/31/76 | 12/31/75 |
| **Monetary Liabilities** Current Liabilities and Long-term Borrowings .............. | $5,508.1 | $4,950.2 |
| **Monetary Assets** Cash, Receivables (both long- and short-term), Customer Financing, Recoverable Costs, Government Securities, and Advances to Affiliates .......................... | −5,045.5 | −4,286.9 |
| Net Monetary Liabilities ............... | $  462.6 | $  663.3 |

The average of net monetary liabilities for the year 1976 was $563 [= .5 × ($462.6 + $663.3) million. The price change for the year was 4.7%. GE's gain from being a net debtor during 1976 when prices increased by 4.7% was, then, about .047 × $563 = $26 million.

loan.) The gain from being in a net monetary liability position, although real in an economic sense, does not produce a current inflow of cash.

The gain or loss from holding monetary items is in many ways the most meaningful of the general price level adjustments. The interest expense reported in the conventional income statements is the actual cost of borrowing. It depends upon the interest rate negotiated at the time of the loan. That interest rate, in turn, depends in part on the lender's and borrower's anticipations about the rate of inflation during the term of the loan. (Interest rates are increased when the lender expects inflation during the term of the loan. The borrower accepts the higher rate because he or she expects to repay "cheaper" dollars.)

Thus, the borrower's conventional income statement shows an interest expense that reflects the inflation expected by both the borrower and the lender. The gain from being in a net monetary liability position in a time of rising prices is, in a real sense, an offset to reported interest expense. It reflects a gain from being a debtor during a period of inflation that both parties to the loan expected. After the fact, who benefited, the borrower or the lender, depends on whether the actual rate of price increase during the term of the loan differed from the rate anticipated by both parties to the loan at the time the loan was made. If the actual rate of price increase turns out to be less than the anticipated rate, then the lender benefits. If the actual rate turns out to be greater than the anticipated rate, then the borrower benefits.

*Shell Oil's GPLA Financial Information (Exhibit 3)*

Shell Oil Company published supplementary general price level adjusted financial information for 1976. This information is reproduced in Exhibit 3. Several items in the supplementary disclosure are worthy of note. First, this information is somewhat more than the FASB once proposed as requirements. Second, Shell shows comparisons of financial ratios based on both conventional and price level adjusted financial statements. Except for the debt-equity ratio, the ratios based on price level adjustments are different from those based on conventional statements in a way that analysts and investors generally consider less favorable. Third, Shell classifies deferred federal income taxes as monetary. The auditors concur (as do we) with this classification, although it is contrary to the FASB proposal. Classifying deferred federal income taxes as monetary increases the gain on monetary items and thus increases price level adjusted net income.

## EXHIBIT 3

# Shell Oil Company 1976 Annual Report

## Supplementary Price Level Adjusted Financial Information

Although the rate of inflation has moderated, it continues to erode the purchasing power of the dollar and distort traditional measurements of income and wealth. During the five years covered by this report the purchasing power of the dollar declined 29 percent. In the last thirty years it has been reduced to less than one third of its former purchasing power. Financial statements prepared under generally accepted accounting principles report the actual number of dollars received or expended without regard to changes in the purchasing power of the currency. Investments made over extended periods of time are added together as though the dollars involved were common units of measurement. Amortization of these prior period costs is deducted from current period revenues in calculations of net income. Since the purchasing power of the dollar has changed materially, this change must be considered for a proper assessment of economic results.

Individual business enterprises are affected differently by inflation. Holders of monetary assets, such as cash or receivables, lose purchasing power during inflationary periods since these assets will purchase fewer goods and services in time. Conversely, holders of liabilities benefit during such periods because less purchasing power will be required to satisfy their obligations. Rates of return and other financial ratios are also influenced greatly by the ages of the investments and subsequent changes in the purchasing power of the dollar.

In the accompanying price level adjusted financial statements all historical dollar amounts have been restated to a common unit of measurement, i.e., the December 1976 dollar. For example, a capital asset acquired in 1966 for $1 is restated to $1.78 in terms of 1976 dollars for each year shown and depreciation is similarly restated. Each year is therefore expressed on a comparable basis which provides a better measure of economic progress.

Profitability ratios for Shell are substantially lower when both income and investments are stated in common units of measurement. Some of the profits reported for 1976 and prior years are therefore not a true economic gain, but merely the result of erosions in the purchasing power of the dollar. One of the principal factors is depreciation, depletion and amortization. When the historical cost of assets is restated in equivalent current dollars, the 1976 depreciation provision increased 30 percent or $194 million. Other meaningful comparisons are the indicated purchasing power gain on long-term debt relative to the interest and discount amortization on this indebtedness. Also, a high proportion of income is absorbed by taxes. Because of inflation, effective tax rates are significantly greater than the rates enacted by legislative bodies.

### REPORT OF INDEPENDENT ACCOUNTANTS

**To the Board of Directors and Shareholders of Shell Oil Company:**

We have examined the consolidated financial statements of Shell Oil Company appearing in the Annual Reports to Shareholders for the five years ended December 31, 1976. Those financial statements do not reflect the changes in the general purchasing power of the U.S. dollar from the time transactions took place. We have also examined the supplementary price level adjusted financial information for the five years ended December 31, 1976 restated for effects of changes in the general price level as described in the Explanatory Note on page 41. In our opinion, the supplementary Summary Statement of Income,

## EXHIBIT 3—continued

Summary Balance Sheet and Per Share Data shown on page 41 present fairly the historical financial information restated in terms of the general purchasing power of the U.S. dollar at December 31, 1976 in accordance with guidelines, consistently applied, recommended in Accounting Principles Board Statement No. 3 and a Proposed Statement of Financial Accounting Standards, except for the treatment, with which we concur, of deferred income taxes as monetary items.

1200 Milam Street
Houston, Texas 77002
February 11, 1977

| HISTORICAL DOLLARS | (Millions of dollars except per share amounts) | DOLLARS OF CURRENT PURCHASING POWER* | | | | |
|---|---|---|---|---|---|---|
| 1976 | | 1976 | 1975 | 1974 | 1973 | 1972 |
| | **Summary Statement of Income** | | | | | |
| $9,309 | Revenues ............................. | $9,495 | $8,885 | $9,042 | $6,375 | $5,593 |
| | Cost and expenses: | | | | | |
| 639 | Depreciation, depletion, etc. ............ | 833 | 781 | 735 | 704 | 658 |
| 780 | Income and operating taxes ........... | 796 | 763 | 563 | 332 | 298 |
| | Interest and discount amortization | | | | | |
| 79 | on indebtedness ................... | 80 | 77 | 71 | 79 | 81 |
| 7,105 | Other costs and expenses ............ | 7,263 | 6,857 | 7,099 | 4,973 | 4,344 |
| | Income before purchasing power | | | | | |
| 706 | gain or loss on monetary items ........ | 523 | 407 | 574 | 287 | 212 |
| | Purchasing power gain (loss) on: | | | | | |
| — | Long-term debt ...................... | 65 | 72 | 131 | 93 | 41 |
| — | Other monetary items ................ | 5 | (17) | (5) | (5) | 3 |
| $ 706 | Net income ........................... | $ 593 | $ 462 | $ 700 | $ 375 | $ 256 |
| | **Summary Balance Sheet** | | | | | |
| $2,465 | Current assets ....................... | $2,615 | $2,738 | $2,429 | $2,195 | $2,163 |
| 244 | Investments and long-term receivables .... | 277 | 130 | 146 | 124 | 119 |
| 5,082 | Property, plant and equipment (net) ....... | 6,650 | 6,154 | 5,782 | 5,513 | 5,532 |
| 45 | Deferred charges ..................... | 51 | 54 | 48 | 69 | 76 |
| 1,653 | Current liabilities ..................... | 1,653 | 1,616 | 1,430 | 1,233 | 1,251 |
| 1,175 | Long-term debt ....................... | 1,175 | 1,269 | 1,097 | 1,257 | 1,382 |
| 417 | Deferred credits-federal income taxes ..... | 417 | 388 | 360 | 382 | 395 |
| $4,591 | Shareholders' equity ................... | $6,348 | $5,803 | $5,518 | $5,029 | $4,862 |
| | **Per Share Data†** | | | | | |
| $10.11 | Net income .......................... | $ 8.50 | $ 6.82 | $10.39 | $ 5.57 | $ 3.80 |
| $ 2.80 | Cash dividends paid ................... | $ 2.85 | $ 2.80 | $ 2.88 | $ 3.10 | $ 3.27 |
| | **Ratios** (see definitions on page 57) | | | | | |
| 18.0% | Net income to shareholders' equity ........ | 10.2% | 8.4% | 13.9% | 7.7% | 5.3% |
| 14.6% | Net income to total capital ............... | 9.0% | 7.6% | 11.7% | 6.6% | 5.0% |
| 7.6% | Net income to revenues ................ | 6.2% | 5.2% | 7.7% | 5.9% | 4.6% |
| 27.6% | Dividends paid to net income ............ | 33.5% | 41.1% | 27.7% | 55.7% | 86.1% |
| 20.4% | Long-term debt to total capital ............ | 15.6% | 17.9% | 16.6% | 20.0% | 22.1% |

*Based on purchasing power of the dollar at December 31, 1976.
†Per weighted average shares outstanding each year.

**Explanatory Note**

The accompanying supplementary price level adjusted financial information, expressed in terms of December 31, 1976 dollars, is based on the historical dollar financial information. Both the supplementary and historical financial information presented here should be read in conjunction with the notes and other financial statement information in this Annual Report. The supplementary price level information reflects adjustments only for changes that have occurred in the general purchasing power of the dollar as measured by the Gross National Product Implicit Price Deflator. The amounts shown, therefore, do not purport to represent appraised value, replacement cost, or any other measure of the current value of assets.

The Accounting Principles Board Statement No. 3 and a proposal issued by the Financial Accounting Standards Board which give general guidance for the preparation of price level financial statements, treat deferred income taxes as non-monetary items. But for purposes of Shell's general price level restatement, such balances were classified as monetary items because Shell believes that when reversals of such tax differences take place, they give rise immediately to taxable income and to additional taxes payable in current dollars at that time. Had Shell followed the non-monetary treatment for deferred income taxes, restated net income would have been reduced by approximately 4 percent or less and restated shareholders' equity would have been reduced by about 2 percent or less in each of the last five years.

*Summary*

The difference between conventional and GPLA net income is caused basically by the five adjustments demonstrated in this section. GPLA income before recognizing the gain on monetary items is smaller than conventional net income for virtually all companies. This reduction is caused by the substantial increase in depreciation and, except for LIFO companies, an adjustment for more than one-half year of price change to cost of goods sold. Almost all corporations are net borrowers of monetary items so that the adjustment for monetary items almost always is a gain, tending to offset the higher depreciation and cost of goods sold items.

## Adjustments for Specific Price Changes

Several approaches to accounting for specific price changes have been suggested, all of which depart from the use of acquisition cost. Among these alternative approaches are proposals for using current replacement cost (entry value) or net realizable value (exit value) as the valuation basis. It should be noted that, in perfectly competitive markets, the spread, or difference, between the current replacement cost and net realizable value of an asset should be relatively small, essentially representing transaction costs. In less active markets, as characterizes the market for many used assets or in markets for highly specialized assets, the spread between entry and exit values could be much larger, reflecting not only transaction costs but also trading advantages by the buyer or the seller.

*Current Replacement Cost Valuation Method*

When current replacement cost is used as the valuation basis, assets are stated on the balance sheet at the cost of replacing the assets in their current condition. Changes in the replacement cost of assets held during the period and not sold by the end of the period are reported as *holding gains* and *losses* in the income statement or in a statement of capital. Expenses are stated at the cost of replacing the asset services which are consumed during the period.

In determining the replacement cost of various financial statement items, several sources of price data might be used. For merchandise inventory, suppliers' catalogs could be consulted. For manufacturing firms with work in process and finished goods inventories, it is necessary to identify the various inputs into production (for example, raw material used, direct labor services consumed, depreciation recorded on factory equipment) and determine the replacement cost of each. There is likely to be greater difficulty establishing the replacement costs of manufacturing overhead components than of direct material and direct labor because of the numerous dissimilar indirect cost elements involved in the determination.

In cases where established second-hand markets exist for assets, such as automobiles, furniture, and standardized equipment, replacement cost can be determined from dealers in those markets. In some cases, the federal government prepares specific price indices for certain types of assets. These indices provide information concerning the change in the price of specific assets in a new condition. Some adjustment is necessary to reflect the used condition of the assets on hand. The current replacement cost of specially designed equipment and buildings is perhaps the most difficult to determine. A combination of suppliers' catalogs, specific price indices, and real estate appraisals is probably required.

Perhaps the major criticism of using current replacement cost in financial accounting reports is the high degree of subjectivity involved in determining replacement cost. Several persons attempting to determine the replacement cost of a specific asset could arrive at widely different replacement cost amounts. Many of these valuations would be difficult to audit effectively.

## Income Based on Replacement Costs

In 1976, the Securities and Exchange Commission (SEC) began requiring disclosure, in reports filed with the SEC, of certain financial statement information based on replacement cost data.[1] The SEC does not require complete financial statements based on replacement costs but merely disclosure of the following items:

1. Replacement cost of goods sold at the times of sale,
2. Replacement cost of inventory on hand both at the beginning and end of the year (for 1976, only year-end amounts need be disclosed),

[1]Securities and Exchange Commission, "Relating to Amendment of Regulation S-X Requiring Disclosure of Replacement Cost Data," Accounting Series Release No. 190, 1976. Disclosure is required of corporations with inventory and plant costing $100 million or more.

3. Replacement cost of plant assets both at the beginning and the end of the year (for 1976, only year-end amounts need be disclosed), and
4. Depreciation based on the average replacement cost of plant assets during the year.

Exhibit 4 illustrates the disclosures of General Electric Company from its 1976 Form 10-K.

## EXHIBIT 4

## GENERAL ELECTRIC COMPANY
## Replacement Cost Disclosure for 1976 Under SEC Requirements (ASR No. 190)

B.  ESTIMATED CURRENT REPLACEMENT COST OF CERTAIN ASSETS
    AND CERTAIN COSTS AND EXPENSES (UNAUDITED)

In accordance with regulations issued by the Securities and Exchange Commission, the Company has estimated the replacement cost, as of December 31, 1976, of property, plant and equipment and inventories. Additionally, in further compliance with the related SEC directive, the Company has calculated the effect of the estimated replacement costs on 1976 cost of goods sold and depreciation expense.

The SEC has noted that the information required must be estimated on the basis of numerous assumptions and untested techniques which may not have been developed fully. Recognizing the experimental character of this requirement, the SEC has cautioned against simplistic use of the data presented, especially the conversion of the estimated replacement cost of sales and depreciation expense to a net income basis.

Amounts tabulated below represent Company management's efforts to comply with the SEC requirements.

|  | SEC Replacement Cost Data | Historical Cost |
|---|---|---|
|  | (In millions) | |
| **At December 31, 1976:** | | |
| Inventories | $ 3,540 | $ 2,265.4 |
| Property, plant and equipment | $12,550 | $ 5,761.0 |
| Less accumulated depreciation | (7,700) | (3,343.5) |
|  | $ 4,850 | $ 2,417.5 |
| **For the year ended December 31, 1976** | | |
| Cost of goods sold | $11,110 | $10,851.6 |
| **Depreciation expense** | | |
| In cost of goods sold | $ 570 | $ 365.4 |
| In selling, general and administrative expenses | 80 | 53.3 |
|  | $ 650 | $ 418.7 |

The current replacement cost data above have been estimated for worldwide operations except for Utah International Inc. Virtually all of Utah's fixed assets are mineral-related and are exempt from the SEC's requirements for 1976. Estimates for Utah's inventories and cost of goods sold have been omitted because any difference between historical and replacement cost is not believed to be material. Following are the pertinent historical cost amounts of Utah which were excluded from estimated replacement cost data:

*(Exhibit Four is continued on the next page.)*

## EXHIBIT 4 —continued

|  | Utah Historical Cost (In millions) |
| --- | --- |
| At December 31, 1976: | |
| Inventories | $ 89.0 |
| Property, plant and equipment | $962.2 |
| Less accumulated depreciation | (242.6) |
|  | $719.6 |
| For the year ended December 31, 1976: | |
| Cost of goods sold, including depreciation | $629.6 |
| Depreciation expense | $ 67.5 |

In addition to the foregoing, manufacturing land and related improvements ($111.7 million historical cost) and manufacturing plant under construction ($119.9 million historical cost) were excluded as not being subject to theoretical replacement cost techniques.

Procedures developed by the Company in determining replacement cost data are described in the following paragraphs.

*Inventories*—For inventories valued on a LIFO basis (principally in the United States) it was generally assumed that adjustment of acquisition costs by application of LIFO indices resulted in a reasonable estimate of current replacement costs. For remaining inventories (principally outside the United States) published inflation indices were used, where available, or specific sample indices were developed to estimate current replacement cost by adjustment of acquisition cost data.

*Property, plant and equipment*—With respect to buildings, several techniques were used to estimate replacement costs. These included use of (1) planning data (adjusted to present productive capacity) in those instances in which plans actually existed for replacement; (2) "reference plants" where an existing design might be usable whenever replacement becomes necessary; (3) insurance appraisal data where the replacement facility would be substantially similar to an existing facility; and (4) engineering estimates of replacements for other facilities which it is probable would not be replaced in kind.

With respect to most machinery and equipment, restatement indices were developed from a sample of the Company's major machinery and equipment accounts and applied to historical costs by year of addition. Planned costs were used where available and specially prepared estimates were utilized where machinery and equipment would not be replaced substantially in kind.

*Accumulated depreciation*—Accumulated depreciation as of the end of the year, and 1976 replacement cost *depreciation expense,* were determined using the service lives used for financial accounting purposes. In accordance with the SEC directive, replacement cost depreciation was calculated using the "straight-line" method rather than the accelerated methods generally used by the Company in its financial statements.

*Cost of goods sold*—With respect to the inventory-related portion of cost of goods sold, no adjustment was generally deemed necessary for LIFO-valued inventories. Cost of goods sold for non-LIFO valued inventories was adjusted to estimated replacement cost at time of sale. The depreciation portion of cost of goods sold was calculated as discussed above.

*Limitations*—Despite the inherent imprecisions involved in determining the replacement cost of the Company's productive capacity, it is management's view that the data shown in the preceding tabulation have been reasonably estimated. It should be recognized, however, that actual replacement of property, plant and equipment occurs in the normal course of business over many years, rather than at a specific point in time. Furthermore, no attempt has been made to estimate the theoretical improvements in operating costs, such as increased labor productivity and reduced maintenance expense, which normally are associated with replacing productive equipment. Finally, in the continued evolution of the Company's strategic planning activities, some fixed assets designated as subject to replacement in current estimates might not be replaced at the end of their useful lives.

The SEC did not require complete financial statements based on replacement cost, perhaps because the SEC did not want to constrain the uses to which the replacement cost data might be put. In England, Australia, and New Zealand complete financial statements based on replacement costs will be required for many corporations starting in 1979. Next, we demonstrate two possible uses of the replacement cost data: (1) segmentation of the income statement into three measures of income, and (2) disaggregation of the conventionally-reported gross margin (sales minus cost of goods sold) into operating margin and realized holding gains.

*Three Concepts of Income*

Using the replacement cost data, the income statement can be segmented into three measures of income, each much different from the others and each with different meanings. The amounts of these income measures are shown in boldface type in Exhibit 5.

*Distributable Income.* Distributable income is equal to conventional revenue less expenses based on replacement costs. It is designed to answer questions such as the following. If price changes were to stop today but physical operations were to continue without change, what income would we reasonably expect of the firm in the future? What dividends could be declared, at a maximum, without impairing the firm's ability to continue operations at current levels? Distributable income measures this capability. General Electric Company's distributable income for 1976 is $645.5 million.

### EXHIBIT 5
### General Electric Company 1976
### Income Statements for the Year 1976 Based on Both
### Historical Costs and Replacement Cost Data Disclosed Because of SEC Requirements

| | Conventional Historical Cost Basis | Adjustments | Based on SEC Replacement Cost Disclosures |
|---|---|---|---|
| | **$ Amounts in Millions** | | |
| Revenues and other Income ............. | $15,971.6 | None | $15,971.6 |
| Expenses: | | | |
| Cost of Goods Sold[a] .................. | $10,851.6 | Increased by $258.4[a] -----┐ | $11,110.0[a] |
| Depreciation (in Selling General and Administrative Expenses) ............ | 53.3 | Increased by $26.7────── | 80.0 |
| All Other Expenses Including Taxes .... | 4,136.1 | None | 4,136.1 |
| Total Expenses ....................... | $15,041.0 | | $15,326.1 |
| **Distributable Income** .................. | — | | $   645.5 |
| Realized Holding Gains: | | | |
| On Inventory ........................ | — | └►$258.4 | |
| On Plant Assets Used in Selling General and Administrative Functions ........ | — | ► 26.7 | |
| Total Realized Holding Gains .......... | — | | 285.1 |
| **Realized Income** (Distributable Income and Realized Holding Gains)............... | $    930.6 | (= Conventional Net Income) | $    930.6 |
| Unrealized Holding Gains: | | | |
| On Inventory ........................ | — | $197.1[b] | |
| On All Plant Assets ................... | — | 72.5[b] | |
| Total Unrealized Holding Gains ........ | — | | 269.6 |
| **Economic Income** ...................................................................... | | | $ 1,200.2 |

a. Includes depreciation charged as product costs. See Exhibit 4.
b. Estimated by authors, because replacement cost at 1/1/76 was not available. Opening balances of replacement costs will be available starting in 1977.

To take an even simpler example, if a retailer buys one toaster for $30 and sells it for $50 at a time when the replacement cost of a toaster is $38, then pretax distributable income is $12 (= $50 − $38). A retailer who paid out more than $12 in taxes and dividends under these circumstances would not retain sufficient funds to buy the next toaster and could not remain in business at current levels.

Changes in the amount of distributable income over time probably measure the growth capability of a firm better than the changes in any other income figure. This is the income number that financial analysts may study in assessing growth prospects for the company and, hence, in assessing potential for price appreciation of the firm's shares in stock markets. For example, if dividend payments are regularly larger than distributable income, then the firm will likely have to contract operations in the long run or raise new capital just to maintain the current activity levels.

*Realized Income.*    Realized income is that portion of economic income (discussed next) that has been realized in transactions with parties outside the firm. It is distributable income plus realized holding gains, $930.6 million during 1976 for General Electric Company. This income amount is always exactly equal to conventional net income. It is less than economic income by the amount of *unrealized* holding gains during the period. This measure of income has meaning to the extent that the conventional measure has meaning, since they are the same. As managers and investors become accustomed to analyzing distributable income and economic income, this intermediate measure will probably be used less often. Realized income reports only those increments to wealth that have been realized in transactions with outsiders during the period. If replacement costs are properly computed and both inventory and plant are stated at realistic amounts, then the distinction between realized and unrealized is artificial.

*Economic Income.*    Economists, following the lead of Sir John R. Hicks, often define income during a period as how much better off a firm is at the end of a period than it was at the beginning of the period. That is, economic income is wealth at the end of the period less wealth at the beginning of the period plus any distributions to owners during the period. We estimate General Electric Company's economic income for 1976 to be $1,200.2 million. This "well-offness" is measured as conventional income plus all holding gains during the period, both realized and unrealized.[1] Whether or not it makes sense for management or investors to pay attention to the measure is questionable because the degree to which this amount can be earned in the future depends to a large degree on future price changes. It is true, however, that economic income measures the increase in the firm's wealth during the period (but not the change in owners' wealth, which depends upon stock market prices).

### Operating Margin and Holding Gains on Inventory

A second use of the replacement cost data required by the SEC is in disaggregating the conventional gross margin into operating margins and realized holding gains on inventory. Exhibit 6 presents this disaggregation for General Electric Company. See also the Glossary at *inventory profit*.

The *operating margin* is the difference between sales and replacement cost of goods sold. For General Electric Company, the operating margin is $4,587.3 million. The operating margin might be viewed as a measure of management's effectiveness in its operating decisions (pricing policy, production decisions, marketing efficiency, and the like).

The realized holding gain on units sold is the difference between cost of goods sold based on replacement cost and cost of goods sold based on acquisition cost. That is, the realized holding gain is measured by the increase in replacement cost between the time goods assumed to be sold were acquired and when they were sold. For General Electric Company, the realized holding gain on units sold is $258.4 million.

The realized holding gain on units sold is difficult to interpret. It may result partially from skillful forecasting and buying decisions by purchasing management and should be rewarded. It may also result, however, from price increases which all purchasing agents expected and therefore does not represent superior performance. In addition, the gain is not distributable to owners since, if the firm is to continue operating, it must replace the item at the currently higher replacement cost to remain in business. (Of course the firm can usually raise new funds with various issues of equity. In measuring distributable income, we assume that future operations at current levels do not require the raising of additional funds.)

### Example Disclosures of Replacement Costs

On the next several pages, we reproduce the replacement cost disclosures from annual reports of five companies. In addition, much of the Sears Roebuck replacement cost data appears in their notes

---

[1]This view of economic income assumes that the measuring unit has not changed in value. Most economists would argue that adjustments for changes in the value of the measuring unit should also be made.

**EXHIBIT 6**
**General Electric Company**
**Disaggregation of Gross Margin Into Operating Margin and Holding Gains for 1976**
**($ Amounts in Millions)**

|  | Conventional Basis | Replacement Cost Basis |
|---|---|---|
| Sales Revenue (excluding other income)........................ | $15,697.3 | $15,697.3 |
| Less Cost of Goods Sold (See Exhibit 4) ..................... | 10,851.6 | 11,110.0 |
| Conventional Gross Margin ................................. | $ 4,845.7 | |
| Operating Margin ........................................... | | $ 4,587.3 |
| Replacement Cost of Goods Sold.............................................. | | $11,110.0 |
| Less Acquisition Cost of Goods Sold ......................................... | | 10,851.6 |
| Realized Holding Gain....................................................... | | $   258.4 |
| Operating Margin Plus Realized Holding Gain (= Conventional Gross Margin).............................................. | | $ 4,845.7 |

reprinted on page 91 of this book. The companies were chosen because they included the disclosure in the report (rather than only in the Form 10-K) and the disclosure itself is, we think, in some respect remarkable. The accompanying Exhibit 7 shows certain historical cost data about the five companies so that you can more readily grasp the message of the replacement cost disclosures. Why have we chosen these companies? Our reasons follow.

*American Telephone & Telegraph*

AT&T has more total assets (and depreciable plant) than any other U.S. company. Yet they are growing so fast that the replacement cost amounts for plant are a smaller percentage increase over historical cost than for most companies. Moreover, the management of AT&T has some novel views about the meaning of the replacement cost data. The views are well stated in the last 3 paragraphs of the AT&T footnote. We tend to disagree with some of them, but they are worth thinking about.

*Commonwealth Edison*

Commonwealth Edison reports its methodology in its footnote and has made, in our opinion, effective use of the method of *functional pricing* (see Glossary). The company defines its *productive capacity* (see Glossary) more broadly (in terms of BTU's of output) and has made good use of this definition in computing replacement costs.

**EXHIBIT 7**
**Historical Cost Data For Example Companies (1976)**
**(Dollar Amounts in Millions)**

| Company | Net Income for Year | Total Assets (Year-end) | Owners' Equity (Year-end) |
|---|---|---|---|
| American Telephone & Telegraph ................ | $3,602 | $86,717 | $37,219 |
| Commonwealth Edison .......................... | 242 | 5,910 | 2,384 |
| Hilton Hotels .................................... | 31 | 409 | 231 |
| Koppers ......................................... | 67 | 763 | 424 |
| Trans Union Corporation ........................ | 43 | 1,413 | 268 |

### Hilton Hotels

Hilton's chief financial officer, John V. Giovenco, realized that replacement cost for a hotel building was not as valuable information to the reader as the fair market value of the entire property. Hilton accepted the SEC's invitation to provide more information than just replacement cost. It gives the fair market value of its properties. Note that the excess of fair market value of the properties over their historical cost, $347 million, is more than one and one-half as large as owners' equity reported in the historical cost balance sheet.

### Koppers

Koppers' annual report is particularly easy to read because the company's chief financial officer, A. William Capone, provides helpful explanations right on the financial statements. Likewise, he provides an easy-to-follow replacement cost footnote.

### Trans Union Corporation

Trans Union uses several different methods in deriving its replacement costs. It uses *functional pricing* for its rail car lease fleet, *indexing* for the ocean vessel fleet and equipment, *unit pricing* for building and leasehold improvements, and *direct pricing* for its inventories. (See the Glossary.) Moreover, in defining productive capacity, the measure of output is dollars of revenue rather than some physical measure. This is the only company we have seen which describes using all four of the techniques generally available for deriving replacement cost data.

## AMERICAN TELEPHONE & TELEGRAPH CO.
## 1976 Annual Report Excerpt

(N) Replacement Cost (Unaudited)—In response to Securities and Exchange Commission requirements, the following figures compare telephone plant investment as shown on the balance sheet at December 31, 1976 with the approximate cost to replace its productive capacity at that date. They also compare accumulated depreciation at that date with the amount that would have been provided had past depreciation accruals contemplated such replacement costs. Additionally, they compare depreciation expense for the year ended December 31, 1976 with depreciation expense computed (using historic depreciation assumptions) on these estimates of replacement costs.

| | Millions of Dollars | | |
| --- | --- | --- | --- |
| | As Stated | At Replacement Cost | Difference |
| Telephone plant investment: | | | |
| For which replacement cost has been determined...... | $90,660 | $130,405 | $39,745 |
| Included at historic cost............ | 3,507 | 3,507 | — |
| Total........... | 94,167 | 133,912 | 39,745 |
| Accumulated depreciation....... | 18,245 | 32,634 | 14,389 |
| Net telephone plant investment........ | $75,922 | $101,278 | $25,356 |
| Depreciation expense.. | $ 4,484 | $ 5,980 | $ 1,496 |

These replacement cost figures are theoretical, based on the assumptions that, as of December 31, 1976: electronic switching systems would replace all electromechanical switching systems; most other telephone plant would be replaced in accordance with present replacement practices; and building space would be reduced because of the use of electronic switching systems. Certain telephone plant categories are included at historic cost: principally land, telephone plant under construction, and telephone plant held for future use.

The difference between historic and estimated replacement cost of net telephone plant investment does not represent additional book value for the Company's stock. . The above replacement cost is an approximation of the amount of capital that could have been required were the Company to have replaced the entire productive capacity of such plant on December 31, 1976. Replacement actually will take place over many years and the funds needed will be derived from sources similar to those available during 1976.

Depreciation expense based on an estimate of replacement cost also is a theoretical figure and not deductible in determining income tax expense. The excess of depreciation on replacement cost over that determined on historic cost is a measure of the extent to which current operations have not been making provision for the higher replacement cost of present plant capacity. Such provision, if made, would provide funds which would be used in lieu of funds from other sources for plant construction.

It would be unrealistic to impute a reduced net income by the difference between depreciation based on historic cost and that based on estimates of replacement cost. New plant is likely to provide largely-offsetting additional revenue-generating services and operating efficiencies. Additionally, replacement of plant will take place over many years. It is true, however, that the earnings of the Company must be high enough to provide some equity capital from reinvested earnings and to attract additional debt and equity to provide funds for any replacement cost in excess of depreciation accruals based on the historic cost of the plant.

# COMMONWEALTH EDISON
## 1976 Annual Report Excerpt

### (16) *Replacement Cost Information (Unaudited)*

Estimates of replacement costs and related data are set forth below. These estimates do not consider all of the effects of inflation on the Company's operations and necessarily require substantial subjective judgments. Moreover, replacement costs are not recognized for tax and ratemaking purposes. Consequently, it would be inappropriate to use these data to adjust reported earnings because doing so would result in a serious mismatch between revenues and expenses. Other limitations are set forth in notes a through g below.

|  | Estimated Replacement Cost Data (Note g) | Original (Historical) Cost Data |
|---|---|---|
|  | —Millions of Dollars— | |
| **UTILITY PLANT AND FUEL INVENTORIES AT DECEMBER 31, 1976** | | |
| Utility plant and equipment (Note a) | $16,140 | $7,398 |
| Less—Accumulated provision for depreciation (Note b) | 6,590 | 1,619 |
|  | $ 9,550 | $5,779 |
| Nuclear fuel (including leased fuel) at amortized cost (Note c): | | |
| Fuel in reactors | 300 | 103 |
| Fuel stocks | 450 | 137 |
|  | $10,300 | $6,019 |
| Coal and fuel oil inventories (Note d) | $    95 | $   126 |
| **DEPRECIATION AND FUEL EXPENSE FOR THE YEAR 1976** | | |
| Depreciation expense (Note e) | $    465 | $   197 |
| Fuel expense (Note f): | | |
| Amortization and lease charges of nuclear fuel in reactors | $    185 | $    51 |
| Coal and fuel oil burned | 330 | 438 |
|  | $    515 | $   489 |

### Notes to Replacement Cost Information

a. *Plant and equipment.* Construction work in progress, land and intangible plant are included in the replacement cost data at their original cost of $1,630 million. The replacement costs of other plant and equipment represent estimated amounts which would be incurred if the plant and equipment facilities were replaced at December 31, 1976 price levels, assuming no cost escalation beyond that date.

Actual replacement of plant and equipment will take place over many years, probably in form and manner different from those assumed in developing these estimates. For these and other reasons, the replacement cost information presented is not indicative of the current value of existing plant and equipment or the Company's future capital requirements.

The estimated replacement cost of our 15,815 megawatts (MW) of generating facilities reflects an increase in the nuclear proportion from its present level of 5,058 MW (32%) to an assumed level of 7,908 MW (50%), an increase of 2,850 MW, with corresponding reductions in coal-fired capacity of 1,951 MW, in oil-fired peaking capacity of 302 MW and in oil-fired steam capacity of 597 MW, to reflect assumed levels of 40%, 10% and zero, respectively, for these three categories. Each kind of capacity was then priced at the estimated average cost per kilowatt of building such capacity at current price levels, reflecting present environmental and safety regulations.

No changes in mix were assumed for transmission, distribution and general plant, for which replacement costs were estimated by using the July 1, 1976 Handy-Whitman Index of Public Utility Construction Costs applied by plant accounts and vintage years, with adjustments to December 31, 1976 price levels.

b. *Accumulated depreciation.* The accumulated provision for depreciation (replacement cost basis) was estimated separately for each of five major classes of facilities—steam-electric generation (nuclear and coal), peaking generation (oil), transmission, distribution and general plant. The method used was to multiply the replacement cost of facilities in each class by a percentage representing the estimated expired life of existing facilities in that class at December 31, 1976. For each of the two classes of generating plant, the estimated expired life was based upon a weighted average for all units in the class, computed by weighting the expired life of each unit according to its net capability. For each of the three remaining plant classes, transmission, distribution and general plant, the estimated expired life was based on the weighted average for all facilities in the class computed by weighting the expired life of each group of facilities according to its replacement cost.

c. *Nuclear fuel.* The replacement cost of in-core reactor fuel represents the current value of the estimated energy content of such fuel which would be required by the 7,908 MW of nuclear capacity contemplated under the replacement cost assumptions (see note a). The method used was (i) to determine the initial energy content (expressed in usable Btu's) of all in-core assemblies which would be required to fuel the assumed nuclear capacity, assuming the same average mixture of initial and re-load fuel as existed in our reactors at December 31, 1976, (ii) to reduce this initial quantity of Btu's by 53%, representing the average percentage of depletion recorded for all existing nuclear fuel cores at December 31, 1976 (calculated by dividing the accumulated per books amortization of nuclear fuel in reactors at December 31, 1976 by the original cost thereof), and (iii) to price the remaining Btu's of usable energy at their estimated current replacement cost. Thus, the number of Btu's of usable energy per kilowatt of in-core fuel is roughly the same, under the replacement cost assumption, as is thought actually to exist at December 31, 1976. Only the

## Commonwealth Edison Excerpt—continued

number of kilowatts and the price per Btu are changed. The replacement price per Btu is based upon $35 per pound of uranium concentrate, $75 per separative work unit (swu) of enrichment service and $100 per kilogram of uranium (kg of U) for fuel fabrication.

These same pricing assumptions (per pound, per swu and per kg of U) have been applied to nuclear fuel stocks on hand and not yet placed in reactors, including uranium concentrate, uranium in various stages of refinement, conversion, enrichment and fuel fabrication, and completed fuel assemblies.

d. *Coal and fuel oil inventories.* Actual inventories of coal and peaker oil on hand at December 31, 1976 were assumed to be reduced in proportion to the respective reductions in coal-fired and peaker fuel usage referred to in note f. The replacement costs of coal and fuel oil inventories were then determined by pricing such reduced inventories at their estimated current replacement values.

e. *Depreciation expense.* 1976 depreciation expense based on replacement cost was determined using the rates and methods used for computing book depreciation based on original cost.

f. *Fuel expense.* To determine 1976 fuel expense on a replacement cost basis, actual fuel usage was adjusted to reflect the changed proportions of nuclear, coal and oil-fired generating facilities referred to in note a. As a result, the quantity of nuclear fuel usage was increased while coal and oil usage was reduced. Actual 1976 operating rates for nuclear generation and oil-fired peakers were used in estimating the output of these two categories of generation under the replacement cost assumption. The remaining output was assumed to result from coal-fired generation. No change was made in purchased power.

Notwithstanding the existence of a number of fuel supply contracts of varying length, fuel expense was restated by pricing the estimated usage of each kind of fuel at its estimated current replacement price.

Nuclear fuel amortization was calculated by pricing the estimated increased nuclear fuel usage (in Btu's) at the estimated December 31, 1976 replacement price (assuming no leasing) plus an allowance for waste disposal cost less salvage. Coal and fuel oil expenses were calculated by pricing the reduced 1976 usage of each such fuel at its average December 31, 1976 replacement cost and adding related handling expenses. This procedure was followed because replacement prices of nuclear, coal and oil fuel at year-end 1976 were estimated to be representative of such prices throughout the year.

g. *General.* If replacement costs were fully recognized for ratemaking and tax purposes, it would be appropriate to record them on the books, at least with respect to the proportion of plant represented by stockholders' equity, in order to partially reflect the effects of inflation. Failing that, however, a modest first step might be to restate depreciation expense to reflect the higher construction costs of recently completed plant. A suggested procedure would be to depreciate the same proportion of plant facilities each year as at present, but to price the depreciation provision (expressed in units of physical plant) at the unit cost of the facilities most recently placed in service and not theretofore depreciated. Under such a "last-in, first-out" (LIFO) approach, depreciation charges would be significantly increased, but not as much as under full replacement cost accounting.

While not departing from the use of historical costs, the LIFO depreciation approach would tend to reflect higher construction costs already sustained and technological changes already embodied in completed plant.

LIFO depreciation was discussed at the 1975 stockholders' meeting. It would have increased the Company's 1976 depreciation expense from $197 million to $345 million, but the increase would be inappropriate unless allowed for tax and ratemaking purposes.

# HILTON HOTELS CORPORATION
## 1976 Annual Report Excerpt

*[10] Information on Replacement Cost (Unaudited) and
Fair Market Value of Property and Equipment*

As part of the Company's compliance with the Securities
and Exchange Commission's Accounting Series Release
190 (ASR 190), the Company had appraisals made of each of
its major wholly-owned and 17% to 50% owned properties.
The appraisals were made by Joseph J. Blake and Associates,
Inc., Valuation Counselors, Inc., and Real Estate Research
Corporation.

Although ASR 190 requires replacement cost data only for
depreciable property, the appraisers were requested also
to estimate the fair market value of the same properties as
well as that of the underlying land.

The replacement cost information represents estimates
of the cost to be incurred at December 31, 1976, if such
assets were replaced at that time. The replacement cost of
buildings, leaseholds and improvements was developed by
estimating construction costs to obtain comparable facilities; replacement cost for furniture and equipment, representing all personal property, was arrived at by applying
current furnishing costs per room to the existing number of
rooms. Replacement cost was developed by the use of indices, units of capacity, and component costing techniques.

Fair market value is frequently referred to as the price
at which a willing seller would sell and a willing buyer
would buy, neither being compelled to sell or buy. Fair market value was arrived at by calculating the present worth
of estimated future income streams accruing to the owner
utilizing rates of return ranging from 9 to 12 percent, and
various terms of financing, and conditions of sale and
profitability factors with respect to individual properties.
It was assumed that the buyers of the hotel properties would
retain management companies to operate the properties
and therefore $3,965,000 in annual pro-forma management
fees were deducted from the estimated future earnings
stream used to value the hotel properties. No management
fee was assumed for the Las Vegas properties since it is not
customary for owners of hotel-casinos to employ third
party management firms.

In the development of the information on replacement
cost and fair market value, various critical estimates and
assumptions were made. Although these estimates and
assumptions are believed to be reasonable in the circumstances, they nevertheless are subjective judgments of management and the appraisers relevant only to the time as of
which the information is furnished. The resulting estimated
replacement cost and fair market value information may
vary therefore from actual future replacement cost or fair
market value because of changed conditions.

The basic replacement cost data presented does not take
into consideration any operating cost savings or additional
revenues which may result from the replacement of existing
properties with properties having improved technology and
facilities. If the Company's income producing properties
were to be replaced in the manner assumed in the calculation of replacement cost of existing properties, many costs
other than depreciation, such as labor costs, repairs and
maintenance and heat, light and power, would be affected.
Although these probable cost changes cannot be quantified
with any precision, the current level of operating costs
other than depreciation and possibly property taxes may be
reduced as a result of the technological improvements
assumed in the hypothetical replacement.

Replacement cost depreciation was calculated on the
straight-line method generally over the historical depreciation lives. The exceptions were those properties which had
been operating prior to the time they were acquired by the

Company. Such properties are depreciated for replacement
cost purposes as new property from the date of construction including the estimated remaining life at December 31,
1976, versus a shorter term as used property for historical
cost purposes.

The following table represents the summary of data described above as of December 31, 1976:

*Hilton Hotels Corporation and Subsidiaries*

| (In thousands of dollars) | Historical Cost | Estimated Replacement Cost Exclusive of Land (Unaudited) | Estimated Fair Market Value Inclusive of Land |
|---|---|---|---|
| December 31, 1976 | | | |
| Depreciable property, buildings, leaseholds and improvements | $233,851 | 634,029 | |
| Furniture and equipment | 77,041 | 118,399 | |
| Total | 310,892 | 752,428 | |
| Less accumulated depreciation | 130,651 | 422,689 | |
| Net depreciable property | 180,241 | 329,739 | |
| Land | 56,720 | | |
| Net property | 236,961 | | 466,937 |
| Reconciliation to Consolidated Balance Sheet: | | | |
| Add operating equipment at cost | 1,908 | | |
| Less cost to acquire leasehold interest in the Waldorf Corporation included in above costs, note 9 | (35,000) | | |
| Total as shown on the accompanying consolidated balance sheet | $203,869 | | |
| Year ended December 31, 1976 Depreciation expense | $ 16,499 | 27,302 | |

*Hilton Hotels Corporation and Subsidiaries
17% to 50% Owned Companies*

| (In thousands of dollars) | Historical Cost | Estimated Replacement Cost Exclusive of Land (Unaudited) | Estimated Fair Market Value Inclusive of Land |
|---|---|---|---|
| December 31, 1976 | | | |
| Depreciable property, buildings, leaseholds and improvements | $125,353 | 238,100 | |
| Furniture and equipment | 21,412 | 33,247 | |
| Total | 146,765 | 271,347 | |
| Less accumulated depreciaton | 47,250 | 101,789 | |
| Net depreciable property | 99,515 | 169,558 | |
| Land | 34,426 | | |
| Net property | $133,941 | | 250,708 |
| Year ended December 31, 1976 Depreciation expense | $ 6,531 | 9,969 | |

The excess of the estimated fair market value of wholly-
owned and 17% to 50% owned property over historical
cost is $346,743,000. The presentation of this information
does not imply management's intent to replace or sell existing properties.

# KOPPERS COMPANY
## 1976 Annual Report Excerpt

### 14. Replacement Costs (Unaudited)

In order to give investors some understanding of the impact of inflation on the operations and financial status of corporations, the Securities and Exchange Commission now requires that large, publicly held companies provide estimates for the effect on financial statements of the current replacement cost of inventories and productive capacity.

Koppers management has consistently recognized that financial statements in the Company's reports to shareholders, which are based on historical costs, do not reflect the effects of inflation. It should be recognized, however, that there are limitations upon the usefulness of the replacement cost information that follows. The required information is not precise and does not give a complete or balanced presentation of the impact of inflation. It does not necessarily reflect management's intent to replace existing inventory or productive facilities. Neither does it reflect any operating cost savings that can result from replacement of existing production facilities with assets of improved technology or of higher productivity.

Management strongly concurs with the SEC's intention that the following replacement cost data not be used to indicate the effect of inflation upon the Company's net income. Simplistic use of the data to restate net income could be greatly misleading. Because of the many unresolved conceptual problems involved, the Company has not attempted to quantify the total impact of inflation. Further, consideration of the following replacement cost information alone does not recognize the customary relationship between cost changes and changes in selling price to maintain profit margins. Competitive conditions permitting, the Company expects to modify its future selling prices to recognize cost changes.

The following section presents the replacement cost information required by the SEC. The final section discloses the methodology used to compute the estimates.

| | ($ Thousands) | |
| --- | --- | --- |
| | Historical Cost From 1976 Balance Sheet | Estimated Replacement Cost |
| If the Company were to totally replace its year-end 1976 inventories, how much would it cost? Inventories, as of 12/31/76 . . . . . . . . . . . . . . . . . | $157,554 | $ 214,000 |

What would 1976 cost of sales have been if the replacement cost of the inventory used at the time of sale had been the basis for determining production costs?

| | | |
| --- | --- | --- |
| Cost of sales, (excluding depreciation) for the year ended 12/31/76 . . . . . . . . . . | $919,954 | $ 921,000 |

What would it have cost at year-end 1976 to replace the Company's productive capacity (its fixed assets)?

| | | |
| --- | --- | --- |
| Machinery, equipment and buildings . . . . . . . . | $522,265 | $1,092,000 |

What would have been the depreciated cost of those assets?

| | | |
| --- | --- | --- |
| Less accumulated depreciation . . . . . . . . . . . . | 256,369 | 687,000 |
| | $265,896 | $ 405,000 |

What would 1976 depreciation expense have been if it had been calculated using the average replacement cost of productive capacity?

| | | |
| --- | --- | --- |
| Depreciation, for the year ended 12/31/76 . . . | $ 35,198 | $ 75,000 |

The Company cautions that the above replacement cost data are not the current value of existing property, plant, equipment and inventories. Rather, they represent the Company's estimates of the costs of replacement that would have been incurred at December 31, 1976 under the hypothetical assumption that such assets had been replaced in total at that time. Accordingly, the difference between the historical cost and replacement cost does not represent additional book value of the Company's common stock.

### METHODOLOGY
#### Inventories

The estimated replacement cost of raw materials has been based on standard cost which approximates current cost. Finished goods and work-in-process have been estimated on the basis of standard costs that approximate current costs and include current material, labor, and overhead variances as well as an allocation of replacement cost depreciation of buildings, machinery and equipment determined on a straight-line basis.

## Cost of Sales

For those inventories accounted for on a last-in, first-out (LIFO) basis, estimated replacement cost of sales, exclusive of depreciation, was based on applying the LIFO method of costing ending inventories adjusted for any decrements during the year. The turnover rate of inventories accounted for on a first-in, first-out (FIFO) basis is fast enough to approximate replacement cost. No attempt has been made to quantify the effects of improved efficiency or reduced operating costs that might occur if manufacturing facilities were replaced.

## Property, Plant and Equipment

The estimated replacement costs for approximately 80-85% of the Company's property, plant and equipment were developed on a functional pricing basis. This utilized updated costs of recent applications of present-day technology. The estimated costs of replacing the remaining 15-20% of total assets, where there has been little or no significant technological obsolescence over the years, were appropriately indexed by year of acquisition at then current price levels.

Replacement cost data have not been provided for mineral reserves, as they are specifically excluded by the SEC from this determination. Depletion expense for mineral reserves is not required to be calculated on a replacement cost basis. Therefore, in accordance with current guidelines, depletion expense has been included in the replacement cost data for inventories and cost of sales at the historical cost amount.

In addition, no replacement cost information has been provided for land, as it is not consumed in the production process. No replacement cost data have been given for timber obtained under long-term Crown leases (Canada) or long-term cutting rights agreements (United States), as current costs for timber removed are matched against current revenue from the sale of such timber.

| | ($ Thousands) | |
| --- | --- | --- |
| | Fixed Assets | Accumulated Depreciation and Depletion |
| Totals as shown in the accompanying Consolidated Financial Statements ........... | $570,552 | $265,355 |
| Less amounts for which replacement cost data have not been provided: | | |
| Mineral reserves ........................ | 13,063 | 2,016 |
| Depletable timber properties ............... | 21,242 | 6,970 |
| Land at cost ........................... | 13,982 | — |
| Historical amounts for which replacement cost data have been provided ............... | $522,265 | $256,369 |

Accumulated depreciation of productive capacity at year end and the provision for depreciation for the year related to the replacement cost of such assets were calculated using straight-line depreciation rates based upon the estimated service lives and salvage values used for financial accounting purposes.This was computed by applying a general or specific index to year-end historical cost balances for cost and accumulated depreciation and then recomputing a ratio of accumulated depreciation to historical cost.

## TRANS UNION CORPORATION
## 1976 Annual Report Excerpt

### Replacement Cost Data (unaudited)

Disclosure of certain replacement cost data is required by regulations of the Securities and Exchange Commission. These disclosures are not intended to reflect current values. No uniform concepts or procedures have been prescribed for determining such data and thus the information reported herein is not necessarily comparable with similar data reported by others. The methods used in our calculations are explained below. By necessity, these methods were subjective and therefore the resulting replacement cost disclosures should not be considered as precise, but rather as rough approximations. While management believes the methods used are reasonable, any number of other methods, which also could be judged as reasonable, could have been employed and such other methods would have produced a variety of different results.

Replacement cost information does not reflect a complete picture of the effect of inflation on the Company's business since it does not consider the inflation hedge provided by leverage and deferral of taxes. Also, a major impact of inflation on the Company's business is generally reflected in the historical cost financial statements through higher interest, maintenance and operating costs.

Following is a summary of the procedures used to estimate the required replacement cost data:

### Rail Car Lease Fleet

The Company's rail car leasing business involves the providing of services (e.g. maintenance, administration and risk of ownership) and capital (e.g. financing the cost of rail cars) to shippers. This latter part of the business involves a substantial investment in the Company's rail car lease fleet. Since the Company has no requirement for shipping services itself, it perceives the capacity of this fleet to be its revenue earning ability, rather than any measure of physical volume.

The replacement cost of the rail car fleet is deemed to be that value which the Company would be willing to invest in new cars to obtain an income stream at a level equivalent to that which the fleet is currently earning. In practice, replacements of retired cars are not made unless a satisfactory rate of return is obtainable under an acceptable lease arrangement with a credit-worthy lessee. The techniques used to determine replacement costs were based on the decision making process applied to new car additions and involve discounted cash flow calculations applied to lease rentals less executory costs such as maintenance.

Rail cars leased in under long-term financing leases were included in the calculations and rail cars leased out under similar arrangements were excluded.

### Ocean Vessel Fleet

The replacement cost of three U.S. flag LASH vessels was estimated by trending historical construction costs, before deducting actual construction subsidy received, with the domestic shipbuilding index prepared by the Maritime Administration, and then deducting an estimated construction subsidy calculated at the current rate. The replacement cost of capitalized interest during construction was estimated to be approximately equivalent to historical cost amounts. The replacement cost of LASH barges was estimated based on recent actual barge costs. Replacement cost for five general cargo C-4 vessels (which are fully depreciated) was not estimated because these vessels will not be replaced when economies of operation finally require their retirement. Replacement cost for two tankers bareboat chartered out through 1994-95 is not required because such charters are equivalent to finance leases. Replacement cost data for the Company's remaining vessels is not required in 1976 because all such vessels are foreign flag vessels.

### Building and Leasehold Improvements

The replacement cost of buildings was estimated using the 1976 median U.S. construction cost per square foot for several general categories of buildings as published by Robert Snow Means Company, Inc. Leasehold improvements were not material and therefore replacement costs were assumed to be equivalent to historical costs.

### Equipment

The replacement cost of equipment was estimated using a combination of various Bureau of Labor Statistics (B.L.S.) wholesale price indexes, insurance appraisals and, in the case of equipment belonging to one operating unit, current price quotations. The B.L.S. wholesale price index considered to be the most appropriate for the equipment at each particular location was selected. Such indexes were used to trend historical costs or past insurance appraisal values to obtain the estimated current replacement cost for the equipment of the applicable location. Such procedures generally yield an estimate of reproduction cost which management believes provides a reasonable approximation of replacement cost for these assets, given the relative immateriality of such assets and the imprecision inherent in the data.

For some locations where historical costs were used for trending, the average age of the equipment account was estimated by dividing the annual depreciation provision into the balance of accumulated depreciation. For other locations, actual aging of the equipment account was available for trending.

## Inventories

Book inventories are determined on the basis of first-in, first-out cost, which is considered to be a reasonable approximation of replacement cost, considering the inventory turnover period and the relatively immaterial cost changes occuring during this period.

The replacement cost of inventories related to long-term contracts was not determined because of the close relationship between the historical cost of such inventories and contractual revenues. Replacement cost data for long-term contracts is generally not relevant as a measure of the effect of inflation because of this relationship.

The replacement cost of inventories located outside North America and the European Economic Community was not required for 1976. The replacement cost of land held for resale has not been estimated because the Company does not intend to replace this land.

## Depreciation

The replacement cost depreciation expense for 1976 was estimated based on the average replacement cost of the related assets as of the beginning and end of the year. Lives and methods used were the same as those used for books. Replacement cost depreciation estimates were made only for those asset categories for which replacement cost estimates were made.

## Cost of Sales and Services

The replacement cost of raw materials and purchased products included in cost of sales was estimated by trending the applicable historical cost of sales with specific B.L.S. wholesale price indexes adjusted for inventory turnover. The most appropriate B.L.S. wholesale price index(es) for each major operating unit was (were) selected for this purpose. Corresponding Canadian indexes were used for Canadian operating units.

The replacement cost of condominium sales was estimated by trending historical costs with the construction index for buildings prepared by Engineering News Record adjusted for inventory turnover.

The replacement cost depreciation expense included in cost of sales and services is an estimated portion of replacement cost depreciation calculated as described above.

The replacement cost of manufacturing labor and overhead charged first to inventory and then to cost of sales was estimated based on changes in hourly labor rates and inventory turnover. The replacement cost of items charged directly to cost of services (e.g. certain rail car maintenance and vessel operating expenses) was estimated to be equivalent to historical cost.

For the reasons discussed above under inventory, replacement cost was not estimated for long-term contract sales. Nor was replacement cost of sales and services estimated for operating units outside North America and the European Economic Community. These latter geographic exclusions include the operations of foreign flag vessels.

Replacement cost of sales and services was reduced by $1,500,000 which was the estimated fuel savings U.S. flag vessels would enjoy if replaced with vessels powered with the most efficient engines now available.

Replacement cost of land sales has not been estimated because the Company does not intend to replace this land.

## Required Data

The estimated replacement cost data and its historical cost equivalent are as follows:

|  | Replacement Cost Basis | Historical Cost Basis |
|---|---|---|
|  | (Dollars in millions) | |
| As of December 31, 1976— | | |
| Productive capacity | | |
| Cost ................... | $1,214.7 | $1,096.1 |
| Depreciated cost ........ | 854.2 | 787.2 |
| Inventories ................. | 63.9 | 62.9 |
| Year ended December 31, 1976— | | |
| Cost of sales and services (including $43,500,000 and $39,200,000 of depreciation, respectively) .............. | 260.5 | 254.7 |
| Depreciation included in selling, general and administrative expense ..... | 2.6 | 2.0 |

## Reconciliation to Historical Cost Amounts

The reconciliation of the historical cost amounts reflected above to those reported in the accompanying financial statements for 1976, is as follows:

|  | Productive Capacity | Inventories | Cost of Sales and Services |
|---|---|---|---|
|  | (Dollars in millions) | | |
| Gross amount for which replacement costs were estimated | $1,096.1 | $62.9 | $254.7 |
| Add/(Deduct) assets or related costs— | | | |
| Located outside North America and EEC ........ | 125.9 | 20.2 | 160.1 |
| Finance leases in ... | (28.6) | — | (1.1) |
| Finance leases out .. | 83.9 | — | — |
| Long-term contracts . | — | 14.6 | 101.7 |
| Not to be replaced .. | 14.2 | — | 12.1 |
| Construction in progress ........ | 20.1 | — | — |
| Amounts reported in accompanying financial statements . | $1,311.6 | $97.7 | $527.5 |

The balance sheet amounts for productive capacity are comprised of the following:

| | |
|---|---|
| Rail car lease fleet .. | $  890.8 |
| Ocean vessel fleet .. | 258.9 |
| Buildings .......... | 53.8 |
| Equipment ........ | 108.1 |
| | $1,311.6 |

# Pronouncements
## Governing Generally Accepted Accounting Principles

(There are about 20 FASB *Interpretations* of the above *Bulletins, Opinions,* and FASB *Statements.*)

**Note:** This list shows pronouncements issued through July 1, 1977.

### Establishing Generally Accepted Accounting Principles: A Brief History

Prior to 1933, there was little regulation of the form and content of published financial statements. The New York Stock Exchange sought to impose certain requirements on listed companies, but their requirements were minimal and not always effective. Basically, the individual companies decided what kind of financial statements, if any, to publish. Some companies, such as U.S. Steel, issued elaborate financial statements audited by a large accounting firm. Other companies only rarely communicated with shareholders; we suspect that some shareholders' only communications from the company were the periodic dividend checks. As a result of the stock market crash of 1929 and certain financial reporting scandals, the Congress enacted the Securities Act of 1933. In that act, Congress in effect gave the power to set generally accepted accounting principles (GAAP) to the Federal Trade Commission. The Securities Exchange Act of 1934 was passed in the following year creating the Securities and Exchange Commission and transferring the power to establish GAAP to it.

Since 1934, the Congress has been relatively silent on accounting matters. In the Revenue Act of 1971, the Congress became involved in the acceptable accounting methods for the investment credit. In 1975, the Congress passed a law requiring that there be uniform accounting standards for the extractive industries by the end of 1977. In recent years, certain legislators (notably Senator Metcalf of Montana and Representative Moss of California) have, on behalf of Congress, taken an increasing interest in accounting and the setting of accounting principles.

*The SEC*

The SEC speaks on accounting matters through Accounting Series Releases (ASR's). There are now over 200 ASR's; the rate of issuance of ASR's has recently accelerated. (ASR No. 150, for example, was issued in 1973.) By the late 1930's the SEC discovered that it had plenty to do without seeking to establish generally accepted accounting principles. (Moreover, we note that most SEC commissioners have been lawyers and they may not have had a taste for setting accounting principles.) At any rate, in 1938 the SEC (in ASR No. 4) delegated most of the responsibility for setting generally accepted accounting principles to the accounting profession. (The SEC stated that it would not accept financial statements in which the accounting procedures lacked "substantial authoritative support". This was generally interpreted to mean that the accounting profession was to set GAAP.)

The SEC is still legislatively charged with the responsiblity for setting the accounting standards for reports, but it has tended to let the Financial Accounting Standards Board (and its predecessors) take the lead. Often, however, the SEC decides that readers of financial statements will find certain additional disclosures helpful and will require companies to supply the information. These required disclosures most often take the form of footnotes; the amount of reported net income or asset totals is not usually affected. An example of such supplementary disclosure is the required replacement cost data called for in ASR No. 190 (1976), which are discussed in this book in the section on *Accounting for Changing Prices*.

### The Committee on Accounting Procedure (1939-1959)

The accounting profession responded to the mandate of ASR No. 4 through its professional organization, now named the American Institute of Certified Public Accountants (AICPA or the Institute). In 1939 the Institute enlarged its Committee on Accounting Procedure (CAP) and gave that Committee the responsibility determining and promulgating pronouncements on GAAP. The CAP spoke on accounting matters through *Accounting Research Bulletins* (ARB's). ARB No. 43 summarized and updated by subject the first 42 ARB's; ARB's 43–51 are listed at the start of this section.

By the 1950's, the CAP found itself struggling to set GAAP without the benefit of any underlying axioms or fundamentals of accounting and without a substantial research staff. Increasingly, the CAP had to decide issues without having a firm theoretical basis for choosing among accounting alternatives. The AICPA decided to replace the CAP with another group and to provide that group with a substantial research staff.

### The Accounting Principles Board (1959-1973)

The Accounting Principles Board (APB) began its operations in 1959. It asked the AICPA's Director of Research to commission studies (called *Accounting Research Studies;* there were eventually 15) of the fundamental foundations of accounting, on which APB judgments could be based. In 1962 Professors Robert T. Sprouse and Maurice Moonitz produced an Accounting Research Study entitled *A Tentative Set of Broad Accounting Principles for Business Enterprises,* which was written to be the fundamental statement that the APB had sought. This particular statement advocated, among other things, that the basis of valuation in accounting ought to be some measure of current value, rather than historical cost. The APB was aghast. It reacted by issuing APB *Statement No. 1* (see the list above) in 1962 which said that the results of the Sprouse-Moonitz study "are too radically different from present generally accepted accounting principles for acceptance at this time."

The APB decided to continue to make pronouncements on GAAP without a fundamental statement of accounting theory. The APB spoke on GAAP through *Opinions*. The list of thirty-one APB *Opinions* is shown above. Note that *Opinion No. 6* affirmed that the outstanding ARB's were to be considered binding until explicitly superceded. The *Opinions* of the APB presented accounting requirements, while the APB *Statements* tended to give accounting suggestions. (Shell Oil Company, but few others, has followed the suggestions of *Statement No. 3* in preparing general price level adjusted supplementary financial statements. These are reproduced in our section on *Inflation Accounting* on pages 96–97.)

Just as the CAP had foundered before it, the APB began to have difficulty in acting because it lacked a fundamental set of accounting principles. Moreover, the organization structure of the APB (part-time members whose paid employment was elsewhere) became politically untenable. By 1970, it was clear that the APB could not function effectively.

### The Wheat and Trueblood Committees

In 1970, a committee, now known as the Wheat Committee (after its chairman, Francis M. Wheat), was formed to devise an alternative to the APB. It devised the structure of the Financial Accounting Standards Board, which is discussed below. Another committee, now known as the Trueblood Committee (after its chairman, Robert M. Trueblood), was formed to make a statement of the objectives of financial statements so that the FASB could have a set of fundamental guiding principles on which to base its *Statements*. The Trueblood Committee Report (*Objectives of Financial Statements*) was issued in 1973.

### The Financial Accounting Standards Board (1973-     )

The Financial Accounting Standards Board (FASB) began operations in 1973. It consists of seven full-time members. The FASB acts in the following fashion:
1. It places an accounting problem on its agenda.
2. It forms a task force to study the problem.
3. With task force approval, the FASB issues a *Discussion Memorandum* on the accounting issue. This is a neutral document discussing all sides of the issue. The FASB asks for comments, on this document and the issue.

**4.** A public hearing is held at which interested parties may comment on the *Discussion Memorandum.*

**5.** As a result of comments, the FASB may issue an *Exposure Draft* indicating the accounting rule that the FASB proposes to issue. The draft is circulated and the FASB asks for comments on it. As a result of the comments, the FASB might issue a revised *Exposure Draft,* as it did in the development of a new standard (No. 13) for lease accounting.

**6.** The FASB may then issue a *Statement of Financial Accounting Standards,* containing new accounting rules.

**7.** From time to time, the FASB issues *Interpretations* of previously issued ARB's APB *Opinions* and FASB *Statements.* (The FASB will send a current list of its pronouncements on request. The address is Publications Division; FASB; High Ridge Park; Stamford, Connecticut 06905.)

One of the items on the original FASB agenda was known as the "Conceptual Framework" project. The purpose of this project is to react to the Trueblood Committee Report and to come up with the accounting fundamentals to be used as a guide in the setting of GAAP. The FASB issued a *Discussion Memorandum* on this subject in 1976. It is likely to be some time before an Exposure Draft on this subject is issued. Meanwhile, the FASB operates like its predecessors, pronouncing on accounting principles in an *ad hoc* fashion. Much of its work, however, has been of a crisis-resolving nature. For example, the near-insolvency of certain real estate ventures provided the FASB with the problem of specifying the proper accounting treatment for banks who had made loans to these ventures and who had renegotiated the loans. Legislation mentioned earlier has required the efforts of the FASB for more than a year in seeking to prescribe uniform accounting standards in the extractive industries.

*Development of Generally Accepted Accounting Principles*

Certain problems in accounting will not stay solved. If you scan the list of pronouncements given at the beginning of this section, you will see that some topics recur. The following discussion traces the development of some of these problems. We do not attempt to give all the examples of this sort that might be supplied.

*Pension Plans.* Note that *ARB No. 47* and APB *Opinion No. 8* both mention pension plans. This is a complex technical issue for which the accounting is still not satisfactory in our opinion. (For a glimpse at why GAAP is still not satisfactory, read our note explaining General Electric's pension plan in GE's note 4 on page 37 of the annual report.) The FASB issued an *Interpretation* of APB *Opinion No. 8* in 1974, a *Discussion Memorandum* on this subject in 1975, and an impending *Exposure Draft* has been mentioned in press releases; the study of the topic continues.

*Earnings Per Share.* ARB No. 49 first dealt with this subject in 1958. It was superceded in 1966 by APB *Opinion No. 9,* which in turn was superceded on this subject by a lengthy APB *Opinion No. 15* issued in 1969. There have been several subsequent official interpretations issued on the subject. This is an extremely complex issue. We have not illustrated the complications in this book, but see the Glossary at *primary earnings per share* and *fully diluted earnings per share.*

*Business Combinations.* Note that *ARB No. 48* and APB *Opinion No. 16* both address business combinations, such as the merger of General Electric Company and Utah International described in GE's note 1 and our explanation. The accounting here is still not satisfactory in our opinion. In 1976, the FASB issued a *Discussion Memorandum* on this subject, but further action will probably await decisions on the conceptual framework.

*Contingencies.* Contingencies, events that might occur, present an accounting problem; see the Glossary at *contingent liability* and see GE's balance sheet at its note 20. Both *ARB No. 50* and FASB *Statement No. 5* address the problem. The current situation seems relatively quiet.

*Investment Credit.* The APB in *Opinion No. 2* required the *deferral* method (see the Glossary). Later, the SEC in ASR 96 indicated that both the deferral and the *flow-through* methods would be acceptable to it. The APB then reversed itself in *Opinion No. 4,* saying that the flow-through method was, in fact, also acceptable. Subsequently, the APB on several occasions indicated it favored the deferral method, but could not enlist sufficient support to issue an Opinion.

*Leases.* The accounting for long-term noncancelable leases was, in our opinion, the single largest embarrassment to the accounting profession between 1964 and 1977. In 1964, the APB in *Opinion No. 5* stated that the tenant (lessee) had not, in effect, purchased an asset and undertaken a liability, when it signed a long-term noncancelable lease. (See the Glossary at *lease, financing lease,* and *operating lease.*) In APB *Opinion No. 7,* issued in 1966, the Board said that the "landlord" (manufacturer or lessor) had, in fact, sold an asset in return for a long-term receivable when it signed a long-term noncancelable lease. Thus there were hundreds of millions of dollars worth of assets (notably airplanes and retail store sites) that were not assets on anyone's books. In its very last *Opinion* in 1973 *(No. 31),*

116116116

116116116

the APB called for certain footnote disclosure by lessees. Finally, in late 1976 the FASB in *Statement No. 13* required symmetric accounting by lessors and lessees. Companies have until 1981 in many cases, however, to bring their financial statements into compliance with respect to leases signed before *Statement No. 13* took effect.

The grace period (applicable only to leases already signed by December 1976) between 1976 (passage of FASB *Statement No. 13*) and 1981 (final date for compliance) arises because of various covenants companies may have entered into. For example, a company might agree in a bond indenture not to let the debt-equity ratio become larger than, say, 60 percent. If the debt-equity ratio becomes larger than 60 percent, then the bond becomes payable immediately, rather than at maturity. Most of these covenants were entered into in good faith while APB *Opinion No. 5* was in effect. Both the borrower and the lender knew that the borrower might sign leases (as lessor) that would not appear on the balance sheet. If the FASB required the immediate recognition of these leases on the balance sheet, then the bonds might become immediately payable, in spite of the intentions of the parties to the loan at the time the loan was made. The FASB granted the grace period to allow borrowers and lenders to solve these and related problems. The SEC re-entered the picture in mid-1977 by granting the grace period only to companies with restrictive loan covenants. The SEC requires companies to show immediately the effects in the financial statements of all leases, if there is no adverse effect on loan agreements. (Companies continue to agree, in borrowing or otherwise, to covenants relating to accounting numbers or ratios. The wise company specifies that the accounting principles to be used in computing the number or ratio be the principles in effect at the time the agreement is made, not at the time the statements are issued.)

# Accounting Magic

Generally accepted accounting principles permit alternative treatments for certain accounting events. Which treatment a company chooses will affect the financial statements that the company issues. In this section, we show how alternative accounting treatments of identical events can lead to reported income figures that are perhaps surprisingly different from each other.[1]

## The Scenario

On January 1, two companies start in business. The two companies are exactly alike in all respects except for their accounting treatment of several events. Conservative Company chooses the accounting alternatives that will minimize its reported income while High Flyer Company chooses the alternatives that will maximize its reported income. Both companies choose, where permitted, accounting methods that will minimize income taxes. The following events occur during the year.

1. Both companies issue common stock to raise the funds necessary to commence a merchandising business.
2. Both companies purchase $7,000,000 worth of equipment that is assumed to have zero salvage value and a depreciable life of 10 years.
3. Both companies make the following purchases of merchandise inventory:

| Date | Units Purchased | | Unit Price | | Cost of Purchase |
|---|---|---|---|---|---|
| January 1 ........................... | 85,000 | @ | $60 | = | $ 5,100,000 |
| May 1 ............................... | 95,000 | @ | $63 | = | 5,985,000 |
| September 1 ........................ | 100,000 | @ | $68 | = | 6,800,000 |
| Total ............................... | 280,000 | | | | $17,885,000 |

4. During the year, both companies sell 210,000 units at an average price of $100 each so that each realizes sales revenues of $21,000,000.
5. During the year, both companies have selling, general and administrative expenses, excluding officers' salaries, of $3,350,000.
6. At the end of the year, both the companies "pay" bonuses worth $120,000 to officers for jobs well done in addition to the $350,000 paid to them during the year in salaries. Conservative Company pays cash bonuses of $120,000 while High Flyer Company awards options for purchasing shares of common stock to its officers. Comparable options have market value of $120,000.

## Accounting Alternatives

At the end of the year both companies prepare financial statements. Both must decide how to report the various events that occurred during the year. The following decisions made by each company are all generally acceptable.

---

[1] The title for this example, "Accounting Magic,' and indeed the inspiration for its preparation come from an article by Leonard Spacek, "Business Success Requires an Understanding of Unsolved Problems of Accounting and Financial Reporting," Arthur Andersen Pamphlet (September 25, 1959), pp. 19-28. Since the time Spacek prepared his illustration, there have been changes in generally accepted accounting principles, but several of the alternatives we illustrate were illustrated by him, too.

*Inventory Cost Flow Assumption.* Since not all goods purchased during the year were sold, each company must make an assumption about the cost of goods sold to be shown on the income statement and, simultaneously, about the cost of ending inventory to be shown on the balance sheet. Conservative Company makes a last-in, first-out (LIFO) cost flow assumption while High Flyer Company makes a first-in, first-out (FIFO) assumption. Since the beginning inventory is zero, the cost of goods available for sale by each company is equal to the purchases of $17,885,000 during the year. Both companies have 70,000 units in ending inventory. Conservative Company, using LIFO, reports a cost of goods sold of $13,685,000 (= $17,885,000 – 70,000 × $60) while High Flyer Company reports a cost of goods sold of $13,125,000 (= $17,885,000 – 70,000 × $68.) Income tax regulations require a company to use LIFO in its financial statements if it uses LIFO for its tax return. High Flyer Company desires not to use LIFO in its financial statements and therefore foregoes the savings in taxes from using LIFO on its tax returns.

*Depreciation.* Conservative Company decides to depreciate its equipment using the double-declining-balance method on both its tax return and its financial statements. High Flyer Company decides to use the straight-line method in reporting income to stockholders but the double-declining-balance method in its tax return. Conservative Company therefore reports depreciation

### ACCOUNTING MAGIC COMPARATIVE INCOME STATEMENTS
#### For the Year Ending December 31

| | Conservative Company | | High Flyer Company | |
| --- | --- | --- | --- | --- |
| | Financial Statement | Tax Return | Financial Statement | Tax Return |
| | *(Amounts in Thousands Except Per Share Amounts)* | | | |
| Sales Revenues | $21,000 | $21,000 | $21,000 | $21,000 |
| **Expenses** | | | | |
| Cost of Goods Sold | $13,685 | $13,685 | $13,125 | $13,125 |
| Depreciation on Equipment | 1,400 | 1,400 | 700 | 1,400[b] |
| **Officers' Compensation:** | | | | |
| Salaries | 350 | 350 | 350 | 350 |
| Cash Bonuses | 120 | 120 | — | — |
| Stock Options | — | — | 0 | 0 |
| Other Selling, General and Administrative Expenses | 3,350 | 3,350 | 3,350 | 3,350 |
| Expenses before Income Taxes | $18,905 | $18,905 | $17,525 | $18,225 |
| Income before Taxes | $ 2,095 | $ 2,095 | $ 3,475 | $ 2,775 |
| Income Tax Expense[a] | 922 | | 955 | |
| Net Income | $ 1,173 | | $ 2,520 | |
| Earnings Per Share in Dollars (500,000 Shares Outstanding) | $ 2.35 | | $ 5.04 | |

[a]Computation of Income Tax Expense:

| | | | | |
| --- | --- | --- | --- | --- |
| Income Before Taxes | $ 2,095 | $ 2,095 | $ 3,475 | $ 2,775 |
| Income Tax on Current Income (20 percent of first $25,000 plus 22 percent of next $25,000 plus 48 percent of remainder) | $ 992 | $ 992 | $ 1,655 | $ 1,319 |
| Less: Tax Credit for Investment in Equipment | 70 | 700 | 700 | 700 |
| Income Tax Expense | $ 922 | | $ 955 | |
| Income Tax Currently Payable | | $ 292 | | $ 619 |
| Deferred Investment Tax Credit ($700 – $70) | $ 630 | | | |
| [b]Income Taxes Deferred by Timing Difference for Depreciation (.48 × $700) | | | $ 336 | |

expense of $1,400,000 (= 2 × 1/10 × $7,000,000) while High Flyer Company reports depreciation expense of $700,000 (= 1/10 × $7,000,000) to stockholders and $1,400,000 on its tax return.

*Officers' Bonuses.* Conservative Company reports expense of $120,000 for the cash bonuses it pays while High Flyer Company reports no expense for the stock options granted. Under generally accepted accounting principles, the fair market value of qualified stock options granted to employees is not shown as an expense. (When the options are exercised, there will be an accounting transaction but the entry will record merely the cash received at the time of exercise.)

*Investment Tax Credit.* Since both companies purchased long-term assets costing $7,000,000, each is entitled to a reduction, or "tax credit," of $700,000 (= .10 × $7,000,000) in its tax bill for the year.[2] On its financial statements to stockholders, Conservative Company chooses to report the benefits of that tax reduction over the ten-year life of the equipment that gave rise to the tax reduction *(deferral method,* explained in the Glossary). On its financial statements to stockholders, High Flyer reports the entire benefit of the tax reduction in the first year *(flow-through method,* explained in the Glossary).

## Published Income Statements

*Income Tax Calculation.* Because Conservative Company reports the same revenues and expenses on both its financial statements and income tax return, its taxable income is the same as reported income before taxes. High Flyer Company shows larger deductions from revenues on the income tax return than it reports to stockholders and one of these differences—for depreciation of equipment—is viewed as a timing difference. That is, in subsequent years, High Flyer Company may report smaller deductions on its tax return than it reports to stockholders. Consequently, High Flyer Company reports a deferred tax expense on its income statement and will show a deferred tax liability on its balance sheet.

The income statements for both companies are shown on the previous page. As a result of its conservative treatment of accounting alternatives, Conservative Company reports net income and earnings per share less than half of what High Flyer Company reports. Both companies used generally accepted accounting principles and each would receive a "clean" opinion from its auditor.

## Comparisons of Fund Flows

Until the time when the two companies paid their respective executive bonuses and income taxes, they were exactly alike in all economically significant respects. Because of the difference in executives' bonuses—Conservative Company paid cash, while High Flyer granted stock options with the same value—Conservative Company paid out $120,000 more cash than did High Flyer for this item. High Flyer Company, in order to report higher net income, had to pay income taxes $327,000 (= $619,000 – $292,000) larger than did Conservative Company. Thus, after tax payments, Conservative Company, in a real sense, is considerably better off than is High Flyer. Overall, then, Conservative Company ends the year with $207,000 (= $327,000 – $120,000) more cash, or other liquid net assets, than does High Flyer.

You might find it instructive to construct statements of changes in financial position for each of the two companies. If you use cash as the definition of funds, you will find that Conservative Company generates $207,000 more cash than does High Flyer. If you use working capital (= current assets – current liabilities) as the definition of funds, you will find that High Flyer generates $353,000 more funds than does Conservative Company. The difference between these two amounts, $560,000, arises from the different cost flow assumptions for inventory. High Flyer uses FIFO; its ending inventory is valued at $68 per unit. Conservative Company uses LIFO; its ending inventory is valued at $60 per unit. The difference in inventory valuation is $8 per unit. Since there are 70,000 more units in ending inventory than in beginning inventory, the difference in the increase in working capital over the increase in cash is $560,000 (= $8 × 70,000). Again, we see the major impact of the inventory flow assumption in times of changing prices on published financial statements.

---

[2]As this book goes to press, the percentage for the investment tax credit is 10 percent, but it changes from time to time. A larger rate will increase the difference between reported earnings of the two companies; a smaller rate will reduce the difference.

**Other Choices Not Illustrated**

The simple illustration for Conservative Company and High Flyer Company by no means exhausts the set of choices between alternative generally accepted accounting principles. Some of the other economic events that can be alternatively reported are briefly described next.

*Revenue Recognition on Long-Term Projects.* If a company engages in long-term projects, such as constructing buildings or machinery for others, it can report all income on the contract either at the time the contract is completed, which may be several years after work on the project commences (conservative), or it can report for each year during construction a portion of the expected income equal to the portion of the project that has been completed during the year.

*Treatment of Past and Prior Service Pension Costs.* Suppose that a company enacts a pension plan at the start of the year, or "sweetens" an already-existing plan, granting retroactive benefits to current employees. The company thus incurs *past service costs* under the new plan or *prior service costs* under the "sweetened" plan. Assume that the interest rate used for these purposes is six percent per year and that the present value of the past (or prior) service cost is $3,000,000. The conservative treatment of these costs for tax purposes, under the Pension Reform Act of 1974, would be to amortize and fund them over ten years, while charging income each year with the interest on the unamortized portion of the past (or prior) service costs. In the first year, the conservative treatment would show pension costs under the new law of $462,000 (= 1/10 × $3,000,000 + .06 × 9/10 × $3,000,000 = $300,000 + $162,000). The less conservative treatment would amortize and fund the past (or prior) service costs over thirty years, while charging income each year with the interest on the unamortized portion of the costs. The less conservative treatment would show pension costs in the first year of $274,000 (= 1/30 × $3,000,000 + .06 × 29/30 × $3,000,000 = $100,000 + $174,000). The more conservative company would show pension costs almost 70 percent larger than the less conservative company.

*Others.* Still other choices not explained here include:
(1) whether to apply the lower-of-cost-or-market valuation basis to individual items in inventory or to groups of items,
(2) whether to capitalize into building costs or to expense interest costs during construction,
(3) intercompany allocation of corporate income taxes,
(4) methods of accounting for franchise income,
(5) accounting for purchase discounts,
(6) treatment of overhead costs on self-constructed assets,
(7) methods of computing deferred income taxes,
(8) treatment of relocation costs,
(9) treatment of coupon redemptions,
(10) consolidation of finance subsidiaries, and
(11) consolidation of foreign subsidiaries.
Note that items (10) and (11) do not generally affect net income, but do affect balance sheet totals.

We think that this list of accounting alternatives is surprisingly limited given the current outcry from some sources about accounting choices.

# An Annual Report for the U.S. Government

On the following pages, we present a set of unaudited financial statements for the U.S. Government. The statements were prepared by the accounting firm of Arthur Andersen & Co. and, as will become apparent, they are based on Arthur Andersen's estimates in many cases. Estimation is necessary because for the most part, the federal government keeps its books on a cash basis, rather than on an accrual basis. Even the cash basis data are not presented by the government in the form of articulated, or linked, balance sheets and income statements. Thus, the Arthur Andersen statements are a significant move toward presenting the financial story of this most important institution in the same form that we are accustomed to seeing in corporate annual reports.

In constructing these financial statements, Arthur Andersen followed generally accepted accounting principles as used by corporations. Some of the weaknesses of GAAP are thereby pinpointed. Land is shown on the balance sheet at historical cost of about $7 billion. Footnote 7 points out that the current value of just a part of this land is about $30 billion.

Aside from these introductory remarks, we have included no further comments. We have not been able to improve upon Arthur Andersen's commentary in the footnotes to the financial statements. Some of the footnotes have been abbreviated or omitted to save space.

## ILLUSTRATIVE CONSOLIDATED FINANCIAL STATEMENTS

### UNITED STATES GOVERNMENT
### June 30, 1974 and 1973

For purposes of illustration, we have collected financial information currently available in several publications of the United States Government and have used this information as a basis for preparing consolidated financial statements of the United States Government in conventional format as of June 30, 1974 and 1973, and for the years then ended.

The amounts reflected in the following illustrative financial statements and notes thereto have not been audited by Arthur Andersen & Co., and accordingly, we do not express an opinion on them. Even though these financial statements may not be complete and accurate in all respects, they do provide the necessary background for discussion of some of the issues involved.

# UNITED STATES GOVERNMENT
## ILLUSTRATIVE CONSOLIDATED BALANCE SHEET
### (Unaudited) (Notes 1 and 2)
### JUNE 30, 1974 AND 1973

## ASSETS

|  | Millions | |
|---|---|---|
|  | 1974 | 1973 |
| CASH AND CASH EQUIVALENTS .............................. | $ 18,127 | $ 22,797 |
| GOLD, at official rate (Note 3) ................................ | 11,567 | 10,410 |
| RECEIVABLES (net of allowances): |  |  |
| Accounts ........................................ | 5,490 | 4,859 |
| Taxes (Note 4) ........................................ | 14,960 | 12,844 |
| Loans (Note 5) ........................................ | 65,836 | 62,985 |
|  | 86,286 | 80,688 |
| INVENTORIES, at cost (Note 6): |  |  |
| Military and strategic system supplies ..................... | 28,019 | 25,173 |
| Stockpiled materials and commodities ...................... | 11,526 | 12,693 |
| Other materials and supplies .. ....................... | 11,026 | 12,012 |
|  | 50,571 | 49,878 |
| PROPERTY AND EQUIPMENT, at cost: |  |  |
| Land (Note 7) ..................... .................... | 6,686 | 6,415 |
| Buildings, structures and facilities (Note 8) ................ | 88,649 | 86,129 |
| Strategic and tactical military assets (Note 9) ............... | 119,913 | 117,670 |
| Nonmilitary equipment (Note 9) ......................... | 39,708 | 37,377 |
| Construction in progress ................................ | 19,400 | 17,169 |
| Other ............................................ | 2,118 | 1,848 |
|  | 276,474 | 266,608 |
| Less—Accumulated depreciation (Note 10) ................ | 129,000 | 122,000 |
|  | 147,474 | 144,608 |
| DEFERRED CHARGES AND OTHER ASSETS ...................... | 15,297 | 15,369 |
|  | $329,322 | $323,750 |

## LIABILITIES AND DEFICIT

| | Millions | |
|---|---|---|
| | 1974 | 1973 |
| FEDERAL DEBT (Note 11): | | |
| Gross debt outstanding ............................. | $ 486,247 | $ 468,426 |
| Less—Intragovernmental holdings— | | |
| Trust funds ................................. | (129,745) | (114,852) |
| Federal Reserve ............................. | (80,649) | (75,182) |
| Other ........................................ | (10,449) | (10,529) |
| Debt outstanding with the public ................ | 265,404 | 267,863 |
| Less—Unamortized discount ........................ | 2,506 | 2,243 |
| | 262,898 | 265,620 |
| FEDERAL RESERVE LIABILITIES: | | |
| Federal Reserve Notes outstanding .................... | 64,263 | 58,754 |
| Deposits of member banks ........................... | 26,760 | 25,506 |
| Other .......................................... | 2,286 | 1,725 |
| | 93,309 | 85,985 |
| ACCOUNTS PAYABLE AND ACCRUED LIABILITIES: | | |
| Accounts payable ................................. | 32,491 | 30,757 |
| Accrued interest, annual leave and other ............... | 11,187 | 11,819 |
| Deferred revenue .................................. | 6,734 | 6,565 |
| | 50,412 | 49,141 |
| OTHER LIABILITIES ............................ | 18,991 | 19,836 |
| RETIREMENT AND DISABILITY BENEFITS (Note 12): | | |
| Civil Service ........................................ | 108,000 | 97,000 |
| Military ............................................. | 80,380 | 70,950 |
| Veterans ........................................... | 110,980 | 110,850 |
| | 299,360 | 278,800 |
| ACCRUED SOCIAL SECURITY (Note 13) ..................... | 416,020 | 340,930 |
| CONTINGENCIES (Note 14) | | |
| Total liabilities .......................... | 1,140,990 | 1,040,312 |
| LESS—ACCUMULATED DEFICIT ........................... | 811,668 | 716,562 |
| | $ 329,322 | $ 323,750 |

The accompanying notes are an integral part of this balance sheet.

# UNITED STATES GOVERNMENT
## ILLUSTRATIVE CONSOLIDATED STATEMENT OF REVENUES AND EXPENSES
### (Unaudited) (Notes 1 and 2)

## FOR THE YEARS ENDED JUNE 30, 1974 AND 1973

| | Millions | |
|---|---|---|
| | 1974 | 1973 |
| **REVENUES:** | | |
| Individual income taxes | $118,952 | $103,246 |
| Social Security and unemployment taxes and retirement contributions | 76,780 | 64,541 |
| Corporate income taxes | 40,736 | 37,588 |
| Excise taxes | 16,844 | 16,260 |
| Estate and gift taxes | 5,035 | 4,917 |
| Outer continental shelf rents and royalties | 6,748 | 3,956 |
| Other (Note 3) | 6,539 | 4,970 |
| Total revenues | 271,634 | 235,478 |
| **EXPENSES (including transfer payments):** | | |
| National defense— | | |
| Military personnel | 23,728 | 23,246 |
| Operations and maintenance | 27,698 | 24,980 |
| Research and development | 8,582 | 8,157 |
| Depreciation (Note 10) | 11,100 | 10,800 |
| Other | 1,371 | 3,091 |
| | 72,479 | 70,274 |
| Other operating expenses, including depreciation of $2,100 million in 1974 and $2,000 million in 1973 (Note 10) | 41,982 | 36,328 |
| Grants-in-aid, primarily to state and local governments | 41,500 | 40,400 |
| Transfer payments to individuals— | | |
| Income security, including retirement, unemployment and Social Security payments made | 69,381 | 60,373 |
| Health care | 11,300 | 9,000 |
| Veterans' benefits and services | 10,400 | 9,700 |
| Other | 6,900 | 4,800 |
| | 97,981 | 83,873 |
| Noncash provision for retirement and disability benefits— | | |
| Social Security (Note 13) | 75,090 | 63,670 |
| Other (Note 12) | 20,560 | 13,360 |
| | 95,650 | 77,030 |
| Interest expense (net of interest income) | 17,148 | 14,146 |
| Total expenses | 366,740 | 322,051 |
| EXCESS OF EXPENSES OVER REVENUES (Note 15) | $ 95,106 | $ 86,573 |

The accompanying notes are an integral part of this statement.

# UNITED STATES GOVERNMENT
## ILLUSTRATIVE CONSOLIDATED STATEMENT OF CHANGES IN CASH AND CASH EQUIVALENTS
### (Unaudited) (Notes 1 and 2)
### FOR THE YEAR ENDED JUNE 30, 1974

|  |  | Millions |
|---|---|---|
| **SOURCES OF CASH:** | | |
| Excess of expenses over revenues | | $(95,106) |
| Add (deduct) items not affecting cash— | | |
| Depreciation (Note 10) | | 13,200 |
| Noncash provision for retirement and disability benefit expense (Notes 12 and 13) | | 95,650 |
| Revenue attributable to change in gold valuation (Note 3) | | (1,157) |
| Increase in accrued corporate income taxes receivable | | (2,116) |
| Effect of other accrual adjustments (net) | | ( 151) |
| Cash provided by operations | | 10,320 |
| Increase in Federal Reserve liabilities | | 7,324 |
| Total sources of cash | | 17,644 |
| **USES OF CASH:** | | |
| Decrease in net Federal debt— | | |
| Increase in gross debt outstanding | $17,821 | |
| Less—Increase in intragovernmental holdings: | | |
| Trust funds | 14,893 | |
| Federal Reserve | 5,467 | |
| Other | (80) | |
| | 20,280 | |
| Decrease in debt outstanding with the public | 2,459 | |
| Increase in unamortized debt discount | 263 | 2,722 |
| Additions to property and equipment | | 16,066 |
| Increase in loans receivable | | 2,851 |
| Net change in other assets and liabilities | | 675 |
| Total uses of cash | | 22,314 |
| **DECREASE IN CASH** | | (4,670) |
| **CASH AT BEGINNING OF YEAR** | | 22,797 |
| **CASH AT END OF YEAR** | | $ 18,127 |

The accompanying notes are an integral part of this statement.

# UNITED STATES GOVERNMENT

### Notes to Illustrative Consolidated Financial Statements
### (Unaudited)
### June 30, 1974 and 1973

1. SOURCES OF DATA

The United States Government does not have a centralized accounting system which would furnish data necessary for the preparation of consolidated financial statements on an accrual basis. The asset and liability amounts included herein were obtained from several sources within the Government. For some agencies, numbers purporting to reflect the same items were available from more than one source and differed as to amount. In such instances, the sources which appeared to be the most reliable were used.

2. PRINCIPLES OF CONSOLIDATION

The accompanying financial statements include the accounts of all significant agencies and funds included in the Unified Budget of the United States Government, plus those of the traditional "off budget" agencies and the Federal Reserve System. Government-sponsored enterprises such as Federal Land Banks have been excluded because they are privately owned. Amounts reflected are as of June 30, 1974 and 1973, except for the Federal Reserve System, which reports on a calendar-year basis and for which December 31, 1973 and 1972, amounts were used. Intragovernmental assets, liabilities and revenue/expense items of significance have been eliminated in consolidation.

The Federal Reserve System (which operates independently from the Executive and Legislative branches of the Government) has been included in the accompanying financial statements because of the interrelationships between the Federal Reserve System and the Treasury.

The effect of including the Federal Reserve System in the consolidated balance sheet as of June 30, 1974, is summarized below.

|  | Millions |
|---|---:|
| Increase total assets | $ 3,089 |
| Reduce Federal debt | $(80,649) |
| Eliminate gold certificate liability | (11,460) |
| Add Federal Reserve Notes | 64,263 |
| Add deposits of member banks | 26,760 |
| Increase other liability accounts | 2,286 |
|  | 1,200 |
| Reduce deficit | 1,889 |
|  | $ 3,089 |

Government trust funds have been included in the accompanying consolidated financial statements. This reporting has been adopted because the trust funds are included in the Unified Budget and because the assets in such funds are almost exclusively Federal debt securities. In substance, the Government trust funds serve as segregated accounts for specific purposes rather than as trusts.

3. GOLD

Gold has been recorded at the official rate established by Congress ($42.22 per ounce at June 30, 1974, and $38.00 per ounce at June 30,

1973). Although the free market rate for gold is currently much higher, a different rate was not used because (1) the official rate is the basis upon which the Treasury uses the gold as security to increase its demand deposits with the Federal Reserve (most of the gold has been utilized in this way) and (2) it is not possible to determine what effect sales of the Treasury's gold would have on the free market price and, therefore, what alternative value would be appropriate. If the free market rate as of June 30, 1974, of $144.50 per ounce had been used, the aggregate carrying value of gold would have been $39,586 million.

The effect of the change in the official rate for gold between June 30, 1973, and June 30, 1974, is reflected as revenue of the Government in the accompanying consolidated statement of revenues and expenses because such a valuation increase allows the Treasury to increase its cash balances.

## 6. INVENTORIES

Inventories include nondepreciable personal property and are generally stated at cost. The major components of inventory are summarized below.

| Classification | Millions | |
| --- | --- | --- |
| | 1974 | 1973 |
| Military and strategic system supplies— | | |
| Ammunition | $ 9,387 | $ 6,944 |
| Materials related to missile, air and weapons systems | 11,293 | 11,167 |
| Repair parts for weapons and vehicles | 2,545 | 2,425 |
| Excess materials awaiting disposition | 2,354 | 2,862 |
| Miscellaneous | 2,440 | 1,775 |
| | 28,019 | 25,173 |
| Stockpiled materials and commodities— | | |
| Nuclear materials | 6,599 | 6,611 |
| Metals and like materials | 4,417 | 5,595 |
| Helium | 510 | 487 |
| | 11,526 | 12,693 |
| Other materials and supplies— | | |
| Electric, industrial and petroleum supplies | 4,094 | 4,141 |
| Clothing, subsistence and general supplies | 1,936 | 1,799 |
| Excess materials awaiting disposition | 2,190 | 2,333 |
| Miscellaneous | 524 | 1,395 |
| Subtotal—Department of Defense | 8,744 | 9,668 |
| Agencies other than Department of Defense | 2,282 | 2,344 |
| | 11,026 | 12,012 |
| | $50,571 | $49,878 |

The inventory accounts do not include the weapons stockpile of the Atomic Energy Commission, since the extent of this inventory is classified information.

7. LAND

Land owned by the Government as of June 30, 1974, is summarized below by predominant usage.

| Usage | Acres (Millions) | Cost (Millions) |
|---|---|---|
| Forest and wildlife | 503.2 | $ 497 |
| Grazing | 163.5 | 26 |
| Parks and historic sites | 25.1 | 477 |
| Alaska oil and gas reserves | 23.0 | — |
| Military (except airfields) | 18.1 | 314 |
| Flood control and navigation | 8.0 | 3,256 |
| Reclamation and irrigation | 7.0 | 305 |
| Industrial | 2.9 | 204 |
| Airfields | 2.3 | 203 |
| Power development and distribution | 1.5 | 272 |
| Other | 5.9 | 979 |
| | 760.5 | 6,533 |
| Outside United States | .6 | 153 |
| | 761.1 | $6,686 |

The outer continental shelf and other offshore land are not included above.

The Government owns approximately 33.5% of the total acreage of the United States, or 761 million acres (of which 352 million acres are located in Alaska). This total includes 704 million acres of public domain land (land vested in the United States by virtue of its sovereignty).

Cost represents cost to the Government, except that the cost of land acquired through donation, exchange, devise, forfeiture or judicial process is estimated at amounts the Government would have had to pay for the properties if purchased at the date of acquisition by the Government. Public domain land is included at no cost.

A committee of the House of Representatives reported as of June 30, 1972, that the estimated current value of the 704 million acres of public domain land was approximately $29.9 billion. No similar reports are available estimating current values for other land, mineral resources or the outer continental shelf.

8. BUILDINGS, STRUCTURES AND FACILITIES

This category includes all real property owned by the Government except land.

9. DEPRECIABLE PERSONAL PROPERTY

Depreciable personal property has been divided into two categories to split out that portion which relates solely to defense of the nation from that which may have nonmilitary applications. The assets are recorded at acquisition cost and include only those which are currently in use or in usable condition.

| Classification | Millions | |
|---|---|---|
| | 1974 | 1973 |
| Strategic and tactical military assets— | | |
| Aircraft and related equipment | $ 51,032 | $ 49,891 |
| Ships and service craft | 36,268 | 36,081 |
| Combat and tactical vehicles | 16,923 | 18,324 |
| Missiles and related equipment | 9,746 | 9,255 |
| Weapons | 1,091 | 509 |
| Other (primarily ground support) | 4,853 | 3,610 |
| | $119,913 | $117,670 |

10.  DEPRECIATION

Most Government agencies do not depreciate property and equipment. Accumulated depreciation as of June 30, 1974 and 1973, for such agencies was estimated based on available information; reported amounts were used for those agencies (e.g., AEC and TVA) which do depreciate property and equipment. The methods used to arrive at accumulated depreciation for the major categories of property and equipment are described below.

Buildings—Acquisition dates and original costs were obtained for all buildings owned by the Government as of June 30, 1974, and accumulated depreciation was determined based on the number of years each building had been owned.

Structures and Facilities—Net additions in this category were obtained for the last 21 years, and accumulated depreciation was computed under the assumptions that the balance as of June 30, 1953, was one-half depreciated as of that date, that such balance would be depreciated evenly over the remaining one-half of the estimated useful life for this classification, and that there were no sales or retirements since 1953 for this category.

Military Assets and Nonmilitary Equipment—Net additions by major category were obtained for the past 20 years for the Department of Defense. Budget outlays for major equipment purchases were compared to net addition amounts to arrive at estimated percentages for retirements, and the available information and estimates were extended to cover all assets within these categories to arrive at gross addition and retirement figures by year. Estimated useful lives were then used to determine the remaining undepreciated portions of gross additions.

Depreciation by year was computed on a straight-line basis with no salvage values.

11.  FEDERAL DEBT

Maturities of the outstanding marketable securities are reflected in the following table.

| | Millions | |
|---|---|---|
| Due Within | 1974 | 1973 |
| One year | $139,942 | $122,803 |
| One to five years | 77,199 | 88,223 |
| Five to ten years | 26,957 | 31,111 |
| Ten to twenty years | 17,403 | 14,477 |
| Twenty years or longer | 5,074 | 6,357 |
| | $266,575 | $262,971 |

12.  RETIREMENT AND DISABILITY BENEFITS

Liabilities for military retirement benefits and for retirement and disability benefits provided under Civil Service have been recorded, irrespective of whether trust funds exist for the programs, because the liabilities are those of the Government and not of the trust funds and since the covered individuals worked directly for the Government. The recorded amounts are based on the estimated present values of vested benefits, which were derived from the actuarially computed present values of future benefits (as computed by the Government) less the present values of future employee contributions, if any.

The liability for Veterans Administration benefits represents the computed present value of annual benefit payments, which have been estimated by the Government to the year 1999.

The noncash provisions for retirement and disability benefits of $20,560 million for 1974 and $13,360 million for 1973 represent the combined changes in the liabilities for Civil Service, military retirement and veterans' benefits between years.

No attempt has been made to record liabilities for several other Government plans providing future benefits, since the total liabilities for such plans would not be significant in relation to those recorded and certain basic information was not readily available.

### 13. ACCRUED SOCIAL SECURITY

The Government computes two estimates of future liabilities for Social Security. These estimates are based on a present-value approach, taking into consideration future contributions and benefits which have been established by present laws. Beginning in 1972, benefits are automatically adjusted for changes in the consumer price index. The first estimate, usually referred to as the Official Actuarial Concept, indicates that the excess of benefits to be paid to present and future participants over anticipated receipts for the next seventy-five years on a present-value basis is $1.312 trillion as of June 30, 1974. The second estimate, usually referred to as the Full-Reserve Actuarial Concept, estimates that the excess of benefits to be paid to present participants over contributions by present participants on a present-value basis is $2.460 trillion as of June 30, 1974. This estimate is based on concepts that more closely approximate those used in the private sector.

An accrual for Social Security benefits is reflected in the accompanying financial statements because it appears that such benefits could not be terminated or substantially curtailed without serious social and political implications. Social Security receipts and disbursements are also included in the Unified Budget. Further, in principle, the consolidated financial statements and the accumulated deficit should reflect a liability for the amount of future benefits that will not be covered by future contributions under present law. Under this principle, inclusion of an accrual would seem to be both proper and required. It is recognized that the Social Security Act states that payments should be made only to the extent of the trust funds and that covered individuals who have contributed to the fund have no contractual right to receive benefits; however, this does not negate the need to accrue a liability.

An argument could be made to support the current accrual in full of the estimated present value of the difference between future revenue and benefits, i.e., $2.460 trillion for the Full-Reserve Actuarial Concept. However, it was concluded that a more realistic approach would be to accrue for such amounts over a reasonable future period. In determining such period, recognition was given to the fact that the estimated average period for present participants to contribute revenue under the Full-Reserve Actuarial Concept would approximate 25 to 30 years; further, the

Government amortizes its prior service costs for Civil Service retirement benefits over a thirty-year period, and any period up to 40 years could be used to amortize prior service costs in the private sector. A period of 30 years was used as a reasonable period in this regard for establishing the amount to be accrued.